Contesting France

Contesting France reveals the untold role of intelligence in shaping American perceptions of and policy toward France between 1944 and 1947, a critical period of the early Cold War when many feared that French communists were poised to seize power. In doing so, it exposes the prevailing narrative of French unreliability, weakness, and communist intrigue apparent in diplomatic dispatches and intelligence reports sent to the White House as both overblown and deeply contested. Likewise, it shows that local political factions, French intelligence and government officials, colonial officers, and various transnational actors in imperial outposts and in the metropole sought access to US intelligence officials in a deliberate effort to shape US policy for their own political postwar agendas. Using extensive archival research in the United States and France, Susan McCall Perlman sheds new light on the nexus between intelligence and policymaking in the immediate postwar era.

Susan McCall Perlman is Professor of History and Intelligence Studies at the National Intelligence University. She has published widely on US foreign relations and intelligence and is the 2020 recipient of the Robert Beland Excellence in Teaching Award.

CAMBRIDGE STUDIES IN US FOREIGN RELATIONS

Edited by

Paul Thomas Chamberlin, *Columbia University*
Lien-Hang T. Nguyen, *Columbia University*

This series showcases cutting-edge scholarship in US foreign relations that employs dynamic new methodological approaches and archives from the colonial era to the present. The series will be guided by the ethos of transnationalism, focusing on the history of American foreign relations in a global context rather than privileging the US as the dominant actor on the world stage.

Also in the Series

Pete Millwood, *Improbably Diplomats: How Ping-Pong Players, Musicians, and Scientists Remade US–China Relations*

R. Joseph Parrott and Mark Atwood Lawrence (eds.), *The Tricontinental Revolution: Third World Radicalism and the Cold War*

Aaron Donaghy, *The Second Cold War: Carter, Reagan, and the Politics of Foreign Policy*

Amanda C. Demmer, *After Saigon's Fall: Refugees and US–Vietnamese Relations, 1975–1995*

Heather Marie Stur, *Saigon at War: South Vietnam and the Global Sixties*

Seth Jacobs, *Rogue Diplomats: The Proud Tradition of Disobedience in American Foreign Policy*

Sarah Steinbock-Pratt, *Educating the Empire: American Teachers and Contested Colonization in the Philippines*

Walter L. Hixson, *Israel's Armor: The Israel Lobby and the First Generation of the Palestine Conflict*

Aurélie Basha i Novosejt, *"I Made Mistakes": Robert McNamara's Vietnam War Policy, 1960–1964*

Greg Whitesides, *Science and American Foreign Relations since World War II*

Jasper M. Trautsch, *The Genesis of America: US Foreign Policy and the Formation of National Identity, 1793–1815*

Hideaki Kami, *Diplomacy Meets Migration: US Relations with Cuba during the Cold War*

Shaul Mitelpunkt, *Israel in the American Mind: The Cultural Politics of US–Israeli Relations, 1958–1988*

Pierre Asselin, *Vietnam's American War: A History*

Lloyd E. Ambrosius, *Woodrow Wilson and American Internationalism*

Geoffrey C. Stewart, *Vietnam's Lost Revolution: Ngô Đình Diệm's Failure to Build an Independent Nation, 1955–1963*

Michael E. Neagle, *America's Forgotten Colony: Cuba's Isle of Pines*

Elisabeth Leake, *The Defiant Border: The Afghan–Pakistan Borderlands in the Era of Decolonization, 1936–1965*

Tuong Vu, *Vietnam's Communist Revolution: The Power and Limits of Ideology*

Renata Keller, *Mexico's Cold War: Cuba, the United States, and the Legacy of the Mexican Revolution*

Contesting France

*Intelligence and US Foreign Policy in the
Early Cold War*

SUSAN MCCALL PERLMAN

National Intelligence University

CAMBRIDGE
UNIVERSITY PRESS

Shaftesbury Road, Cambridge CB2 8EA, United Kingdom

One Liberty Plaza, 20th Floor, New York, NY 10006, USA

477 Williamstown Road, Port Melbourne, VIC 3207, Australia

314–321, 3rd Floor, Plot 3, Splendor Forum, Jasola District Centre, New Delhi – 110025, India

103 Penang Road, #05–06/07, Visioncrest Commercial, Singapore 238467

Cambridge University Press is part of Cambridge University Press & Assessment, a department of the University of Cambridge.

We share the University's mission to contribute to society through the pursuit of education, learning and research at the highest international levels of excellence.

www.cambridge.org
Information on this title: www.cambridge.org/9781316511817

DOI: 10.1017/9781009053907

First published 2023

A catalogue record for this publication is available from the British Library.

ISBN 978-1-316-51181-7 Hardback

For my family

Contents

Acknowledgments

The writing of history is a solitary task but one that requires a community. I would like to thank the many who have undertaken this journey with me and who have been critical to its successful completion.

I have the deepest gratitude for the librarians and archivists who enabled my research. In Washington, DC, they include the marvelous library staff of Bender Library at American University and the excellent archival staffs at the Library of Congress and the National Archives in College Park. Outside Washington, DC, the archivists at the University of Louisiana at Lafayette and Clemson University were especially accommodating of my quest for insight into the lives of Jefferson Caffery and James Byrnes. Likewise, the archivists of the Truman Library in Independence, Missouri, were attentive and valuable collaborators. In France, I'd like to express my sincerest thanks to the superb archival staffs at the National Archives at Pierrefitte and the Foreign Ministry Archives at La Courneuve; they could not have been more welcoming or helpful. Thank you, too, to Cambridge University Press and series editors Paul Chamberlain and Lien-Hang Nguyen for agreeing to publish this book, and to editor Cecelia Cancellaro for her kind, patient, and expert shepherding of this project to completion.

This study has benefited from the generous support of numerous American University research grants, awards, and fellowships; I am also grateful to the Truman Library and to the Society for Historians of American Foreign Relations for financing research, travel, and seminars. I am likewise obliged to the journals – Cold War History and Intelligence and National Security – that published some of my work related to this book.

I am deeply appreciative to all who contributed to this book by reading and commenting on parts or the whole. Kaeten Mistry, Simon Rofe, Ken Osgood, Giles Scott-Smith, Hugh Wilford, Richard Immerman, John Prados, Mark Stout, Thomas Boghardt, Francesco Cacciatore, Sarah-Jane Corke, and two anonymous reviewers all provided excellent feedback that made it better. Former professors and colleagues at American University – Richard Breitman, Anton Fedyashin, Eileen Findlay, and Lisa Leff – seeded this project and provided invaluable guidance and support over the years. A very special note of gratitude is reserved for my doctoral adviser and mentor, Max Paul Friedman, who taught me the importance of conscientious, deep research and exploring the vantage points of those voices not always heard in traditional renderings of the past. My fellow graduate students at American University were, to quote Dean Acheson, "present at the creation."[1] Nguyet Nguyen, Lindsay MacNeill, Maddie Orser, Andrew Chatfield, Allen Pietrobon, and Johanna Neuman read first drafts of this idea in research seminar and have provided excellent feedback and advice ever since. Thanks, too, to my colleagues at the National Intelligence University for their interest and support. Lastly, I would like to thank David Capitant, professor at the Sorbonne Law School and grandson of René Capitant, a minister in Charles de Gaulle's provisional government and later minister of justice in the Fifth Republic. By chance I rented David's flat in Paris while there to research this project and found his company delightful and his insight into de Gaulle's France invaluable. All translations in this book are my own as are any errors therein.

Finally, I have relied on the abiding love and support of my family throughout the many years of this project, and it is to them that this book is dedicated. My father and mother, Jim and Sandy McCall, were believers and unabashed supporters from the beginning, but most importantly I learned from their example to love books and history. From my father I learned that intellectual pursuit is freedom, and it is a gift not to be wasted. My brother, Patrick McCall, has been steadfast in his support, as have my parents-in-law, Abbye and Gene Perlman. But by far my biggest debt is to my husband, Todd Perlman, who has read and heard every word of this book many times over the years, who has graciously picked up the slack when I needed time to think and write, and who has loved me and championed this book better than anyone could; and to my son, James, who has lived with Charles de Gaulle and French communists for more than half of his life and counting. When the words won't flow, he is a reminder of what matters most in life, and he is my greatest joy.

Abbreviations in Text

AFL   American Federation of Labor
AMGOT   American Military Government of Occupied Territories
AML   Amis du Manifeste de la Liberté (Friends of the Manifest of
           Liberty)
BCRA   Bureau Central de Renseignements et d'Action (Central
           Bureau of Intelligence and Operations)
CFLN   Comité Français de Libération Nationale (French Committee
           of National Liberation)
CGT   Confédération Générale du Travail (General Federation
           of Labor)
CIA   Central Intelligence Agency
CIG   Central Intelligence Group
CNR   Conseil National de la Résistance (National Couincil of the
           Resistance).
DGER   Direction Générale des Études et Recherches (General
           Directorate for Studies and Research)
ERP   European Recovery Program
FBI   Federal Bureau of Investigation
FFI   Forces Françaises de l'Intérieur (French Interior Forces – Free
           French)
FTP   Francs-Tireurs et Partisans (Irregulars and Partisans)
GPRF   Gouvernement Provisoire de la République Française
           (Provisional Government of the French Republic)
IRIS   Interim Research and Intelligence Service, State Department
JICANA   Joint Intelligence Collection Agency, North Africa

MRP	Mouvement Républicain Populaire (Popular Republican Movement)
MVD	Ministerstvo Vnutrennikh Del (Ministry of Internal Affairs)
NKVD	Narodnyĭ Komissariat Vnutrennikh Del (People's Commissariat for Internal Affairs)
OIR	Office of Intelligence and Research, State Department
OSS	Office of Strategic Services
OWI	Office of War Information
PCA	Parti Communiste Algérien (Algerian Communist Party)
PCF	Parti Communiste Français (French Communist Party)
PCI	Partito Comunista Italiano (Italian Communist Party)
PPA	Parti Peuple Algérien (Algerian People's Party)
PRL	Parti Républicain de la Liberté (Republican Party of Liberty)
PSB	Psychological Strategy Board
R&A	Research and Analysis Branch, OSS
RGR	Rassemblement des Gauches Républicaines (Rally of the Republican Left)
RPF	Rasssemblement du Peuple Français (Rally of the French People)
SDECE	Service de Documentation Extérieure et de Contre-Espionnage (External Documentation and Counter-Espionage Service)
SFIO	Section Française de l'Internationale Ouvrière (French Section of the Workers' International)
SHAEF	Supreme Headquarters Allied Expeditionary Force
SSU	Strategic Services Unit
SWNCC	State–War–Navy Coordinating Committee
UPS	Union Patriotes Soviétiques (Union of Soviet Patriots)

Abbreviations in Notes

ADG   Archives du Général de Gaulle (Archives Nationales, Archives
        of General de Gaulle)
AIDF   Army Intelligence Document File
AN   Archives Nationales (France National Archives, Pierrefitte)
CREST   CIA Records Search Tool
CU   Clemson University (Byrnes Papers)
DDF   *Documents Diplomatiques Français* (French Diplomatic
        Documents)
DDRS   United States Declassified Document Reference System
FDRL   Franklin D. Roosevelt Presidential Library
FRUS   *Foreign Relations of the United States*
GCMP   George C. Marshall Papers
HSTL   Harry S. Truman Presidential Library
LOC   Library of Congress
MAE   Archives de Ministère des Affaires Étrangères (France Foreign
        Ministry Archives, La Courneuve)
MID   Military Intelligence Division
NARA   National Archives and Records Administration (College
        Park, MD)
NYT   *New York Times*
ORE   Office of Records and Estimates, CIA
PSF   President's Secretary's Files, HSTL
ULL   University of Louisiana at Lafayette (Caffery Papers)
WDIR   War Department Intelligence Review
WMD   weapons of mass destruction
WP   *Washington Post*

Introduction

On the River Seine, on a cold December day in 1947, dark waters lapped against barges anchored into a blockade against the passage of coal and other supplies from the north to the south of France. The normally bustling Central Market in Paris lay idle, empty carts lining the street like skeletons stripped of their verdant produce and local goods. On the Avenue de Clichy, near where Parisian volunteers under Marechal Bon-Adrien Jeannot de Moncey had held back advancing Russian armies in 1814, it was quiet but for the shuffling feet of the bundled hundreds waiting in a bread line, trying to keep warm against a bitter north wind. Now, helmeted National Guardsmen patrolled the freight yards nearby, deserted since the rail workers had gone on strike. Outside of Paris, strikes directed by the communist-led trade union paralyzed every major industrial center. Violence had erupted in the coalfields north of Paris and the southern port of Marseille, belying the uneasy calm elsewhere. Rumors circulated that the strikes – and the violence – were directed from abroad. It is unlikely that, preoccupied by their own concerns, the beleaguered Parisians in the bread line that December day stopped at de Moncey's memorial, but they too must have wondered if the Russians were again on the march. At the very least, they might have pondered how, less than three years after the end of the Second World War, France seemed poised for the second catastrophic collapse in a decade.

From Paris, *New York Times* Paris Bureau Chief Harold Callender portrayed dark images of the strikes for American readers: "France has become in the last few weeks a storm center of the Western World." The Soviet Union, he said, seemed determined to carry out a "gigantic test of mobilization of the indigenous forces at its disposal – a dress rehearsal for some ambitious potential project which some describe as that of an internal political revolution and others describe as that of transforming these two Western countries into Soviet satellites."[1] US officials also viewed the situation with alarm and sought to push through an interim aid package to bolster the French government.[2] Secretary of State George Marshall wrote members of Congress that there was a serious risk they would lose France without it, for the communist-inspired agitation was a "flagrant attempt to seize power."[3] Another senior official noted that a communist Europe, run by the "graduates of Moscow's Comintern," would bring about a "tight alliance" between the Soviet Union and Europe, an alliance "far more powerful than any seen on earth before," encompassing 330 million Europeans and 200 million Soviets, bound together by hostility to the United States.[4] Disturbed by the paralysis gripping both France and Italy, President Harry Truman told administration and Congressional leaders assembled at the White House that month that the United States faced "the greatest challenge to its security in its history, even including the two world wars."[5]

Not long after, journalists Joseph and Stewart Alsop detailed White House thinking in their *Saturday Evening Post* exposé, "If Russia Grabs Europe," noting the heightened alarm evident in the demeanor of Truman and his senior experts. The two brothers, who were close to Truman and administration officials, wondered "What could have driven the mild-mannered, cheerful, unimaginative man from Missouri to this dark conclusion?" The answer, they claimed, lay within the intelligence reports that crossed Truman's desk every morning: he was "inescapably and daily confronted with the facts."[6]

Though the Alsops recognized the influence of intelligence at the time, there has been no analysis of its effect on American perceptions of France in histories of Franco-American relations, nor an appreciation of its role in American foreign policy during the uncertain and dangerous period from the months before Liberation in 1944 until the culmination of the French strikes – the height of Cold War tension in France – in late 1947. *Contesting France* is the first study of Franco-American relations to offer comprehensive examination of the US intelligence that shaped American perceptions of France in the early Cold War. By internationalizing intelligence – situating it within a broader international and transimperial context that decenters Washington and accounts for French and colonized, official and non-state actors operating in France and its empire – this book demonstrates how French and American images of the French Communist Party (PCF) as anti-American, foreign, and bent on revolution developed and took flight before the end of the Second World War, fed by a constant stream of warnings by French factions who used their contacts with American diplomats and intelligence experts to influence American foreign policy to suit their needs. For a time, this intelligence was deeply contested by US intelligence officers and diplomats depending on their vantage point, and it fed competing visions about France and its empire. Ultimately, though, intelligence that suggested that France was on the verge of collapse prevailed, and it lent urgency to the situation by stoking fear and a sense of foreboding. Above all, *Contesting France* shows that the images conjured by the reports that flowed across Truman's desk profoundly influenced American analysis and all but dictated US responses to the crisis.

OLD FEUDS

It did not take long after the end of the Second World War for Americans to forget Soviet contributions to the war and to ignore the utter devastation visited upon Europe during six years of total war. And while the degree of carnage and material destruction varied, "common to all European experiences and memories was the cost of war in lives lost, families torn apart, hopes crushed, morality tarnished, politics discredited, economies devastated, and economies destabilized."[7] The beginning of the Cold War in Europe played out most visibly in places like France, Italy and Greece, where the general transition from war to peace between 1944 and 1947 overlaid pseudo or real civil wars, which pitted communist resistors against former regimes and collaborators. Tony Judt once noted the immense impact of these European civil wars; indeed, their very nature meant that war in Europe was not over in 1945 with the defeat of the Nazis. "It is one of the most traumatic features of civil war," he wrote, "that even after the enemy is defeated, he remains in place and with him memory of the conflict."[8] Internecine battles between factions only eroded the legitimacy and authority of the governments, which projected weakness and instability to American officials observing from abroad. Those same officials were especially alarmed by communist-led efforts to transform the Second World War into a "social revolution."[9] In France and Italy, the communist parties earned their best showings with 28.6 and 19 percent of the vote in postwar elections, buoyed by their participation in the anti-Nazi Resistance and Marxism's appeal to masses left hungry and destitute by the war. At the same time, the violence that had characterized the war continued in these partisan struggles and, in France's case, extended into its colonies and overseas territories. Thus, the Cold War emerged not as a discrete break with the past, but as a continuation of wartime score-settling and a new phase in European democracies' struggle against communism.[10]

The effects of this violence and the legitimacy vacuum the war created were especially profound in France, as various factions jockeyed for power in the Liberation and immediate postwar eras. After the war, members of the PCF enjoyed new strength and influence due to their prominent role in the Resistance. For a time, they supported General Charles de Gaulle, leader of the Free French and the French Committee of National Liberation (CFLN) in Algiers. Other groups on the far right, military elements loyal to de Gaulle's rival General Henri Giraud, prewar political figures, and a vocal émigré community in the United States all opposed de Gaulle, arguing that he would be a complicit partner in communist attempts to seize power or foment revolution after Liberation. Eventually de Gaulle consolidated his power within a provisional government, which welcomed PCF officials for the first time in history. Fragile and uncomfortable, this temporary alliance between the general and the communists soon soured.

Convinced the PCF was maneuvering for his ouster, de Gaulle resigned in January 1946, leaving a series of coalition governments to inaugurate the Fourth Republic on the most inauspicious of terms. By the end of the year, the PCF had become the strongest and largest political party in France. Observers in France and abroad feared that the communists, acting on orders from Moscow, would sabotage other parties, paving the way for authoritarian rule. With growing tension between the Soviet Union and the United States, and growing anti-communism in the West, de Gaulle reemerged at the head of an anti-communist movement in the spring of 1947. The Socialist-led government finally broke with the PCF, expelling them from the ruling coalition in May. As the communists moved into opposition, many feared they would launch an all-out assault on the government. American leaders, acutely aware that their plans for European recovery hinged on events in France and Italy, announced the Marshall Plan that summer.

The autumn before the strikes, Soviet and Yugoslav officials, in the first meeting of the new Communist Information Bureau (Cominform), reprimanded the PCF and its Italian counterpart, the Italian Communist Party (PCI), for opportunist policies and parliamentary tactics since Liberation. Not long after, the PCF stoked social unrest and encouraged strikes to force their reentry into the government. By December, strikes had broken out across the nation in key industries, including the railroads and mines;

at their apex, nearly three million workers stayed home. The unusual violence of the strikes and the creation of ad hoc worker committees resembling "soviets" led many to fear that a communist insurrection was underway.

Alarmed by the deteriorating situation and perceived French incapacity, American officials did much more than offer financial assistance to prop up France's economy during the crisis years from Liberation to the French strikes in December 1947. They engaged directly in French internal affairs to bolster noncommunist groups, weaken the PCF, and break the communist Confédération Générale du Travail's (CGT) hold over labor. They encouraged an anti-Soviet foreign policy orientation and pressured French leaders to align with American interests in an emergent Cold War. Against American anti-imperial discourse, US officials also came to support and assist French retention of its overseas empire. The American belief that France was a vital but weak ally imperiled by an insidious communist threat persisted well beyond the immediate postwar period. So too did American intervention in French affairs. Those perceptions and images, and indeed the high emotions aroused by the French crisis, shaped Franco-American relations for the rest of the century.

Contesting France examines the genesis of American perceptions of France through analytic focus on the intelligence that the Alsops argued had driven US responses to the crisis in France that unfolded in 1944 and climaxed at the end of 1947. In doing so, this book makes three interlocking arguments. First, while Truman understood the situation to be dire, he may not have appreciated the provenance and nature of the reports on his desk. Despite the appearance of consensus and the persistence of an alarmist narrative that held that France was weak, anti-American, and on the verge of a communist revolution, the reality was more complex. In fact, the intelligence was deeply contested by US intelligence officers. Second, a vast transnational – at times transimperial – web of factions and sources in America, France, and the outposts of empire quietly passed information to their contacts in US intelligence and diplomatic circles and influenced US policy in important, yet unrecognized ways. That intelligence embodied those sources' aspirations and fears, and sometimes, their bald financial ambitions. Conservative French factions, in particular, successfully used intelligence to play up the communist threat and focus American attention. Third, *Contesting France* contends that the intelligence pointing to an imminent and existential communist threat was often overblown, part of campaign to encourage intervention in the affairs of America's oldest ally.

CONTESTING INTELLIGENCE

Historians have long assumed that US officials were largely united in their perception of postwar France as weak and lurching toward revolution. *Contesting France* reveals that US intelligence officials were often bitterly divided in their assessments of France and the threat posed by communism. There was some ideological fluidity within American officialdom on French affairs, but there were core beliefs that coalesced into two camps. While US military intelligence, the Central Intelligence Group, and US embassy officials in Paris viewed France as weak, unreliable, and wreathed in communist intrigue, officials in the wartime Office of Strategic Services (OSS) and its successor organizations in the State Department pointed to France's resilience and initiative. This book argues that these differences were often a reflection of the distinctive intelligence cultures of the organizations and the personal pedigrees and experiences of their analysts. To borrow from Barbara Rosenwein, their effects created an "emotional community" of like-minded officials who perceived France through a similar lens.[11] OSS analysts tended to be less dogmatic than military intelligence officers and State Department officials, the product of their academic training, diverse viewpoints, and their intimate knowledge of France and its empire. Many of them shared Franklin Roosevelt's liberal outlook, including his anti-colonial sentiment and willingness to work with communists, and but they did not share his antipathy for de Gaulle or sense that France was finished as a great power. By contrast, military intelligence and State Department officials in Washington and embassy analysts in Paris were more conservative and reflexively anti-communist in their outlook. Unlike pro-Gaullist OSS "liberals," these "conservatives," for a time, saw de Gaulle as illegitimate and France as weak, beset by a communist peril. Over time, however, as the Cold War deepened, conservatives came to view de Gaulle as a potential anti-communist partner and French strength – bolstered by restoration of its empire – as a necessary precondition for its critical role as an anti-Soviet bulwark. Not surprisingly, the views of these liberal Gaullist and conservative anti-Gaullist factions of US officials dovetailed with likeminded factions in metropolitan and overseas France with whom they were in contact. Yet there were also significant divergences within the same organizations that sometimes made for contradictory assessments. State Department officials posted in French colonies, for example, often viewed communist-inspired liberation movements there with less suspicion than their counterparts in Paris and Washington, DC. Even within the nascent Central Intelligence Agency

(CIA), there was some evidence of a divide over the nature and degree of the communist threat in France.

The competition among American intelligence organizations and State Department officials in the United States, France, and in France's overseas empire underscores the fact that both intelligence and policymaking at the end of the Second World War and early postwar period were often improvised, the product of changing presidential administrations in Washington, DC, a gap in American intelligence structures between the war and the postwar, and ever-shifting dynamics in France and its empire. This instability helps to explain, as Richard Immerman once asked, how intelligence often shaped American perceptions [of France] and why, at other times, it failed to have an effect.[12] For a time, this tension likely moderated US policy. Yet the alarmist narratives cultivated by US military intelligence and embassy officials ultimately emerged victorious in these intra-agency battles in the immediate postwar era.

This study traces, how, in the end, US officials minimized early differences and dissenting views. With the OSS's disbandment, the marginalization of the State Department's nascent intelligence bureau, and the apparent preference for military intelligence in the new Truman administration after the war, analysis emanating from the embassy in Paris and the US military quickly coalesced around a conservative, anti-communist Cold War consensus. Instead of offering alternative scenarios and nuanced appraisals of the complex situation in postwar France, this analysis stoked the administration's worst fears about France and legitimized hardline US policy. It also foreclosed the possibility of splitting the PCF from the Soviet Union before the party's hardline turn in 1947 and garnering communist support for a peaceful, gradual devolution of power in France's empire. While one narrative ultimately prevailed, the fact that there were bitter lines drawn over the nature of the threat shows that there was nothing inevitable about the course of Franco-American relations in the immediate postwar era.

CONTESTING FACTIONS

While these disputes could be partially explained by the worldviews and experience of US intelligence officers and diplomats, this book argues that the intelligence that made its way to Truman's desk was profoundly influenced by a transnational and transimperial web of informants, who also contested narratives about France. These informants were not a monolithic group but instead represented various factions[13] along the political and ideological spectrum, within and outside of the public space, state and nonstate actors, as well as foreign nationals and other groups with vested interests. These sources gathered, sometimes invented, and often distorted intelligence on the role and activities of communists in metropolitan and overseas France. In many cases, the intelligence was tailored to grab American attention and reflected the political aims of the source.

During the war, the State Department and military intelligence's French sources came almost entirely from among well-placed ex-Vichyites, conservative military and industrial circles, colonial authorities, anti-communist groups and former politicians clamoring for a role in liberated France; many were émigrés living in the United States. To their American interlocutors, these high-level informants represented tradition and a bulwark against radical change, and their claim to speak for France lent credibility to administration policies. One Resistance official wryly referred to this anti-communist, anti-Gaullist grouping as "les américains" for their close alignment with the United States.[14] These sources expressed genuine concern about communist influence, and their repeated references to the horrors of the Paris Commune and the Terror of 1793 reflected the real trauma that those events engendered for many French. They were, however, also astute observers of American politics, and they realized that on this point – fear of Bolshevism – they enjoyed common ground with their contacts in the Roosevelt and Truman administrations. They thus played up French weakness, disunity, and the communist menace to convince the US to intervene in France, a move that they hoped would protect their own economic and political interests. They also supported French control over the empire in order to strengthen metropolitan France – especially in the event of another war – and cast national liberation movements as components of an international communist conspiracy. Over time, these conservative factions played an important role in persuading their American counterparts, against their anti-imperial instincts, to side with colonizers.

By contrast, the French sources of OSS and a successor agency in the State Department, the Interim Research and Intelligence Service (IRIS)[15] often emerged from Resistance circles – including Gaullist and communist elements – and from local contacts with colonized populations. In Resistance circles, this loose grouping was referred to as "les nationaux,"[16] those who belonged to Free France and attached great significance to the preservation of French sovereignty.[17] They were also united by a focus on defeating Germany and the recognition that the prewar status quo was untenable. These French sources challenged the claims of "les américains" and presented an alternative vision of France that came to dominate OSS analysis. To OSS experts, the value of these sources lay in their position in the heart of Resistant France, upon which Americans would rely for support and intelligence in an invasion. Instead of a hostile and apathetic nation on the verge of revolution, "les nationaux" suggested that France was a sturdy, worthy ally for the United States; they also warned against any foreign intervention in French domestic affairs. While not united by political ideology, many in this grouping understood the popularity of communism and questioned the continued viability of France's *mission civilisatrice* overseas.

After the war, these factions further organized along Cold War lines. No longer was it a question of nationalism or alignment with the United States; it was a question of East and West. By 1946, right-wing and conservative factions, Gaullists, and elements of the non-communist left coalesced under an anti-communist banner, opposed to communists in the PCF. It seems, perhaps, that US ambassador to France Jefferson Caffery had been correct; in the Cold War, "il faut choisir."

In unearthing the activity of these myriad actors, this book builds upon recent efforts to emphasize French agency and contributions to the development of the Cold War and French influence on US policy.[18] William Hitchcock and Michael Creswell have shown how the French were able to compensate for the power imbalance with the United States through careful diplomacy and manipulation of American strategic goals. They challenged Geir Lundestad's notion of "empire by invitation,"[19] but moved beyond simple resistance; these historians suggest that French leaders "finally succeeded in altering the structure of international relations in order to defend their interests more effectively."[20] Likewise, *Contesting France* argues that webs of informants shaped US perceptions of the situation in France, and, in doing so, displayed initiative and created remarkable room for maneuver even as France became more dependent on the United States. Even as some US officials seemed determined to retire from the continent after the end of the Second World War, French factions – in touch with US intelligence – played an important role in refocusing American attention toward Europe and, later, the Global South. These actors thus played a crucial role in constructing the contours of American empire and the postwar global order.

Further, by raising the critical role of French factions level with national diplomatic apparatuses, this account shows how the French desire to show strength (as oft-noted by US officials) was not just about prestige as Alessandro Brogi has suggested, but about outmaneuvering political rivals and establishing legitimacy in a France where the leadership and soul of the nation appeared to be up for grabs.[21] The exchanges between these factions and their American interlocutors, whether a formal discussion or a whispered aside, were diplomatic acts. They were also sources of power and influence that have been overlooked in accounts that focus on foreign ministries as the sole locus of diplomacy. From the bottom up, these everyday exchanges created the substructures upon which formal (and official) Franco-American relations rested.[22] At the same time, *Contesting France* underscores the agency of the colonized and those factions who argued against French restoration, and whose voices, for a time, echoed in the reporting of the OSS, intelligence officers in the State Department, and other US officials on the ground. As Jeffrey James Byrne points out in his important study on Algeria's Cold War, these actors understood that they could leverage Cold War competition to draw in the superpowers to their own advantage.[23]

CONTESTING COMMUNISM

That one narrative prevailed had consequences for Franco-American relations that cannot be fully appreciated without consideration of the intelligence behind it. The intelligence on Truman's desk conjured images of impending French collapse and revolution, but, as this book argues, it was overblown, the product of the misjudgments of embassy and intelligence analysts and the political agendas of their sources who played up the communist threat to encourage American intervention in French affairs. These assessments often rested on a flimsy evidentiary basis, and too often had to be adjusted when their worst predictions failed to materialize. This was a problem that increasingly disturbed mid-level analysts in the State Department and CIA even if, from above, these doubts failed to sway their leaders.

Taking its cue from Maxwell Aderath, Jacques Fauvet, and Irwin Wall, *Contesting France* argues that the PCF in this period was, as Wall put it "first, foremost, and most fundamentally French" rather than Soviet stooges. Likewise, it denies the charge inherent in the more recent work of Philippe Buton, Stéphane Courtois and Marc Lazar, who argue that new sources reveal PCF intent to seize power, in two distinct periods: once during Liberation, and again in late 1945 to early 1946.[24] This account directly challenges this neo-orthodox view by showing how French officials perceived the threat posed by French communism – as an adept political rival rather than an existential threat – and how this often differed from more alarmist public announcements and conversations with their American partners. The PCF criticized its political rivals and offered stinging rebukes of the prewar establishment and Vichy collaborationists, as all sides jockeyed for position in postwar France. Some of this criticism reflected the desire of many French, including, for a time, non-communist leftists, the moderate right, and Gaullists, to turn the page on the decadence of the past that had contributed to France's ruin in 1940. Some criticism, like that levied by local communist parties in North Africa, was highly expedient, meant to seize upon the spirit of the age and the movement toward freedom for the colonized to bolster their political fortunes. In this immediate postwar period, however, there were no signs that the PCF was ready to reject its newfound status and prestige in the heart of the French government in favor of an illegal seizure of power. And, for a time, the party resisted the calls of the colonized to support their push for complete separation from France. Once out of government, the incentive to participate in France's reconstruction disappeared. Party leaders tacked closer to the Soviet Union and undertook dangerous measures to force their return, efforts that would leave them decades in the wilderness. This revolutionary turn, however, happened only after 1947.

This account makes use of the minutes of the Cominform to demonstrate that, until that point, the PCF had followed a legal, parliamentary path since Liberation, that the party was not yet controlled by Moscow, and that the harsh criticism of the party at the Cominform meeting did not encourage an illegal seizure of power. This is not to suggest that Soviet influence over a domestic political party in France – which is undeniable even if "direction" is not – should not have concerned French and American officials in the immediate period after Liberation. The point, rather, is that the PCF remained a uniquely French political party throughout the early postwar period. Despite the hundreds of warnings about coups, seizures of power, and revolution, the PCF had no intention of illegally seizing power in the immediate postwar years. Over time, however, hardening international tensions, Soviet pressure, and growing French anti-communism reinforced the Stalinist wing of the party and ensured the PCF's isolation for decades to come.

INTERNATIONALIZING INTELLIGENCE

How are we to understand these images and their persistence? Most accounts of Franco-American relations rest on the conventional terrain of the traditional diplomatic record. This approach privileges the views from Paris and Washington, DC, and the beliefs and actions of senior officials on both sides of the Atlantic. American assessment of France appears as the product of disbelief over the shocking French collapse in the face of the German Army in 1940, a contentious wartime relationship between Franklin Roosevelt and Charles de Gaulle, and fear of a communist France after the war. American perceptions of French weakness drove US officials to feminize France and view it as emotional and unstable, in need of a more masculine oversight.[25]

To fully appreciate US policy for France, however, we must identify the key assumptions and uncertainties underpinning the relationship. As the Alsops had suggested in the *Saturday Evening Post*, nowhere were they more apparent than in the intelligence channeled to US officials from diplomats and intelligence officers reporting from American missions in places like Paris and Marseille and from outposts as far flung as Saigon, Algiers, and Rabat. Thus, *Contesting France* represents a continuation of broader scholarly efforts to situate America in the world. More specifically, this book, part of a nascent body of scholarship that seeks to internationalize intelligence and incorporate it into the study of US foreign relations, deploys the diplomatic record alongside previously untapped intelligence reporting, thus illuminating new findings out of numerous American and French archives and reassessing more traditional sources. In doing so, *Contesting France* offers keen insight into how the French government and various factions viewed the situation in France. There were, in fact, French actors who better appreciated the real threat posed by French communism and, at the same time, American vulnerability to anti-Communist disinformation. Rather than an occasional, if supportive, aside to diplomatic reporting, intelligence emerges in these pages as another fluid category of evidence that was deeply intertwined with the diplomatic record in unexpected ways.[26] Likewise, *Contesting France* decenters focus from Washington, DC, and emphasizes perspectives of US observers on the ground and from France and its colonies and overseas departments; it also recognizes the myriad voices calling from across Europe – Polish exiles, anti-Soviet émigrés, Hungarian businessmen, and British spies, to name a few – all weavers of the web of US contacts. In this way, *Contesting France* reflects the aim of *histoire croisée*, to examine the intersection of these different perspectives and worldviews, and their relationships to each other, in order to illuminate their effects on Franco-American relations.[27]

This book recognizes, indeed argues, the intelligence that informed US policy, and the images of France it fostered, were not the output of a mechanical process but instead the product of embodied people with emotions and cultural and ideological affinities that shaded their perceptions. Recognizing the role that emotions play in the making of foreign policy, this book borrows key insights from emotion history to help explain the influence of intelligence in American perceptions of France. First, it recognizes the historical and socio-cultural contexts that shaped the mood in France and collective emotions.[28] The atmosphere in France was already supercharged, the product of war and a German occupation that required choosing sides. To many observers, it now appeared that France was the last bulwark against Soviet expansion, the frontline in another existential battle between East and West. This was the kind of struggle that provokes passion and intensifies emotions like suspicion, hatred, revenge, and above all fear and betrayal. Often the contradictions and fears evident in intelligence analysis were deeply emotional. Second, it recognizes the connection between the personal and the public domains.[29] For many US intelligence officers and diplomats, personal investment in the struggle fed bitterness, intolerance of the other side, and obsession. The fear of a fifth column only further nourished a hysteria that at times led some to question the mental health of those deeply enmeshed in the struggle, not to mention the collective health of nations. Others, however, viewed France and their French counterparts with affinity, understanding, and admiration. These private sentiments, often shaped by personal experience, informed their reporting, eventually spilling into the public domain. Third, in this way, emotion – both feelings deeply held and those artfully deployed by US officials and transnational factions to "grab attention" – suffused the intelligence that ultimately shaped master narratives about France.[30]

Expanding the lens beyond France and the United States to consider dynamics in the French empire, *Contesting France* also applies many of the insights of the global[31] and transimperial turns in the history of US foreign relations. As Kristin Hoganson and Jay Sexton note in their compendium *Crossing Empires*, the transnational turn twenty years ago – and its attendant focus on flows of people, goods, and ideas across borders – was an important intervention in the ways scholars think about US foreign relations, but it does not fully account for an important political formation – the empire – and the larger interconnected webs and routes that fed them.[32] In the aftermath of Liberation, there was considerable emotion wrapped up in perceptions of France's empire – the fear of losing something precious to something sinister – a concern very closely tied to the communist problem in France. French officials were preoccupied by desires to reestablish control over France's vast empire, particularly in Indochina, North Africa, and the Levant. This account argues that these imperial concerns were hardly separate and indeed intertwined with domestic fears of a communist takeover in metropolitan France. The colonies churned with restlessness after the war, as national liberation movements – some communist-directed or inspired – agitated to change or sever relationships with France. Early on, American officials believed that the French government had badly managed its empire and no longer deserved to govern the colonized. *Contesting France* shows how transimperial webs of French sources used their contacts with US intelligence to tie anti-colonial nationalism to Soviet communism and persuade their American counterparts to support the postwar restoration of France's empire. Those multidirectional dynamics between imperial center and colony drove France to both collaborate and clash with other imperial powers, those then emerging in novel forms as with American and Soviet expansionism and those former European powers gravely weakened by the destruction wrought by the Second World War. Indeed, developments in the empire affected the imperial center just as developments in the metropole profoundly affected US policies and activities in North Africa and Indochina.

At the same time, rather than privilege the nation-state above all else, a transimperial approach accounts for those state *and* nonstate actors in official and nonofficial capacities, French and colonized, operating in and across empires, as well as the flow of the knowledge and information they carried with them. In this way, intelligence is a new line of inquiry in the transimperial approach and a product that followed imperial routes and circuits as intelligence sources in Paris, Algiers, and Saigon passed their information among the outposts of empire and Paris, Washington, DC, and even Moscow. *Contesting France* conceives of these flows, circuits, and relationships as a web to illuminate those multidirectional flows of intelligence from colony to imperial center, between imperial centers, and among only vaguely connected sources across Europe. In this way, a web is a more apt construct than the network, which implies linearity and can be easily confused with a bounded group of intelligence operatives. Instead, web here is used to depict connections through multiple points – for example, the intelligence merchant who sells his wares to multiple intelligence services and diplomats. Finally, global circuits of intelligence often flowed through and mirrored transimperial webs of complex relationships. *Contesting France* recognizes the role that the transimperial transfer of intelligence as a form of knowledge (and the images, stereotypes and narratives contained therein) played contesting narratives about France, and eventually, harmonizing orientalist views between French and American officials convincing the United States to, as Mark Atwood Lawrence puts it, "assume the burden" of fighting communism in France and its empire in the early Cold War.[33]

This book uses the general term "source" to describes the actors from whom US intelligence officers and diplomats gathered information on the communist threat in France. It uses the terms "informant" and "contact" in the same sense, as confidential sources of information. While distinctions between source, informant, contact, asset, and even agent can be made based on whether they were remunerated, their proximity to the activities described in the intelligence provided, and the relationship with the intelligence officers and diplomats with whom they had contact, they are not applied in these pages. "Intelligence officer" is also a general term to denote Americans engaged in the profession of intelligence, whether as a servicemember or as a civilian representative of one of the nascent intelligence organizations of the time. However, as *Contesting France* points out, the distinction between intelligence officer and diplomat – and indeed intelligence and diplomacy – were often blurred. While this book refers to those who gathered information in the US embassies and missions abroad as "embassy analysts" or "embassy officials," they, too, often *acted* as intelligence officers and gathered information that fed intelligence reports, even if they were not officially part of a profession that was still taking shape in the immediate postwar era.

This book begins by exploring the contest over images of France and perceptions of the threat posed by communism during the Liberation era between American diplomats and intelligence officers, and among French factions vying for legitimacy and authority in postwar France. The chapters then examine the evolution of "the communist threat" with the PCF's emergence as a leading party in the government and its relationship with the Soviet Union in the immediate postwar period, and American and non-communist French actors' understanding of the role of the PCF in French life. Next, this story moves to the far reaches of the French empire, interweaving the dynamic of growing unrest in Algeria and tension in Indochina as it affected the metropole and presented an intelligence challenge for French and American officials. Subsequent chapters examine the period following de Gaulle's resignation, as the PCF reached the height of its power and rumors of a communist coup abounded just as war erupted in Indochina. They trace growing anti-communism in US and French governmental circles, which coincided with increasing tensions with the Soviet Union. In this vein, these chapters chart certain developments of capital importance for France – the Truman Doctrine, Marshall Plan, and the founding of the Cominform – alongside significant colonial and domestic events like the insurrection in Algeria and the outbreak of war in Indochina, the PCF's expulsion from the government, the return of de Gaulle and the creation of his anti-communist movement, and nationwide strikes and unrest at the end of 1947.

* * * * *

When communist officials finally halted the strikes in December 1947, American officials celebrated the two-week old French government's success in unmasking the PCF as a Stalinist party and defeating what they viewed as an attempt to seize power. PCF leader Maurice Thorez indicated that the retreat was tactical, and that they would continue to use work stoppages and strikes against the implementation of the Marshall Plan in future attempts to show that France could not be governed without them. American officials remained concerned because they could not imagine a scenario in which the PCF and the Soviets would not renew the struggle.

Additionally, certain French sources kept up the drumbeat, warning their American interlocutors that the battle, not the war, had been won. The next time, they argued, the communists would be better prepared, and they would be armed. For the previous four years, American embassy and intelligence analysts and their French sources had warned that the PCF aimed to seize power; the strikes of 1947 were only their latest attempt. This book argues that they misjudged communist intentions and overestimated the threat – with repercussions for French domestic affairs and Franco-American relations in the decades to come – based upon flawed intelligence. There were, however, people in France who saw the reality more clearly than the French sources who participated in the hysteria. This is the story of how the narrative of France as weak and prone to revolution prevailed; it is also the story of important challenges to this entrenched view, and about other missed possibilities. Alarming as they were, disturbing images of a France poised to tip into revolution did not appear for the first time that December but were the logical culmination of years of perceived French weakness and communist intrigue, images fostered by factions on both sides of the Atlantic. Playing to stereotype, thy set the stage for a showdown over intelligence, politics, and history.

Liberation

For many people in France, 1944 was the harshest year yet of the Occupation. As the war shifted in the Allies' favor, German treatment of the French people steadily worsened. Supply lines that had fed Paris for four years were cut. Parisians ate less than at any time before. Electricity dwindled, available only a few hours of the day. Emotions ran high as neighbors denounced one another and resistants exacted revenge upon suspected collaborators. At the same time, Allied bombs targeting war-making factories fell over the city's northern, working-class suburbs, killing almost 2,000 people.[1] Kathleen Channel, a former writer for the *New York Times*, remarked in March, "the Paris air is more highly charged with menace than at any time since the French Revolution. Invasion, civil war, siege, famine, prison – whatever form the future may take – Parisians are minutely expecting the deadliest phase of the war."[2] Most, whatever their feelings about Vichy, were anti-German and eagerly awaited the roar of American and French tanks. Many who mingled in resistant circles and lost friends to Nazi deportations and concentration camps also welcomed and cheered the militants gathering to chase the Germans from the city.

Others, however, hesitated. Gazing over the Parisian landscape from the protected cloisters of their stately homes, these wealthier French feared that the mobs of youthful toughs and communists roaming the streets aimed for more than a German defeat but to take over Paris in the ensuing chaos.[3] They hoped that the Americans would arrive in time to save them from another French Revolution.

On August 26, 1944, liberation finally came. Charles de Gaulle's triumphant promenade down the Champs-Élysées with General Philippe

Leclerc's Second Armored Division sealed his authority as the heart of Resistant France and head of the new provisional government. Spontaneous celebrations erupted all over the city as the war-weary denizens of Paris greeted their liberators streaming in from the west. But these heady days did not last. The French people faced critical shortages as German soldiers retreated and Allied efforts remained focused on a final confrontation building in the east. They also faced the mammoth task of reconciling the past and rebuilding a nation devastated by occupation and war. American GIs who entered the city after August grew frustrated with high prices and French indifference, and they fell back on well-worn stereotypes of French weakness, apathy, and duplicity to express their aggravation.

US officials had alienated many French with schemes to deal with Vichy Chief of State Marshal Philippe Pétain and Admiral François Darlan[4] and the hope that General Henri Giraud would somehow outmaneuver Charles de Gaulle to become the leader of Fighting France. These missteps cast a pall over US–French negotiations on the two major issues of 1944 – military plans for an Allied invasion of Western Europe and arrangements for the civil administration of France after Liberation. Both issues were shot through with growing concerns about communism; both also carried with them major implications for the future of Franco-American relations.

Watching the drama unfold from his station in Paris, William Koren, an intelligence analyst for the OSS, feared that the antagonism evident in encounters between the French and the Americans could damage Franco-American relations. In October, Koren, a Rhodes Scholar and doctoral student in French history before the war, wrote to Dr. William Langer, under whom he had studied at Princeton and who now headed the OSS's Research and Analysis (R&A) Branch in Washington, DC. Koren complained that American officers in France held a jaundiced view of their French allies, believing "1. The French squawk but haven't really suffered. 2. The French are not in the war effort. 3. The French are bent on revolution. 4. The French don't really like us."[5] Koren attributed these US impressions to a number of factors such as American ignorance of French conditions and history, the distant past as well as more recent years under German occupation. But he also argued that some of America's French partners had played a crucial role in perpetuating these impressions. US military officers, he claimed, were subjected to "a veritable barrage of propaganda over Rightist dinner tables concerning a plot for an armed uprising which is prevented only by the presence of

Americans in Paris."[6] These same French groups – conservative, privileged, and often linked to collaboration – suffered most under purges after
Liberation. They were also, Koren contended, "those in the easiest
position for transmitting their alarm to American officers."[7]

Many in the Roosevelt administration shared the views that Koren
ascribed to American military officials. Historians routinely attribute this
impression to Franklin Roosevelt's personal antipathy for de Gaulle and
his sense that France had crumbled from decades of decay associated with a
confused multiparty system and imperial overreach. Some scholars rightly
point to deep-seated anti-Gaullist sentiments in the State Department,
while others suggest that de Gaulle's difficult personality and behavior
were at least partially responsible for Franco-American tensions. But
what of Koren's claim that French informants whispering in the attentive
ears of American officials were also responsible for this prevailing image of
France?

Koren's report suggests four important issues that challenge the usual
story. First, he argued that French associates from specific political circles
with calculated agendas exercised influence over American officials.
Second, this influence was not limited to a few familiar French observers
but was exercised by a myriad of French contacts on a much larger scale.
Nor was this pressure confined to the State Department and White House;
there was also notable exchange between French sources and US intelligence circles. Third, Koren demonstrated that American perception of a
communist threat in France was already shaping Franco-American relations well before the end of the war. And finally, he dismissed the
prevailing image of France as inaccurate and biased, suggesting the possibility, at least, of an alternative. Indeed, just as French sources bolstered
the image of France predominant within White House, State Department,
and military intelligence circles, other contacts shaped OSS analysis of the
situation in France. Both sides actively contested the other's perception
based upon the information and images transmitted to them by their
French informants.

LES AMÉRICAINS

Koren had a point. Military and State Department officials *were* barraged
with rumors of communist plots prevented only by American intervention
in France. And many, if not most, of these stories originated with the
faction General Charles Luguet, a member of the Free French delegation
in Washington, DC, had called "les Américains" – a set of French

informants from right-leaning political, industrial, and military circles with clear agendas for liberated France. A few claimed that France had not really suffered under German occupation, and many offered arguments to suggest that communist elements of the Resistance viewed defeat of the Germans as only secondary to furthering their own postwar aims. Some went so far as to suggest that communist activity might compromise American supply and lines of communication.

By far the most common claim, however, was that France was on the verge of a communist revolution. Almost entirely anti-Gaullist in their orientation, these sources attempted to link de Gaulle and his Algiers Committee to the communist menace to demonstrate his unsuitability to govern France. They also disparaged the Resistance inside France as communist-dominated and ineffective. Only American intervention in French affairs, usually in connection with their own political pretensions, could stave off civil war and protect postwar stability in Europe. At the same time, they denounced PCF members as unpatriotic and anti-Anglo-American and argued that de Gaulle's criticism of American policy was due to his own pathological anti-Americanism and pro-Soviet tendencies. These charges, fostered by these contacts and reinforced by other reporting, became part of a basic formula employed to influence US policy.

In their American interlocutors these sources found a receptive audience. But more importantly, their claims echoed in the attitudes and beliefs held by conservative US officials, many of whom already distrusted de Gaulle – the product of a difficult, disputatious relationship since 1940 stemming in part from the gaping disparity between his vision of an independent, restored France and their belief that France was weak and in decline. American officers also naturally identified with their French military counterparts. One Office of War Information (OWI) officer complained that US military officials were largely ignorant of French affairs and that they were "more comfortable with the Vichyssoise [*sic*] crowd, the Nazified Frenchmen, than those who for their convictions of liberalism either had to leave France or were put in prison, etc."[8] Moreover, officers with no specialized expertise often staffed Army and Navy intelligence units.[9] This made it much more likely that their analysis would reflect the ideology and policy prerogatives of their services.

For their part, State Department officials and diplomats emulated the courts of prewar Europe, and they privileged panache, good breeding, and the intimacy of male camaraderie.[10] Throughout the war, many of these diplomats remained close to their German counterparts and deeply opposed to the Soviet regime and communist ideology. Journalist Edgar

Ansel Mowrer, who eventually resigned from OWI to protest the US's Vichy policy, once described American diplomats as members of a conservative international elite for whom it was natural to trust their "own kind" abroad. Thus, they believed "Frenchmen who tell them that whereas in America democracy means Henry Ford and Rockefeller Center, Palm Beach parties and church-going, in France it means just the forty-hour work week, atheism and revolution."[11] Deeply suspicious of revolutionary tendencies in France, they saw France in emotional and gendered terms, as feminized, both as a victim in need of assistance and, at the same time, as an unstable "pétroleuse" threatening to burn down the prewar edifice upon which their fortunes and reputations rested. They also resisted analysis from more liberal, pro-Gaullist observers, the "radical boys" in newer wartime agencies, including the OSS.[12] The gates of the gentlemen's club, to be meaningful, had to be strictly patrolled.

State Department and military officials were in regular contact with a number of groups who shared their anti-Gaullist, anti-communist perspective. This included elements inside Pétain's regime, despite the break in official relations after November 1942. US Ambassador to Portugal Henry Norweb, for example, met in January 1944 with the Vichy air attaché to Spain, then convalescing in Lisbon. Lieutenant Colonel André de Gorostarzu was a rising star in Pétain's entourage and member of his military cabinet charged with delicate negotiations with Franco's regime in Spain. De Gorostarzu was also associated with "La Cagoule," a far-right fascist and anti-communist movement responsible for several violent attacks and bombings in interwar France.[13] Members of La Cagoule – "the hood" – often came from the rarefied reaches of society – senior military officers, wealthy businessmen, and descendants of the aristocracy – and swore their allegiance to "the greater glory" of France in secret ceremonies. They were also well represented among informants of US diplomats and intelligence. From his sickbed in Lisbon, de Gorostarzu told Norweb that de Gaulle had courted the Soviets and entered an alliance with the PCF to consolidate his position. French workers already had communist tendencies, he said, and "he and his friends" feared that any Gaullist government would "pander to the Red-leaning of the French proletariat."[14] The message to the Americans from Vichy was clear: Arming the Resistance or supporting de Gaulle would lead to an unstable, communist France.

Administration officials also met regularly with former members of prewar French governments, now out of office and often very bitter about their misfortune. Alexis Léger, Horace Crocicchia, Jacques Lemaigre-Dubreuil, and Camille Jean Fernand Laurent were among the many who repeated the same basic charges against de Gaulle and the PCF and appealed for American intervention in French affairs.[15] These exchanges represented thinly veiled attempts to attack political rivals and maneuver into positions of authority. Léger, a former high official in the French foreign ministry who enjoyed routine access to State Department officials and Roosevelt, repeatedly warned against recognition of de Gaulle on the grounds that he was a Soviet sympathizer with authoritarian tendencies. To this, he added the charge that de Gaulle harbored deep and abiding anti-Americanism. In one conversation with H. Freeman "Doc" Matthews, a former first secretary at Vichy, now the State Department's chief of European affairs and himself a bitter critic of de Gaulle, Léger further argued that de Gaulle's advocacy of democracy was a farce, and that the United States "would be guilty of a breach of faith with the French people if [it] allowed [him] to enter France ... as a provisional leader."[16] These were remarkable claims from a man who had expressed no enmity toward the general until several years after moving to the United States in 1940. As de Gaulle's biographer Jean Lacouture describes it, Léger's transition to "active hostility" toward Free France coincided with de Gaulle's appointment of René Massigli, Léger's sworn enemy, as the head of foreign affairs.[17] Whatever his reasons, Léger had Roosevelt's ear.

Other disgruntled officials soon joined the chorus repeating the basic formula. The former Governor of French Guinea Horace Crocicchia, who was upset about his removal from office for his Vichy ties, claimed that if de Gaulle continued in power after the Liberation, "inevitably he would be dominated by the Communist Party, which will press for French entry into the Moscow Commonwealth of Soviet Republics."[18] In a startling dismissal of two key aspects of French nationhood – sovereignty and free elections – he also called for American intervention *before* elections could be held because of the possibility that they might seat a communist regime.[19]

In mid-February, Jacques Lemaigre-Dubreuil, a notorious vegetable oil manufacturer with close connections to La Cagoule and Giraud, sought out Admiral William Glassford, the US representative in Dakar, to pass a secret letter to Roosevelt. Lemaigre-Dubreuil, an energetic man with dark eyes, a square Gallic jaw, and a receding hairline, was rumored to have provided "valuable services" to the Franco regime during the Spanish Civil War; he was also deeply involved in the intrigue surrounding Allied landings in North Africa.[20] Known for his hostility to de Gaulle, he enjoyed routine access to American envoy Robert Murphy and Secretary of State Cordell Hull during negotiations with Giraud.[21] Lemaigre-Dubreuil warned that the communists, well-organized and determined, were the only group in position to seize power, and he denied de Gaulle's ability to unify France. Instead, he advocated a new "apolitical" Committee of National Safety to be established in Spain or Portugal, to assume authority from Pétain and act as the provisional government. In a remarkable expression of self-promotion, he suggested that "this organization should be as adept as to details as was the landings of the Allies in North Africa,"[22] an event that he loudly and often credited himself with facilitating. After Liberation, a Spanish informant passed information to the US military attaché in Madrid detailing Lemaigre-Dubreuil's continued efforts in Spain to fight de Gaulle "by all means, supported by the Americans."[23] Despite these efforts, Lemaigre-Dubreuil eventually fell out of favor. An intriguing character and natural conspirator who could change his stripes when opportunity beckoned, Lemaigre-Dubreuil died violently in 1955, the victim of an assassin's spray of gunfire in Casablanca.

Matthews also spoke with Camille Jean Fernand Laurent, another former member of the French Chamber of Deputies living in America and an erstwhile informant of US military intelligence. Fernand Laurent had been a prewar business associate of Lemaigre-Dubreuil. Like Lemaigre-Dubreuil, he rejected de Gaulle's leadership of Free France. Fernand Laurent, Matthews reported, was bitter at the CFLN for having deprived him of his parliamentary status, which he attributed to his refusal to be subservient to de Gaulle. He echoed earlier charges about the CFLN's worthiness as an ally; he also reminded his American colleague that he was a loyal friend who had supported American policy. In a nod to American tradition, he noted that the National Assembly and the apparatus of a democratic government "by the people and for the people" still existed in France; they (and he among them) still had the capacity to appoint a provisional government. If, however, the Allies installed de Gaulle's regime in the wake of their armies, he claimed, elections would be a sham and civil war more likely.[24]

Certain French military elements also remained in frequent communication with US officials. General Henri Giraud had been the administration's choice to lead Free France. The mustachioed Giraud, who had famously escaped German captivity, cut a dashing figure and appealed to US officials who detested the imperious de Gaulle. But by early 1944, he was locked in the last throes of a bitter struggle over political leadership of the CFLN. Despite ill-fated attempts to unify the Free French, Giraud had maintained his own intelligence organization. Some of its efforts were directed away from anti-German resistance, and it increasingly worked to delegitimize Giraud's rivals.

In one clear attempt to use intelligence to undermine de Gaulle, a representative of French General Staff and Giraudist groups in France delivered the "Dossier Mornay" to the State Department and US Army intelligence in late 1943; by January 1944, it reached the desks of two of de Gaulle's most ardent detractors and skeptics of French grandeur, Franklin Roosevelt and Admiral William Leahy, the former ambassador to Vichy, now Roosevelt's powerful chief of staff. Leahy was a striking figure with a stern demeanor and the visage of a "snapping turtle." According to Charles "Chip" Bohlen, a department expert in Soviet and French affairs, Leahy spoke very little but "very much to the point in salty, pithy expressions."[25] These informants again employed the basic formula to discredit de Gaulle, the CFLN, and the PCF; in another obvious power play, they recommended that an independent secret service under Giraud be established to coordinate with the Allied chiefs of staff for invasion planning.[26] Subsequent reports from these elements reiterated the same charges, amplifying fears of civil war and feeding images of France prostrate, awaiting salvation from the United States.

While Giraud ultimately failed to overcome de Gaulle, the dossier did have an impact. Roosevelt seemed intrigued by the report, and he asked Leahy to look into it. Leahy, a staunch conservative and anti-communist who maintained affection for Pétain, had already thwarted a planned conference with de Gaulle in 1943. Heavily invested in earlier schemes to deal with Darlan, Leahy detested the upstart Frenchman. State Department Europeanists routinely fed him reports about de Gaulle's alleged sympathy for communists, to which he often added the gloss of "military necessity" in support of their policy recommendations.[27] Leahy saw no way to act on the dossier at present but suggested that it might still have some use. War Department officials had begun to pressure the administration for some recognition of the CFLN to ease the Allied landing expected in late spring. Leahy, like Roosevelt, remained unconvinced, and he suggested that they might use the dossier to bolster their arguments against proposals to recognize de Gaulle's committee as the de facto government of France.[28]

Many of these allegations were buttressed by intelligence reports passed from the Polish government-in-exile to US representatives in London. Early in the war, the Poles had created covert networks to gather Polish elements and help them escape France for England. However, these units soon evolved into a sophisticated espionage network directed against German activities in France. While Polish officials managed intelligence operations in other nations, French agents staffed Polish networks in France.[29] Anti-communist and anti-German, they reportedly worked closely with Giraud's staff in North Africa and with American intelligence in Lisbon.[30] Their reports also employed the basic formula to deny de Gaulle's legitimacy through charges of collusion with the PCF, to disparage the Resistance and its true aims, and to warn of growing anti-Americanism and communist influence in French affairs. Time and again, they reported that "an atmosphere of pre-revolutionary tension" prevailed in France, and that French communists were already openly planning to provoke a social revolution during liberation and establish close union with the Soviets.[31] Secretary of State Cordell Hull, for one, wrote that he found the reports "extremely interesting" and requested copies be sent to his representatives in Algiers.[32]

Prominent French émigrés in the United States also sought to shape American policy. While these contacts did not necessarily represent the majority view of the French colony in the United States, they were well-placed and noisy proponents of their perspective on French affairs. That spring, Paul Vignaux, a philosophy professor (for a time at Notre Dame) and member of the Catholic Labor Movement reiterated the basic formula to agents with the US Army's Military Intelligence Division (MID).[33] Vignaux, a prolific informant of American intelligence, was close to Alexis Léger. He did not have right-wing sympathies but instead represented a strain of anti-communist leftism that was hostile to de Gaulle.[34] And in late May, the MID reported the views of another influential member of the French colony, Michel Pobers, editor of the anti-Gaullist (and pro-Giraud) newspaper *Pour la victoire*, a weekly created and directed by Geneviève Tabouis, a close confidant of Eleanor Roosevelt and a frequent visitor to the US embassy in Paris before the war.[35] Determined to avoid a Gaullist government in France, Pobers levied charges identical to those whispered by other French sources to their American intimates.[36]

These groups – military, industrial, political, and émigré – also took advantage of their connections with US military attachés to influence American views of the French. Many of these contacts took place through US missions in Madrid and Lisbon – notorious centers of reaction and fascist intrigue – and in Paris. On April 14, 1944, for example, the US military attaché in Madrid, Colonel Frederick Sharp, reported intelligence from Paris Police officials alarmed by communist terrorism and the growing influence of the PCF. There were, these sources claimed, hundreds of thousands of PCF militants ready to rise up during Liberation, against which the police would be powerless, a foreboding situation reminiscent of the Paris Commune.[37]

One former military attaché, eighty-year-old retired General T. Bentley Mott, contributed to this atmosphere of crisis. Mott, who had married a French woman and whose best man had been World War I hero Marshal Ferdinand Foch, spent nearly two decades in France after the turn of the century as an attaché. He now claimed that he had recently toured Unoccupied France.[38] Afterward, he remained in Paris for six months, where he tried to ascertain what Frenchmen thought about Giraud, de Gaulle, and the CFLN. Of his sources, he said: "I know intimately people in every walk of life – very old friends who trust me as one of themselves."[39] Mott's informants again echoed other contacts who denied de Gaulle's legitimacy through expressed fear of a communist France wrought by purges, reprisals, and civil war. And like many of the administration's French sources, Mott implied that his informants wanted American protection because they were "broken" and unable to manage events themselves. In another remarkable claim, he declared that nine-tenths of the French public would support American control over French affairs. Mott indicated that he had discussed these points with Colonel Robert Solberg, the military attaché in Lisbon, who expressed full agreement. Neither of them, Mott wrote, "thought on March 4th that the subject we were discussing was going to become so critical on April 4th,"[40] the day de Gaulle assumed commander-in-chief powers previously exercised by Giraud and invited communists Fernand Grenier and François Billoux to join the CFLN.

Mott's memo enjoyed wide circulation among senior US officials. Yet it soon became apparent that Mott had not been forthcoming about his French sources. Army Chief of Staff George Marshall discovered that Mott had stayed at the Bristol Hotel while in Paris. German military and Gestapo officers largely occupied the hotel during that time, and Mott's sources turned out to be "old French Army friends, career civil servants, and important businessmen who were producing war material for the Germans."[41] Mott, somewhat chastened when confronted with the issue, nevertheless reiterated his belief that there were between 60,000 and 100,000 communists running loose in France, just waiting to make trouble.[42]

Mott's colleague Colonel Solberg also deserved further scrutiny. The son of a Polish general of the Czar's army, Solberg had himself been a Czarist cavalry officer in the First World War. After the Russian Revolution, he escaped to the United States. In December 1940, he joined US Army intelligence and later Donovan's precursor to the OSS, the Coordinator of Information. He was deeply involved in the Lemaigre-Dubreuil intrigues in North Africa but was dismissed from the OSS by

Donovan in June 1942 after an unauthorized trip to North Africa. He returned to Army Intelligence and served out the rest of the war as a military attaché in Lisbon and, after the war, in Brussels, a position from which he continued to warn of communist revolution.[43] In spite of these circumstances, Mott's claims were long-lived. Two days after Marshall's letter to the president, the MID issued a report relaying Mott's earlier claims, with no mention of Marshall's disqualifying memo.[44]

Given this climate, it is not surprising that relations between the Algiers Committee and the United States hardly improved, even as the invasion drew near. In mid-March, Roosevelt provided Eisenhower his directives for the upcoming landings. While he allowed him to deal with the CFLN, Roosevelt instructed Eisenhower to do nothing that constituted recognition of the committee.[45] May and June were dominated by further disputes over recognition and currency arrangements after the invasion. Roosevelt refused to formally invite de Gaulle to Washington, DC, because he was not a head of state, but leader of a committee, and he forbade united nations radio from broadcasting the term "provisional government" after the CFLN adopted the title on June 3. French representatives continued to demand clarification of the US government's relationship with the now Gouvernement Provisoire de la République Française (GPRF) and to denounce Allied plans to issue currency after the invasion, a direct contravention of French sovereignty. Still the administration refused to adjust its policy, despite the efficacy of the Resistance after the landings. De Gaulle finally visited the US in July, but he came away with little more than Roosevelt's promise to consider "de facto" recognition, a bromide that meant very little. In France, however, Eisenhower recognized de Gaulle's importance and the necessity for French administration of liberated areas. With this in mind, he turned over the liberation of Paris in August to de Gaulle and General Philippe Leclerc's Second Armored Division.[46] Nevertheless, throughout that spring and summer conservative Europeanists in the State Department, military intelligence, and their French partners kept up the drumbeat.

In the weeks after Liberation, many in the State Department came to realize what Eisenhower and OSS analysts already knew, that there was no alternative to de Gaulle. Even those who embodied his most serious opposition – including Matthews and Hull – began to soften their position and pressure Roosevelt to recognize the GPRF. Their French sources also noted shifting winds and refocused their efforts from delegitimizing de Gaulle, who now seemed inevitable, to an area in which they had enjoyed substantial success – awakening the United States to the red menace threatening France and Europe.

In September, State Department representatives in Paris reported conversations with prewar French friends, who now indicated acceptance of the GPRF, but widespread concern about communist influence and postwar intentions. Rather than admitting the error of previous claims of Gaullist fellow-traveling and an imminent communist coup, these French sources asserted that this had been prevented only by the invasion and swift arrival of American and French troops.[47] Meanwhile, French informants continued to warn about communist activity and appeal for American intervention. One French military official in Spain told the US Naval attaché that there were tens of thousands of Spanish "reds" along the border with France and recommended sending US troops to prevent the emergence of a "completely Communistic France."[48]

As opinion on de Gaulle and the GPRF evolved, Hull finally wrote to Roosevelt recommending recognition, stating that many of their fears about de Gaulle had been allayed. Still Roosevelt refused. Lord Halifax, the British ambassador to the United States, blamed concerns about communism and de Gaulle's strength – the same issues put forward by French sources in their contacts with US intelligence. "Admiral Leahy had so constantly predicted to the president that the liberation of France would give signal for civil war," he said, "that Mr. Roosevelt, until recently, did not believe that de Gaulle could firmly establish his authority in France."[49] These predictions were unrealized, but Roosevelt was not done drawing conclusions about events in France.[50] By mid-October, however, international developments intervened. Eisenhower wrote the joint chiefs that it was in their military interest to have a strong French government that could prevent disturbances in rear areas, especially with another hard winter approaching. Whatever they thought of de Gaulle, he argued, there was no one stronger. He further advised that if de Gaulle fell, chaos would ensue and spread to the rest of Western Europe, leaving one superpower – the Soviet Union – dominant over the continent.[51] Acceding to pragmatism, Roosevelt finally relented and recognized the GPRF on October 23, 1944. Despite this reevaluation of policy, the American perception of France as weak and fertile ground for communist intrigue remained unchanged.

This image of France persisted, in part, because entrenched views among American officials continued to be massaged by their French associates. The administration's refusal to entertain assessments that challenged these views also contributed to their inflexibility in the face of evidence that contradicted the accepted line. One episode in mid-November 1944 illustrates the trend. By then, France was liberated, de

Gaulle was in power, and the PCF maintained a prominent position within the government. Echoing this reality, in October, Selden Chapin at the embassy in Paris submitted a report describing a commemorative ceremony honoring resistance martyrs at the Père Lachaise cemetery, hosted by the PCF. The memo, and the source – "a reliable observer who attended the ceremony" – painted a positive picture of the event as disciplined and patriotic. Other observers further noted that the communists would not now risk their position by hasty action, and that, to the contrary, they would work to demonstrate their honest desire to cooperate in France's restoration and avoid any impression that they were operating in the interests of the Soviet Union.[52] Senior State Department official Raymond E. Murphy was incredulous. He quickly dismissed any suggestion that the French situation was not dire or that the PCF had less than revolutionary aims. In November, he wrote the department's French experts and demanded that they suppress the memo.

Murphy, a natural conspirator and ardent anti-communist, was a specialist in international communism who reportedly ran a secretive office within the European division dedicated to rooting out worldwide communist subversion. He had already worked closely with the FBI on the domestic communist threat.[53] Murphy's letter was a direct challenge to anyone who was too sanguine about French communism. In a cover note to a harsh rebuttal of Chapin's memo, and despite US representative to the CFLN Jefferson Caffery's similarly optimistic assessment of French political conditions, Murphy surprisingly discounted the use of personal interviews as being "non-productive." Though Chapin only mentioned the presence of Marcel Cachin, the editor of communist newspaper *l'Humanité*, at the event, Murphy seized on the possibility that US officials might talk to a communist; artful schemers like Cachin, he grumbled, "always present a picture at variance with the facts."[54] Rather than engage PCF sources, Murphy now advocated for close readings of communist tracts and papers. He pointed out that a like-minded expert in the Paris embassy, Norris Chipman, had recently employed this type of analysis and that since then, "the data from Paris presents a different picture."[55] Subsequent reporting seemed to reflect renewed emphasis on textual analysis of communist papers as the true source of communist intentions; again, it repeated the same formula to discredit the PCF.

Analysis emanating from the White House, State Department, and military intelligence and based, in part at least, on information provided by French contacts, thus acted as critical support of the administration's policy rather than the other way around. Here, the risk of politicization of intelligence was acute. State Department and White House officials, in particular, sought to justify their French policy. At the same time, their French sources sought to defend their pretensions to be members of the same team as their American counterparts. Moreover, Murphy's treatment of a rather benign alternative explanation of communist behavior further highlighted the tendency to reinforce conventional wisdom and suppress other conclusions.[56] While there were occasional caveats placed upon the qualifications and intentions of a particular source and acknowledgment of their grievances, State Department and military intelligence too often did not link these issues to the evidence and claims presented by their sources.

On December 2, journalist Walter Lippmann, newly returned from France, wrote that he wished he could report that "the tragic muddle" of official US relations with France had been clarified by recognition of the GPRF. This had not been possible, he argued, because "the staff of the embassy in Paris is the same staff that so completely misjudged the French Resistance when Admiral Leahy was at Vichy, and when Mr. Murphy was at Algiers."[57] While Lippmann did not question their desire to see the GPRF succeed, he argued that their records precluded them from contact with important elements in post-Liberation France.[58] Gravely wounded by US policy choices and flirtation with discredited French groups, Franco-American relations ended the year as they had started – anxious, uncertain, and decidedly chilly.

LES NATIONAUX

Koren's memo suggested that the entrenched view of a weak France, bred by contact with a certain French milieu, was neither the only one nor an accurate one. In fact, there was another image bubbling up from exchange between other French sources and OSS intelligence analysts. These contacts – *les nationaux* – contested the predominant view, especially the suggestion that France had no stake in the war, that it was bent on revolution, and that it was churning with anti-American sentiment. In doing so, they also challenged the very premises upon which American policy rested. While other French sources painted a rather unambiguous view of de Gaulle's association with French communists, these informants suggested that the situation was less clear-cut. Most argued that de Gaulle was the only possible leader of liberated France and that any criticism of American policy was grounded in the reality of the French situation, not in deep-seated hostility to the United States. These informants also underscored American misapprehension of the communist threat; to them, PCF militants were patriots who sought expulsion of the German invader, reform of a corrupt system, and their rightful place in French politics. In turn, these sources offered a more hopeful image of France as a strong and reliable ally.

The OSS's heterogeneity and its challenge to the State Department's monopoly on foreign information meant that its analysts routinely clashed with the department's Europeanists. Many in official Washington, DC, viewed OSS R&A as a "cadre of academic radicals incapable of producing objective intelligence estimates in the context of an intensely politicized war," and they were routinely accused of harbouring sympathy for socialist parties and trade unions.[59] However, as Barry Katz points out, there were actually three intellectual communities that worked together under the banner of OSS analysis: mid-career scholars with a conservative outlook but deep hatred of fascism, a cohort of graduate students and newly minted PhDs who routinely challenged established avenues of inquiry, and a "community of the uprooted" – "refugee scholars of a theoretical disposition, leftist orientation, and massive erudition."[60] Despite military and State Department protestations to the contrary, the reality was that R&A spanned a broad political spectrum, but they represented a broader liberal tradition that eschewed vulgar anti-communism and appreciated the desire for change among the war-weary French in France and among their colonized subjects in France's empire.[61] Moreover, documentary evidence and post facto testimonies confirm that OSS analysts successfully submerged their ideological diversity within a set of overriding principles and goals. Without a powerful patron and facing hostility from rival agencies, they knew they would influence policy only if US leaders had confidence in the impartiality and quality of their products.[62]

Many of the OSS's connections came from among those groups dismissed by the administration, namely Resistance circles in Algiers and metropolitan France. In some cases, their sources' political and personal motivations are difficult to distinguish, because these were not recognizable, well-placed informants. But their lack of prominence suggested that they reflected prevailing sentiment in France in ways that French pretenders to power could not, even if they had a stake in American support for de Gaulle and the Resistance. In fact, these informants had a much closer understanding (both in proximity and in reality) of de Gaulle's authority and PCF intentions than the administration's other more influential contacts. Moreover, their associates in the OSS – many of them experts in French culture and history – carried with them their own enduring ties to France and a rigorous academic appreciation of French conditions.

These academic credentials often served them well. H. Stuart Hughes, a Brown University historian and expert in European intellectual history before the war, reported to Washington, DC, that many of the important French political and Resistance leaders in North Africa were university professors and that they had found it "very helpful to get in touch with them in our capacity as scholars."[63] French academics helped the OSS to navigate Resistance politics. From this vantage point, OSS analysts understood that de Gaulle, "supported by a coalition of leftists and intellectuals, was the political force with which the Americans would have to deal."[64] Subsequent trips into southern France also confirmed the importance of the Resistance and their belief that communists posed no threat to stability and order.[65]

From the outset, OSS analysts noted that de Gaulle's detractors and the critics of the CFLN tended to come from a particular French milieu. One report in January indicated that those who disputed de Gaulle's pretensions to represent French authority or lamented the "pro-Russian tendencies of [his] political maneuvering" tended to be certain high officials now out of office but hoping to be called back after the war.[66] OSS analysts further noted that the most pessimistic assessments of France's future and the belief that revolution was imminent came from industrial leaders frightened by the prospect of communist influence on their workers. Seeing through these schemes, the report authors maintained that ostracism of de Gaulle by elements who had contacts with Vichy or a role in North Africa in 1942 "appears at present as excessive and dangerous."[67]

Other reporting denied suggestions that France was lurching toward extremes or that it was not actively in the war. The OSS office in Bern, a clandestine center of resistance activity due to its proximity to the French border, described France in early 1944 in positive emotional terms. It was "a completely different France from that of the years after the armistice. It is a France united in its resistance to the force of occupation. It is a France that has got a hold of itself, a France that appreciates the gravity of coming events, a France that is morally ready to play its role."[68] The French people, they argued, desire neither a military dictatorship nor a dictatorship of the proletariat. The report concluded with an appeal to France's allies to recognize this spirit of France and to help it recover from the trials of the prewar and wartime years. While the immediate period after Liberation could witness some violence among the dispossessed, there would be no bloody revolution in the sense feared by American officials but instead a movement to help the state best the trusts that had contributed to French decadence and defeat.[69]

Subsequent OSS analysis questioned the bases behind anti-communist whisper campaigns, the same rumors that PCF leaders protested in letters to the CFLN. One analyst noted the PCF's vehement denial that they hoped to discredit American officials in North Africa or that they planned to organize a movement hostile to the American army at the time of Liberation. Communist leaders were, the analyst continued, "strictly practical men ... [with] a desire to get the business in hand over with as quickly and efficiently as possible"; in other words, to free France from the Germans, to punish traitors, and ensure the French people have a government of their own choice.[70] The analyst further noted the communists' moderate line of foreign policy, and their positive statements about the United States and appreciation of the important role the United States would play in postwar France. While communists used "revolution" as a political slogan to appeal to disaffected groups who sought deep reforms in postwar France, there was no evidence, he argued, of communist plans to seize power in France. The real danger of revolution would come only if the Allies tried to prevent the French from reaching a democratic solution to their problems.[71]

In early March, while fantastic rumors about a communist uprising swirled in other governmental circles, OSS Bern reported information received from a representative of Northern Zone Resistance on the communist role in the underground. This source noted that the PCF had transformed as new faces replaced old and more patriots joined its ranks to fight the Germans. Communists were not a group apart hoping to further their own ends but an integral part of the Resistance that recognized the authority of de Gaulle and the CFLN. They showed no capacity or desire to transform the Resistance into a revolutionary party. "It is entirely wrong to suppose," he argued, "that in arming the French Resistance you are arming a revolution."[72] The source's OSS contact confirmed his claim about communist methods; it may be surprising to American observers, the American analyst wrote, but there was no evidence of PCF efforts to establish separate Resistance organizations.[73]

Another Resistance leader reiterated that internal politics had been submerged by the reality of the dangers they faced. He denied charges that France was moving toward extremes. He also reminded his interlocutor that the desire for reform of French society emanated not solely from communists but from many other popular elements longing for a more just and responsible system. The French people would oppose dictatorship under any guise, but that it was also inconceivable to return to the status quo before the war.[74] The same source echoed widespread distrust of prewar political and military leaders – the same circles that enjoyed profound influence among the American governing elite – and positive views of de Gaulle. He maintained the Resistance's devotion to the United States, but he did not whitewash current sources of tension in Franco-American relations including reluctance to arm the Resistance, American bombings over France, and the French belief that any Anglo-Saxon interference in French civil affairs originated with the United States. This informant insisted that it was necessary to immediately install a strong French power that could mete out justice and prevent a spiral into civil war. Above all, he said, "it is essential that no foreign administration of the AMGOT type be established in France as it would be taken as a symbol of national humiliation."[75] This was, of course, in direct contrast with the administration's other contacts who denied de Gaulle's popularity and actively sought American intervention in French affairs.

In April 1944, OSS Chief William Donovan forwarded Roosevelt a memo from one of his representatives in Spain who had just met with an important Resistance leader, code-named "Delphi." Delphi also reported increasing disillusionment with the United States and growing admiration for the Russians, then seen as bearing the brunt of the war in Europe. However, he said that this would change once a second front was opened in France.[76] Aware of American contact with prewar politicians and reactionary French, he argued that these exchanges had caused American hesitation toward de Gaulle and damaged Franco-American relations. The French, Delphi argued, overwhelmingly wanted de Gaulle and not a return to the previous regime.[77]

When Charles de Gaulle invited two communist leaders to join the CFLN as ministers of air and state on April 4, certain circles took this as evidence of collusion between Gaullists and communists. OSS analysts in Algiers, however, scrutinized de Gaulle's statements and came to another conclusion entirely. His comments on March 18 and on April 4 demonstrated, they argued, "the chief results of the news that General Eisenhower would have complete liberty of action to make political arrangements in France appear to have been a stiffening of French nationalism, and a greater unity among Frenchmen loyal to de Gaulle and the committee."[78] Furthermore, their information suggested that American policy had achieved the opposite of the desired effect. News of the noncommittal policy, they said, was at least partially responsible for the participation of communist representatives in the government for the first time in French history.[79] On March 18, de Gaulle merely indicated his desire that the committee represent all groups, but it was only after announcement of Eisenhower's authority that two PCF deputies joined the CFLN.[80]

Other resistance elements in the metropole met with OSS representatives later that spring. On May 1, the head of the OSS Bern (and, many years later, director of Central Intelligence) Allen Dulles, reported that recent arrivals into Switzerland from France detailed great suffering among the maquis at the hands of the Germans and Vichy militia, including liquidating individuals and entire centers of resistance, giving lie to any suggestion that the French people remained outside of the war. It was no wonder that they felt abandoned by the Allies, Dulles said, especially since material support for the Resistance seemed inadequate.[81] In this context, bewilderment over US hesitation in arming the Resistance was hardly a sign of anti-Americanism but rather an indication of the harsh realities that American policies engendered inside France.

On June 1, 1944, just days before the Allied invasion of France, an OSS Airgram detailed Franco-American tensions, then at their lowest state since the creation of the CFLN. In a remarkable departure from military and State Department analysis, which usually blamed Gaullist and communist anti-Americanism for any difficulties, OSS analysts again underscored potential blowback from current policy. Moderate French, they argued, had begun to question the good faith of the United States. This was, the authors asserted, a new development informed by old issues – the US and British refusal to recognize the Algiers Committee, continued bombing of French cities, and the lack of agreement about civil administration of France after Liberation – and aggravated by new ones, including the lack of American interest in the British invitation to de Gaulle to discuss Franco-Allied relations in London and failure to reach an agreement on exchange rates after the invasion. Emboldened by American hesitancy, colons – the French population in Algeria – had also stepped up efforts to discredit the government and its reform program for Muslims in North Africa. At the same time, pervasive suspicion of American dealings with Lemaigre-Dubreuil and the Orléanist pretender to the defunct French throne, the Comte de Paris (which many took to show US support for rightists), and rumors of secret meetings with General Giraud only fed fears of an American conspiracy. "It must be recognized," the analysts concluded, "that one consequence of current American policy toward French affairs has been a steady loss of goodwill of 'solid' French whose primary desire in international affairs is to be pro-American."[82]

Other analysts further underscored the errors of American policy and their consequences for Franco-American relations. That summer, OSS

Lieutenant Colonel Roger Griswold wrote that German and Vichy propaganda claiming that the Resistance was made up entirely of fanatical communists and criminals who want to deny all private property and individual liberty was causing undue apprehension. He further opined that perhaps this was why more arms had not been delivered to Resistance groups. If one believed certain military circles in France, he continued, a "savage campaign of liquidation" would be unchained after Liberation and that great excesses would be committed by the elements of the fanatical left.[83] Griswold himself believed that this possibility was small; it was more likely, he wrote, "that the minority which has borne the brunt of persecution, has manned most of the Resistance, and, perhaps, sacrificed the most in order to liberate France, believes that it deserves to have the largest voice in the new government of its country."[84] In contrast to most State Department observers who were appalled by the prospect of purges and reprisals in France, Griswold expressed sympathy for the desire to punish traitors. The death penalty for treason, he wrote, "will, quite justifiably, be exacted in a great many cases," and he warned these events were likely to be distorted by an American press catering to an audience craving headlines.[85]

Griswold further highlighted the damaging effects of American misapprehension of the situation in France. Popular condemnation of the French Revolution in the United States was likely rooted in high school readings of *A Tale of Two Cities*, which, he argued, had served to "discredit French social manifestations for well nigh a century in the eyes of Anglo-Saxons, and has left in many a subconscious readiness to accept derogatory reports of French internecine savagery."[86] He concluded that "irreparable injury to Franco-American relations can be done now by false, one-sided, or sensational reports of violence and bloody revolution in Liberated France," not only in implanting stubborn false impressions in American minds but also in intensifying bitter feelings among the French. The United States should recognize France as a full and willing partner in any postwar framework and avoid any intervention in French internal affairs; failure to do so, he wrote, might lead a humiliated France to turn to xenophobia after the war.[87]

OSS reports, like internal French memos, suggested a pragmatic relationship between Gaullists and Communists, rather than a secret alliance. In late June, another OSS Airgram from Algiers reported that the opening of a land front in France had crystallized differences between communists and the more conservative "official" Resistance. While de Gaulle and his cabinet members in the GPRF preferred concerted military operations to expel the Germans, communists preferred a popular uprising, which other Resistance leaders claimed they would use to consolidate their political position. Yet the Airgram also revealed that communist Resistance elements, especially the Francs-Tireurs et Partisans (FTP), continued to follow the orders of the Forces Françaises de l'Intérieur (FFI) command, where military and conservative elements predominated. It further argued that indications (some of which originated with sources admittedly hostile to the PCF) that communists were beginning to oppose official policy were "still too fragmentary to be conclusive."[88] Communists in the GPRF continued to cooperate loyally with their colleagues even if their differences over methods remained unresolved.[89]

At the end of June, Harvard professor Ramon Guthrie reported his impressions to Donovan and Roosevelt. Decorated for military service in France during the First World War, Guthrie was also a French-trained expert on Marcel Proust and a member of expatriate literary circles in interwar Paris.[90] Now an OSS officer in North Africa, he took direct aim at the administration's French policy. He reported that his sources in Algiers and the metropole agreed that Roosevelt should personally clarify his policy and assert America's desire for France to retake her place among the great powers, a position at odds with the president's belief that France was finished as a global force. Guthrie boldly added that the US should admit mistakes in handling French issues. And again, he reported his sources' belief that American dalliance with rightist elements had only increased de Gaulle's prestige as a symbol of "revolutionary faith."[91] His informants also believed that American reluctance to arm Resistance groups and failure to recognize de Gaulle were due to the fear "they might become powerful enough to set up a government too democratic for our liking in postwar France."[92]

Most of all, Guthrie and his sources directly contested the administration's assessment of French history and recent developments. The Resistance was not composed of criminals hoping to exploit wartime chaos; *the Resistance was France*. Revolution in the French context was not necessarily a bad thing; there were "legitimate revolutionary aspirations" in a nation still divided between the Blacks (Bourbons) and the Reds (Jacobins),[93] ambitions that Guthrie believed the US should make clear it had no intention to thwart.[94] His French contacts believed that the policy of the United States thus far had been to support the "Blacks" against the "Reds," and that the US had been "consistently ... less intent on crushing Fascism than on combating European democracy and returning France to the control of the '200 families' ... responsible for the downfall of France."[95] Guthrie also pointed out that communism had been a "firmly established political doctrine in France for over a century." It is not a foreign "ism," he said, "and it is not promulgated by foreign agitators."[96] He was careful to distinguish between PCF leaders who were more prone to doctrinaire theories and expressions of hard-core Marxism, and rank and file members who were less motivated by ideology and held fast to revolutionary (and democratic) virtues "Liberty, Equality, Fraternity." Noncommunist members of the Resistance inside France confirmed that communists were generally adhering to the various resistance organizations, rather than keeping separate, as other reports had suggested. These sources told Guthrie that they did not believe that France would ever "go communist," although they assumed that the PCF would rightfully constitute a large minority in postwar France. The United States, Guthrie concluded, should avoid interfering in French domestic affairs, allow the French to participate in their own liberation and reconstruction, and encourage the formation of a democratic government "that the overwhelming majority of the French people seem to desire."[97]

After Liberation, William Koren's memo further highlighted the continued ignorance of Supreme Headquarters Allied Expeditionary Force (SHAEF) officers in Paris about the actual situation in France. To start, he argued that they circulated in very restricted social circles and parts of Paris that were "grossly atypical of the city and France as a whole."[98] He contended that many had drawn the wrong impression that the French were hopelessly divided from cursory readings of party newspapers; they were also wrong, he said, in criticizing FFI groups in Paris for being idle, forgetting SHAEF refusals to arm them. Moreover, American officials, feigning alarm over the jockeying between different Resistance factions in Algiers and London and between old Vichyites, again failed to remember the cutthroat rivalry among wartime agencies in the United States. He also pointed out that the idea that the French were swinging toward a bloody revolution rested with US military officers, who as a group were "not much for social change."[99] For them, the word "revolution" conjured images of the Paris Commune, but to most French it was a good thing, a "vote-getting word."[100]

By late October, OSS reporting also reflected a changing mood after Liberation characterized by growing anxiety over communist postwar intentions and division between governing factions. Allen Dulles' sources inside the hexagon maintained that France was not communist, and that the PCF was really a minority group struggling to maintain its influence. He also reported that French political leaders were far from meekly accepting communist dictates; "the red is fading out of the old political parties," he said, "and the Socialists are now just a respectable left-center group, and the Radicals have become practically conservative."[101] However, Dulles' associates tread a fine line that foreshadowed later French efforts to win American aid and support. On one hand, they reassured their American colleagues that de Gaulle was master of the situation, but they also warned against underestimating the communist danger. While de Gaulle's adversaries had argued that American recognition of the CFLN would invite a "socialistic dictatorship," Dulles' informants now suggested that hesitation toward his provisional government might well do the same. "If not strengthened," Dulles warned, "the Provisional Government ... may not be able to meet the determined threat of the communist minority, and elections held by a partially discredited unrecognized government might well lead to a communist victory."[102]

While their counterparts in the State Department challenged reports that seemed to suggest that communism was not the menace they believed it to be, OSS analysts contested the vision of France presented by contacts who had clear political aspirations like many of those who found an attentive ear in State Department and White House circles. These were hardly similar approaches. In Raymond Murphy's case, he dismissed the observations of a source offering a view contrary to his reading of the situation and responded by insisting on a move away from personal interaction toward a hard reading of communist tracts by analysts in the US embassy. By contrast, OSS experts specifically challenged the credibility of sources themselves because of their obvious personal grievances, political ambitions, and connections to the past that undermined their claims. They did not deny circulation to the information reported but offered critical analysis of the composition and motivations of these sources; occasionally, they recommended against entertaining their schemes.

OSS analysts clearly understood that administration sources were attempting to use contact with US intelligence to lobby for their interests and shape American policy, often through fear-mongering and self-promotion. On October 31, 1944, Donovan sent the president a copy of a memo from Colonel Jean Fabry, a former French minister of war who had voted full powers to Pétain in 1940, in which he waved the red flag of revolution and seemed to appeal for American intervention in France. OSS analyst (and prominent Harvard historian of France) Crane Brinton responded to the memo in an attachment sent to Roosevelt. Brinton bluntly dismissed Fabry's memo as "nothing new" and "entirely an attempt at 'international lobbying' by 'ex-Giraudists.'"[103] He continued:

These people still, no doubt, continue to try to influence the American government, but I believe OSS ought not to allow itself to become a channel of communication between this group – or any French pressure group – and the American government. A document of this sort has a certain value as indicating the state of mind of the author and his group. But we have other ways of obtaining this sort of information, ways less compromising to us than the formal acceptance for transmission to Washington of what amounts to a request that the American government should intervene in French domestic politics.[104]

Brinton further denied Fabry's contention that the PCF was a strong revolutionary party "ready at the slightest chance to seize power by violence," and he reminded Donovan and Roosevelt that the fear of the PCF was still of "nightmarish strength" among most of the propertied classes including businessmen, what was left of the aristocracy, the higher clergy, and the rentier classes.[105] The real problem, he said, was to find out how legitimate this fear was. Moreover, he pointed out that the PCF was not the only political party in France; the Socialists were probably stronger than the PCF and a real rival for leftist votes. Millions of Frenchmen, Brinton said, want above all "order, security, peace; most of them want these ends achieved by a strong government, which can make economic and social reforms according to (roughly) the Scandinavian pattern rather than the Russian pattern."[106] Most French are, he concluded, certainly as eager as Fabry to avoid a bloody civil war.[107]

The OSS assessment of the situation in France thus differed dramatically from the administration's analysis. Because many of its sources were not high-level functionaries with clear political agendas, the risk of politicization was not as grave. Where the risk did exist, OSS analysts often noted when political agendas seemed to drive the evidence presented by these sources. Many OSS liberals espoused leftist views and sympathized with the Resistance elements they encountered in France and North Africa. OSS analysts were not entirely objective or immune to the same forces that colored the views of other administration officials; however, the effects of mind-set rigidity are often mitigated by depth of experience.[108] In this way, many OSS analysts had a profound advantage over their counterparts, for Crane Brinton, William Koren, Ramon Guthrie, and others like them had decades of contact and experience in France. Conversely, Roosevelt's own understanding of French affairs was limited, and many of his conservative advisors' views had been conditioned by their common membership in elite circles, narrow engagement with specific elements of French society, and a well-developed disdain for anything communist. These were the days before the aim of "policy neutral" analysis was paramount, and OSS analysts often criticized the adminis-tration's shortsighted policies.[109] In doing so, they offered clear dissent from the conventional view, and they led the way in fostering another lofty and time-honored goal in intelligence circles, speaking the truth to power.

THE COMMITTEE AND THE COMMUNISTS

While administration officials and their French contacts stoked the image of France as weak and simmering with revolution, and OSS analysts and their sources argued the contrary, CFLN and PCF leaders confronted a more complex situation. In fact, their internal memoranda belie any claims of anti-Americanism, apathy, or real collusion between the two factions beyond a desire to unify the Resistance and expel the Germans. Gaullists, while recognizing the necessity to work with all French factions, remained wary of communist postwar intentions and closely monitored their activity. They did not foresee communist revolution after liberation, and they noted that present communist plans seemed to align with de Gaulle's call for national insurrection.[110] Gaullist officials envisioned a situation in which the PCF, rather than fomenting civil war through an uprising, would gain from their adherence to unity and criticism of CFLN policy to bolster electoral strength and to position themselves as the most powerful political party in postwar France. The PCF, alarmed by anti-communist rhetoric circulating in collaborationist circles and within more conservative elements of the CFLN, dedicated much of its energy toward Resistance unity and defending itself against charges of anti-Americanism and fomenting civil war. Any Gaullist-Communist alliance represented the common aim to expel the Nazis and extirpate Vichy. Their rivalry was not part of a civilizational battle with an existential threat; it was part of a political struggle among Resistance factions jockeying for influence. It was a question of authority, a concern that extended beyond the metropole into the empire, with implications for France's status and place in the postwar world.

Gaullist officials, for example, feared that communist agitation in North Africa undermined France's position with its traditional allies. Anglo-American recognition of the CFLN as the provisional government of France, one correspondent argued, "depends too much on the recog-nized authority of this committee by our allies for this authority to be placed in question, especially in North Africa."[111] Others feared that communist activity might alienate certain loyal segments of Muslim populations who considered France "a dog pound of communism," and drive them into the arms of the Allies.[112] Some suggested that native leaders of protectorate nations might use the communists' bitter criticisms of the CFLN against them. "This is not about fighting ideology," one report said, but about preserving France's colonies "from a perhaps mortal danger."[113] Several pointed out that reactionary colons were also using the threat of communism to damage the government (and its reform agenda); if the CFLN failed to dominate the PCF in Algiers, they claimed, then it could not be expected to act effectively against it in France in the event of an insurrection.[114] To CFLN officials, communist criticism was hardly constructive, another rhetorical weapon handed to the committee's detractors.

CFLN officials also feared that communist agitation among the colonized would stir up anti-French sentiment and give sustenance to burgeoning independence movements. Many acknowledged that communist activity among colonized peoples could be well-intentioned, but it was dangerous. "Consciously or not," Léon Muscatelli, the Prefect in Algiers argued, "believing they play their own game, they are also playing that of nationalist Muslims who are more concerned with demands for autonomy than communist ideology."[115] In early February, General Charles Mast, the resident general in Tunisia, reported that communist speakers there had extolled the virtues of the Soviet method of incorporating 40 million Muslims into the USSR. He warned that while the Tunisian Communist Party (PCT) seemed to support some vague link between Tunisian and French people, their program looked quite a bit like the nationalist Neo-Destour platform a decade before the war.[116]

Other reports acknowledged the communists' belief that their activity served French interests by drawing native populations away from nationalist parties. The problem was not communist propaganda itself, one analyst noted, but the fact that nationalists might eventually adopt the same methods used by communists to interest the masses.[117] Whatever the PCF's intentions, another report noted, it was certain that communist agitation among the colonized made the government's duties much more difficult.[118] While communist militants bravely fought the Nazis in France, one report said, in places like Tunisia they threatened to undermine the delicate political balance.[119] In November, Mast noted that the local party in Tunisia had adopted a much more aggressive tone, recommending direct action against the government. He suggested that this was likely due to PCF instructions and tied to developments in the metropole.[120] Ten days later, GPRF representatives in Algeria recommended that officials in Paris draw PCF leaders' attention to "exaggerations" in local communist propaganda and suggest that they keep tighter rein on the Algerian Communist Party (PCA).[121]

While North Africa remained the focus of GPRF concerns about communism among the colonized, there were a few indications by late 1944 of communism's growing influence in Indochina. Until then, much of the government's focus was on reestablishing French control of the area through participation in the Pacific War and on blunting the propaganda of a disparate group of nationalist parties clamoring for independence. On July 24, 1944, General Zinovi Pechkoff, the GPRF delegate in China, wrote to the Commission on Foreign Affairs noting a recent report on revolutionary Annamite groups. It had suggested that the communists in Indochina seemed to be the most moderate and skillful; it was this group, he believed, that would become the most formidable opponent of the colonial regime.[122] Here, as in North Africa, communism appeared as political opposition rather than a revolutionary ideology. "Although it is inspired in its grand lines by Moscow propaganda," the author wrote, "communism in Indochina must not be considered as a doctrine but above all as a party of opposition to a government regime which groups all of the discontent."[123] Their focus on social questions had earned them widespread support among all native classes.[124] By December, there were further indications of an attempted connection between the metropole and communists in Indochina. GPRF intelligence services reported that they had intercepted a message from French communists in Indochina to the PCF, asking the party to interest itself in Indochinese political issues and to establish methods for transmitting party directives and effecting close liaison.[125] While communist agitation among the colonized was not yet a major concern for American officials, French anxiety over this potential challenge to their authority foreshadowed future efforts to use anti-communism to gain American support for the retention of France's empire.

While the committee was clearly concerned that communist agitation would diminish its authority, internal CFLN memos also showed that the PCF was actually on the defensive and went to great lengths to counter anti-communist currents within the CFLN and among France's Anglo-Saxon allies. Time and again, PCF correspondents reiterated their commitment to expulsion of the invader, and they denied working to carve out a special role in the resistance or having a policy apart from the committee. They maintained their loyalty to de Gaulle and determination to wage a national insurrection inseparable from national liberation.

They were, they claimed, "like all groups, with responsibilities and rights" they hoped to exercise. Anti-communism, they argued, only undermined the union of the French people.[126]

Letters from the PCF to the CFLN reiterated these arguments but also addressed rumors spread by elements hostile to communism. In February, communist leaders roundly and openly rejected charges that they were preparing for civil war, and they denied attempts to discredit France's Anglo-American allies or plans to battle American soldiers during the invasion. They argued that their preparations for the national insurrection were part of a plan of action; after all, had de Gaulle not condemned "attentisme" as a crime?[127] They also denied charges (contained in a CFLN letter then circulating in London) that they hoped to make de Gaulle into a Kerensky and reserve the "October Revolution" for themselves. "No one in France," the letter argued, "dreams of opposing any government to the CFLN which the French anticipate as the provisional government of the French republic and which is an expression of all of the French energies participating in the fight for Liberation."[128] They further explained that their outreach to communist parties in North Africa was an attempt to counter the pernicious influence of German agents and to develop better understanding between New France and native populations.[129] Aware of CFLN surveillance, PCF leaders suggested that the committee "would be better informed in addressing themselves directly ... to the communist parties in North Africa than in sending in provocateurs who report the worst lies and nonsense."[130] After having publicly denied rumors of disloyalty and plans for an uprising, PCF leaders surely appreciated that any change in position would have fatally damaged the party's credibility and appeal to French voters.

Beyond domestic and colonial concerns, GPRF officials also displayed a shrewd understanding of the geopolitical situation unfolding in 1944 and a forward-looking agenda to assert French interests in a polarizing world. Internal memos hardly showed a desire to cozy up to the Soviets,[131] except as required to assert French interests in the face of the apparent Anglo-American desire to "treat old allies as quasi-defeated and old enemies as quasi-allies."[132] In fact, GPRF reports warned that the Soviets were playing the Resistance against the government.[133] They demonstrated their growing appreciation that relations between the Big Three were deteriorating and that their allies had not yet grasped the implications of this development. In contrast to the lethargy and uncertainty inherent in Anglo-Saxon policy, one report noted the Soviet Union's dynamism and its rapidly increasing preponderance upon the

European continent. "The face and destiny of postwar Europe may," it said, "... be determined well before the end of hostilities."[134] The authors further noted the weakness of French means to have their voice heard but argued that they must do all possible to express France's interests. Far from suggesting that France throw in its lot entirely with the Soviet Union, the same report reflected an early push toward a western bloc to balance Soviet strength on the continent.[135] Indeed, de Gaulle's visit to the Soviet Union that December showcased difficulties with the Soviets. In addition to tense exchanges over the future of Poland, there was a stark reminder that France stood on the precipice. After showing a fictional war film in which the Russians emerge victorious and revolution breaks out in Berlin, Josef Stalin turned to de Gaulle with a sly smile and remarked that this image "must not be pleasing to General de Gaulle." With pursed lips, de Gaulle retorted, "in any case, it hasn't happened yet."[136]

Finally, the obvious disparity between the administration's French sources and Gaullist and communist officials demonstrates that French national identity was tied up with competing views on the obviously increasing dependence on the Americans. Gaullist and PCF officials were troubled by the continued influence of "les américains" and others tainted by collaboration and defeatism. Communist leaders wondered aloud if US officials were dreaming of "being able to use leftover parliamentarians who have no honor or courage, a pile of sous-Chautemps who carry before history the responsibility for capitulation in the face of the enemy."[137] General Luguet wrote in January that the general atmosphere in the US was characterized by "harmful actions on French and American milieus by persons occupying or just occupying posts," a reference to some military men close to Giraud and Pétain and former politicians known for their attachment to Vichy.[138] He noted the lack of moral unity among the French colony, which only weakened the nationalist position and strengthened the other side. US officials, he said, continued to see the CFLN as internally divided into opposing elements that were dangerous for order, and as representing only the French outside of France. To Luguet, it was therefore important to demonstrate "the force represented by France in Europe and in the world"; an accord with the Soviet Union offered one opportunity.[139] American obsession with communism in France had thus led the French to consider use of force to display strength, and it had driven their ally toward, rather than away from, the Soviet Union.

At the same time, GPRF representatives vied to shape intelligence on France and counter the narrative of French weakness and communist revolution cultivated by "les américains" and administration officials.

Days after Liberation, FBI Director J. Edgar Hoover informed the State Department and military intelligence that French representative to the United States Henri Hoppenot had forbidden CFLN representatives from having any contact with several of the administration's French sources, including Alexis Léger, Geneviève Tabouis, and Camille Chautemps, a former prime minister and Vichy's vice premier. [140] Tried and convicted in absentia in for collaboration after the war, Chautemps had chosen to stay in the United States after a visit in 1940 and became another émigré source for US intelligence. It thus seemed that continued American contacts with reactionary circles reinforced the GPRF's belief that they must challenge the prevailing narrative with displays of French power and influence. In 1944, the French desire to project strength was not only about substituting prestige for power and restoring grandeur,[141] it was also about outmaneuvering "les américains" and demonstrating the legitimacy of "les nationaux" as the voice of New France.

As the year drew to a close, Hoppenot wrote that the pervasive influence of certain French factions coupled with a set of views then entrenched in the Roosevelt administration had led to "a total ignorance of the state of mind in France, of the absence of any national basis for the authority of General Giraud, and an obstinate misunderstanding of the dynamism emanating from the Fighting French movement and its connections to the French Resistance."[142] Despite these constraints, relations had improved because US policy had succumbed to "realities stronger than itself."[143] As Koren had before, Hoppenot suggested that the actual situation in France differed dramatically from the image put forward by administration officials and their French counterparts.

*****

In the end, there was something to Koren's criticism of American policy and the sources upon which it seemed based. He raised the issue because the views he ascribed to American officials in Paris were typical and he believed they might affect US policy on France.[144] It is notable that these sources came from specific circles with political agendas, that they had access to important American officials, and that their views at least bolstered US policy and reinforced a particular vision of a defeated, emotional France in need of American tutelage. Moreover, the claims of these sources dovetailed in remarkable ways with the criticisms of the French that Koren had highlighted.

The persistence of this image – fed by French informants and their American contacts – did affect Franco-American relations. In an ironic twist, it was a both a blow to French unity and its catalyst. The failure to recognize de Gaulle meant that pressure groups of all sorts continued to jockey for power even when the focus should have been on practical questions of support for the invasion and the civil administration of France. Ultimately, however, American hostility only galvanized de Gaulle's support and led to lingering bitterness between France and the United States. OSS analysts recognized this, and so did those military leaders concerned with operational details, including Eisenhower. Alarming reports about communist influence in the underground and their post-Liberation intentions also fueled American hesitation in arming the French Resistance, another blow to Allied unity and French partisans. These sources thus reinforced prevailing American views at the same time that they introduced and perpetuated Cold War stereotypes of a communist threat more than a year before the end of the Second World War.

The importance of Koren's memo, though, extends well beyond his critique of American attitudes and policy. The tenor of his memo, and his own arguments against the major complaints, suggested that this image of France was not the only one. Indeed, other French sources in contact with OSS analytical circles contested American policy and the image of a weak and defeated France. It also demonstrated that there were real choices and options here; this was not about anonymous sources and analysts who toiled in the shadows and never broke through. We now know that their views and criticisms made it to Donovan and the highest reaches of American authority – Secretary of State Hull, Admiral Leahy, and President Roosevelt. Through their exchange with OSS analysts, these sources provided an important challenge and counter-narrative to prevailing views.

As Henri Hoppenot suggested, this image of France – battered but steady, tending toward moderation, ready to assume global responsibility, a worthy and valuable ally – more clearly reflected the situation and circumstances inside France; internal French memos bear this out, and subsequent events proved it true. The vast majority of French people accepted de Gaulle as their leader in 1944. SHAEF officials estimated that Resistance action resulted in "an average delay of two days on all German units attempting to move to the battle," while the OSS concluded that the tactical intelligence provided by the underground had been of "enormous importance" to the success of American operations.[145] Just weeks after D-Day, Eisenhower himself lauded Resistance contributions to allied advances and rewarded their efforts with a dramatic increase in supply drops to the maquis throughout France.[146] The communists did not attempt to seize power at Liberation. Nevertheless, the pattern of Franco-American engagement was set for the foreseeable future; driven by fear of communism, US officials continued to interfere in French affairs while their French counterparts adeptly maneuvered to protect their own interests.

Civil War

By January 1945, the celebratory haze of Liberation had worn off as the French people set about reconstructing their devastated nation. As the war shifted to German territory, Charles de Gaulle and the provisional government faced monumental tasks: how to alleviate suffering and misery, how to reconcile the past and prepare for a future divorced from the prewar status quo, how to build an effective governing coalition based upon the disparate elements of the Resistance unified only by their opposition to the Nazis, and how to convince France's allies that it was a worthy partner deserving a place among the great powers. Many of the cleavages in French society lay bare that year, as all sides continued to jockey for influence and power. Increasingly, de Gaulle and the PCF, for a time maintaining a veneer of Resistance unity, found themselves pitted against one another in a struggle over the complexion of postwar France. "Beneath the surface of French life," journalist Russell Davenport wrote, "flashing forth here and there like heat lightning on an August night, there exists all the potentials of a civil war." France, he argued, "is a cauldron in which the great issues of our time are being smelted and perhaps refined: socialism from Eastern Europe, and human liberty, which has its being chiefly in the Atlantic community." Davenport underscored the nation's certain importance in the postwar era: "If France succeeds in transforming them into a new doctrine then they will have an effect on the stability of the world; if they fail, we will have lost a bastion of liberty."[1]

The perception of a communist threat was hardly new, as we saw in the last chapter. However, in 1945, this danger, for many in the French government and their American allies, became more acute as new variables complicated relations and intensified the feeling of crisis. The PCF's

growing strength and popularity in domestic politics and France's deteriorating relations with the Soviets brought the threat to the forefront and
conditioned French domestic affairs and foreign relations. French factions
that year continued to warn of communist subversion and intrigue through
their exchanges with US diplomats and American intelligence. These contacts – both informal and formal – acted as powerful constraints on
American policy and explain in sharper relief how the United States was
drawn into French affairs even as American soldiers returned home.

French officials knew that they depended on the United States for
vital economic aid and assistance with recovery. They understood that
American support hinged on a non-communist France and French support
for US plans for postwar Europe. On the international level, they tied
growing fears of Soviet expansionism to their claims in Germany and other
postwar issues. Acutely aware of rising anti-communism in the United
States, French officials thus offered their own formula in dealing with their
American counterparts: France is pro-American, largely anti-communist,
and resolved to manage the threat posed by the PCF and its loyalty to
Moscow; while France remains strong and determined, it was weakened by
the war and requires American assistance to assume its responsibilities and
rightful place among the great powers.

There were, of course, many legitimate concerns about PCF methods
and connections to Moscow; de Gaulle routinely received intelligence
reports from his secret services about communist plans to discredit his
government and eliminate him from the political scene. There was also
justifiable outrage over Soviet atrocities at home and scrutiny of their
postwar objectives abroad. However, internal documents suggest that
even French officials still viewed the PCF as a political rival, pursuing
an electoral instead of a revolutionary strategy. US and French experts
also acknowledged that the Soviet Union still desired good relations with
its alliance partners in 1945, contemporary views borne out by post–Cold
War revelations from Russian archives. American diplomatic and intelligence analysis thus had to constantly adjust to account for the disparity
between their gravest fears and the reality of the French situation.

Other important developments also influenced the administration's
understanding of the communist threat that year. Franklin Roosevelt's
death on April 12, 1945, elevated former Senator Harry S. Truman to the
presidency. A machine politician from Missouri, Truman was a compromise candidate for vice president on Roosevelt's winning ticket in 1944. He
assumed office in January 1945 only to be excluded from the president's
inner circle and discussions of foreign policy during a momentous period

when the great powers contemplated the complexion of the postwar world.[2] Three months later, as he reflected upon the nation's loss, Admiral William Leahy lamented Truman's complete lack of experience in international affairs, especially in light of the staggering burdens of war and peace that he would now bear.[3] Gone was Roosevelt's personal diplomatic apparatus; instead, Truman relied on close advisers and delegated foreign policy responsibilities to subordinates. Like Roosevelt, he had no particular affinity for the French, but neither was his disdain for de Gaulle pathological. And while he was greatly troubled by the Soviet regime and doubted its trustworthiness and sincerity, immediately after the war Truman still hoped to maintain workable relations with the Soviets even as he advocated a firm stand.[4] Meanwhile, his new administration struggled to present a coherent foreign policy to meet changing international circumstances.

Truman's advisers were overwhelmingly hostile to communism and suspicious of the Soviets. The State Department's European Division, long a bastion of anti-communism, made gains after Roosevelt's death. Officials who had been quietly sidelined during the war now returned to favor. Loy Henderson, a fervent anti-communist, returned to State as the new head of the Division of Near Eastern and African Affairs, a position from which he exercised influence far beyond his regional expertise. Henderson and Acting Secretary of State Joseph Grew now led a campaign – through staffing of like-minded partisans and encouraging loyalty investigations of dissenters – "to rid the department of unwelcome opinion."[5] State Department officials consolidated their control over foreign policy and successfully, as Martin Weil has argued, "converted [their] control of the cable traffic to overseas embassies into a presumption that the content of official cables reflected an objective view of reality in postwar Europe."[6] These cables, he further noted, "almost uniformly portrayed communism on the march throughout Europe, directed by Moscow and intent on subjugating the entire continent."[7] Truman and his aides consumed those cables each morning.

Perhaps Truman's closest adviser on foreign and military affairs was Admiral William Leahy. Truman assumed that Leahy had been one of Roosevelt's key advisers on foreign policy. This was not true, but it "inclined Truman to give the admiral's views great weight."[8] Leahy, not Secretary of State James Byrnes, filtered the intelligence that came to Truman and discussed foreign affairs with him each morning in the Oval Office. Washington's journalists also noticed the growth of Leahy's power. "No one has more influence, and at the same time is less known to the public, than Admiral William D. Leahy," wrote the United Press's Marquis Childs.[9] Perhaps because of his service in Vichy or his grudging acknowledgment of France's strategic importance, Leahy retained great interest in the French situation. Soviet and French expert Chip Bohlen commented that he visited Leahy's office nearly every day and that they invariably discussed France.[10] Through it all, Leahy remained largely disdainful of de Gaulle and French postwar pretensions, and deeply suspicious of communism in any form.

American analysis of an internal French and international communist threat came to Truman, often through Leahy, from analysts in the newly reopened US embassy in Paris, military attachés, and reporting emanating from other intelligence agencies under the War Department. OSS analysts in Paris also continued their work but were soon overshadowed by the flowering of competing agencies. With de Gaulle firmly in power by 1945, there was no longer a stark delineation between pro-Gaullist OSS assessments on one hand, and more conservative, anti-communist State Department and military intelligence analysis on the other. Yet France remained a contested idea within the American administration and among French factions.

Some historians have suggested the subtlety and moderation of embassy analysis during this period.[11] Indeed, Jefferson Caffery, who was formally appointed ambassador to France on November 25, 1944, portrayed the situation in optimistic terms in his first reports from Paris.[12] Yet, exposed to shifting political currents, the entreaties of myriad factions, and the fervent anti-communism of his advisers, Caffery's views began to harden as the war came to an end and France's importance to American designs grew.

Born in Lafayette, Louisiana, on December 1, 1886, Jefferson Caffery entered the Diplomatic Corps in 1911 after a brief stint as a chemistry teacher and track coach. By the time Caffery arrived in Paris in October 1944 to become the ambassador to France, he was a seasoned diplomat, having served in posts in Europe, Latin America, and the Middle East, and the previous seven years as the US ambassador to Brazil. Caffery was a Roman Catholic convert and well known as a rigid disciplinarian who reportedly kept his mind "supple ... by perusing church dialectics."[13] However, like many in his milieu, Caffery was less capable of fully appreciating the currents in postwar French politics. He routinely attributed French complaints of American heavy-handedness in emotion-laden terms as "irrational," "manifestations of temperamental French malaise," and indicative of "post-Liberation neuroses."[14] While Caffery may have offered more qualified assessments of PCF intentions than military attachés in other European capitals and War Department intelligence analysis, he was not substantially more moderate in his judgment of the threat posed by communism; this role fell instead, for a time, to OSS analysts and the new military attaché in Paris.

OSS analysts generally remained more optimistic about France's strength, political future, and PCF intentions, and more sanguine about friendly relations with the United States; embassy analysts and department Europeanists routinely complained about anti-Americanism and French sensitivity and irrationality – an implicit contrast to American strength and vigor – and they remained skeptical about communist goals and continued to view PCF activity within the context of international communism. These analysts also disagreed on the sources of communist popularity and strength, a reflection of their historical attachment to differing images of France as either weak or resilient, the PCF as revolutionary or a legitimate political adversary.

Roosevelt's death in April 1945 had left OSS Chief William Donovan's efforts to transform the OSS into a peacetime intelligence agency unresolved, as his bureaucratic rivals (especially those in the military services) moved to kill the proposal.[15] In late May, Supreme Allied Commander Dwight Eisenhower had argued for retention of the OSS and its "high class and reliable personnel."[16] The head of OSS Paris likewise pleaded to keep trained personnel with valuable experience and unique contacts built during the war. Moreover, he pointed out, the OSS continued to monitor communist activity and to maintain communication with groups the embassy could not discreetly contact.[17] Nonetheless, Truman ignored Donovan's entreaties and ordered disbandment and the division of OSS functions between the State and War Departments. New Secretary of State James Byrnes was not happy to absorb OSS personnel because of their alleged pro-Soviet sympathies. This was hardly propitious for the continuation of R&A – now reconstituted as the Interim Research and Intelligence Service (IRIS) in the State Department – influence in foreign affairs.[18] Ultimately, Truman approved a Joint Chiefs of Staff plan to consolidate intelligence into a new centralized agency directly under the president, a reality that was, in 1945, still several years away. Meanwhile, an important wellspring of moderation and dissent left behind a void, and the administration's image of France and understanding of the communist threat coalesced around the State Department's more alarmist anti-communist view, bolstered by War Department intelligence analysis and its French sources.

American and French officials were gravely concerned about the growing popularity of the French Communist Party and its undeniable role in
French political life. As they had the previous year, French informants
continued to warn the US government about the domestic communist
"threat," and they sought to capitalize on the perception of crisis to
influence US policy. French communists, they argued, intended to foment
revolution and seize power; hostile to the United States, the PCF would
thus pave the way for Soviet expansion into Western Europe. Groups
outside government also continued to denigrate de Gaulle, shifting from
accusations of his communist sympathies to charges of weakness contributing to communist strength in France. These exchanges represented
attempts by various factions to assault the legitimacy of rival groups
and assert their own authority in postwar France. The provisional government had an obvious interest in securing American support and
financial aid to bolster them against the PCF; other informants had been
disqualified for political office (usually for collaboration) and hoped for
US assistance in their rehabilitation. They also, perhaps unwittingly,
perhaps as an accepted risk, reinforced American images of France as
weak and ripe for communist intrigue.

Not surprisingly, these charges strongly resonated with US officials
fearful of communist inroads in France, especially as the interpretive range
narrowed with the ascendance of anti-communists in the State Department
and within Truman's entourage, and with the marginalization and eventual disbandment of the OSS later in the year. Until that autumn, however,
and despite the anti-communist clamor progressively drowning them
out, analysts in the OSS continued to defend de Gaulle's authority, to
offer critical context for sources of unrest, and to dispel myths of anti-
Americanism; they also underscored critical distinctions between their
analysis and administration reporting on communist capabilities and
intentions, specifically over the meaning of government "takeover" or
"seizing power." Where others viewed any PCF political maneuver as a
potential coup, OSS analysts recognized normal political competition.

RESISTANCE TO THE RESISTANCE

As the war in Europe wound down, French informants from outside the
government continued to use the communist threat to undermine potential rivals and encourage US intervention in French affairs. Those without
access to American diplomats found another way to put forward their
views by approaching US intelligence with information on the communist

threat, virtually guaranteeing their rapt attention. A report from the Military Intelligence Service's (MIS) Information Group, based on contact with French sources, for example, indicated in late May that large PCF gains in municipal elections were the result of deception and government acquiescence. Communists won, they said, because the PCF had astutely employed "anti-fascist" rather than communist labels; they also had the benefit of funds stolen by the FFI and the "very strong pro-Russian propaganda" of the current government. Moreover, they claimed that elections had been poorly organized and managed, opening the way to vote fixing.[19] Another report from the Security and Intelligence Division in June reported comments by Guy de Saint Perier, the nephew and colleague of Nobel Prize-winning surgeon Dr. Alexis Carrel whose reputation had been tainted by charges of collaboration with Vichy and association with Jacques Doriot, the notorious French fascist and Nazi supporter. According to journalist David le Bailly, de Saint Perier was himself a "compulsive anti-communist" who later lived in Argentina with the support of Juan and Eva Perón.[20] De Saint Perier denied de Gaulle's authority, called him weak, and claimed that his allies would have no future influence in French affairs. "With the strong grip the communist party has on de Gaulle," he said, "it is quite probable that before anyone realizes it France will have become entirely Communist."[21]

On July 21, the embassy reported similar conversations with former French officials recognized as discredited collaborators and anti-communists who had been frozen out of postwar politics, among them former ministers Paul Faure, Anatole de Monzie, Lucien Lamoureux, and Léon Barety.[22] Unanimously hostile to de Gaulle, they charged him with bowing to revolutionaries. They encouraged a more active American role in France, criticizing what they characterized as the US's "hands off" policy and warning that "the peak of the crisis is still to come." Moreover, they suggested they would do their part as a burgeoning "Resistance to the Resistance."[23]

Ambassador Caffery further echoed charges of government weakness and incompetence benefiting the PCF, noting that "underlying uneasiness and confusion in the minds of the French people has greatly increased in the past two months as has criticism of the government and de Gaulle."[24] In general, he reported, criticism was directed at government ineptitude in solving France's basic problems. Even people who support de Gaulle, he argued, expressed concern about de Gaulle's disconnect with the French people; many blamed his lack of political experience and inept advisers, and warned that government would face grave difficulties unless de Gaulle showed flexibility and willingness to institute needed reforms.[25]

On June 6, Caffery cabled that "qualified observers" in Paris reported PCF influence within, if not control of, the National Federation of Prisoners of War and Deportees and that "owing to the incompetence of French authorities [the communists] are finding a large following."[26] For proof, Caffery pointed out that communists and fellow travelers in the Federation had staged a well-organized demonstration of 50,000 ex-prisoners in Paris the previous Saturday.[27] Such assessments contributed to the belief (and hope) among certain administration officials that de Gaulle might be ousted. In early June, Joseph Grew told Leahy that he believed that de Gaulle was likely to resign or be removed as the head of the provisional government. Leahy wrote in his diary, "Such an event would be of the greatest advantage to the future of France and very pleasing to all the Allied governments."[28] More importantly, this analysis perpetuated a cycle of blame for France's condition, rather than acknowledging the appeal of the PCF or the impact of the war on French political life.

Despite the administration's doubts about de Gaulle's staying power, some American officials began to appreciate the role of the communist threat in galvanizing domestic support behind the French government. Caffery argued that upcoming legislative elections had evolved into a plebiscite on communism and de Gaulle. Most parties had become more overtly anti-communist due to PCF attacks on the Socialists (SFIO) and the Mouvement Républicain Populaire (MRP), and its recent stances on foreign policy issues that seemed contrary to French interests, such as the Soviet desire to exclude France from Balkan peace negotiations. Caffery believed that many moderates and conservatives would vote for the SFIO or MRP in the October elections, believing they would be a better defense against communism than the old rightist parties. Those who disliked de Gaulle would vote for the PCF or Radical Socialists. The upcoming constitutional referendum was also viewed as a test of anti-communist sentiment and PCF strength. The first question, whether the elected assembly should be "constituent," reflected the widespread desire to give more power to the people and avoid a return to the prewar status quo. The second question, regarding the sovereignty of the elected assembly, was more politically charged. De Gaulle remained opposed to a sovereign elected assembly that would limit the powers of the presidency; the PCF and left-wing Socialists, however, hoped to imbue the assembly with as much power as possible.[29]

Two days after the October 21 national elections, Caffery reported heartening news to Washington, DC. While the PCF had captured the most seats in the assembly, the MRP enjoyed an unexpected level of success. The results of the referendum also showed a great victory for de Gaulle, with 95 percent voting yes on question one – which denied a return to the Third Republic – and 65 percent voting yes on question two – limiting the powers of the elected assembly.[30] Caffery's analysis and a later report that voter turnout had been a record high 79 percent marked a remarkable evolution in political reporting, which had only months before lamented French weakness, voter apathy, communist strength, and predicted de Gaulle's demise, claims denied by OSS analysts years earlier.[31]

While they expressed growing confidence in de Gaulle's grip on power, embassy and MIS analysts remained convinced that the PCF was strong enough to seize power and intended to do so at the first opportunity. Often French informants provided specific details through contact with intelligence experts, which lent credence to more general fears expressed in diplomatic exchanges. One Security and Intelligence Division memo in late April, for example, reported that French factory owners – all of whom expressed fear of the PCF – claimed that the growth of communism would climax in the next few months with armed activity. There were, they argued, semi-military organizations made of young men and embraced by the PCF. The communists would use any future disturbances, they said, to further their policies.[32] Guy de Saint Perier also told MIS analysts that a communist takeover was already evident in nationalization of the mines and the anticipated nationalization of banks and commerce.[33]

Not surprisingly, Raymond E. Murphy viewed the situation in similar terms. In a letter to H. Freeman Matthews and French Desk Director James Bonbright, he argued that word out of Paris (a reference to one of Caffery's telegrams) "clearly indicates that the French Communist Party is now prepared to strike out politically against de Gaulle."[34] He further claimed that once the PCF could dominate the largest trade union, the Confédération Générale du Travail (CGT), it could use a general strike to gain political power. This claim, that the CGT was the main weapon in the PCF's arsenal, would preoccupy US officials in the years to come and drive their determination to break the communist hold on French labor. Moreover, Murphy warned that the presence of "a hostile element in France at the back of our Army of Occupation" made the threat more foreboding.[35] The European Division's French sources agreed. Bonbright scribbled on Murphy's note that Madame Geneviève Tabouis – a familiar source with connections to US military intelligence – told him the previous Thursday that she had heard that "the Communists would try to seize power around the time of Bastille Day" in July.[36]

Other officials offered variations when their predictions of a coup failed to materialize. Based on anti-communist sources "close" to the PCF and trade union movement,[37] Caffery reported that the party could intend to exploit dissatisfaction to discredit the government and force de Gaulle to enlarge communist representation in cabinet posts. Another informant close to the PCF, Caffery said, indicated that Moscow did not desire civil strife in France but would welcome PCF attempts to gain more influence in the government. The source further suggested that the PCF had failed to seize power in August 1944 due to its weakness within Paris Police ranks, and that the party's new strategy was to "bore from within" all branches of the government.[38]

The infiltration or "bore from within" theory was a convenient way to subsume all communist activity within a larger conspiracy, thus denying the possibility that the party's action was anything other than a veiled attempt to seize power in France. Later that summer, Caffery further reported that a "former and important member of Comintern" told him "the present tactics of the PCF remind him of the policy pursued by the Bolsheviks in 1917 in conquering the Leningrad Soviet."[39] In another adaptation of the "infiltration" thesis, a high official in the Interior Ministry suggested to Caffery that communists were positioning them-selves as a party in, but not of, the government; they could thus continue to undermine the regime through spreading influence in the bureaucracy while avoiding blame for government failures. Caffery noted with interest that PCF instructions to its officials insisted that while it is the most capable of governing France, the PCF "is not a party of the government" and that its members "should exert every effort to destroy the capitalist regime of which the present government is the representative."[40] Thus, the PCF had apparently undergone no essential changes since the war, and had only returned to its prewar methods. Such reporting showed that the perception of an ever-present threat of a communist coup could be readily adapted to evolving circumstances, and contradictions in reporting could be easily explained away as mere changes in PCF tactics.

Most administration officials agreed that the PCF intended to "seize power" in France, regardless of the method. But they arrived at this conclusion often by committing fundamental errors in intelligence analy-sis: conflating capabilities with intentions and failing to recognize inherent contradictions in their logic. At the end of July, embassy analyst Norris Chipman reported his observations about the PCF. Outspoken in his beliefs, Chipman was one of Raymond Murphy's allies and a former colleague of Loy Henderson and George Kennan in Riga. Although he was assigned to the embassy in Paris as second secretary, Chipman's wife Fanny later remarked that Chipman had very specific duties at the embassy; his main responsibility there was to report on communist activities.[41] Chipman was unsurprisingly pessimistic about France's future and about PCF intentions in postwar France. And, like other hardliners, Chipman assumed that the Soviets controlled PCF activity. To prove his claims of Soviet direction, Chipman pointed to PCF homages to Stalin and defense of Soviet policies, internal statutes (dating from before the war) stating party membership in Comintern, and failure to repudiate prewar Comintern decisions. Furthermore, he pointed out that communist dogma still insisted upon destruction of "the machine of the State" and a "dictatorship of the proletariat." Chipman suggested too, as right-wing French elements had, that the tactics of the PCF remained the same as prior to the war; "the party platforms announced to the public may appear patriotic and democratic, but the party line given to militants," he said, is that "real patriotism requires primary loyalty to the Soviet Union and real democracy can be achieved only through the dictatorship of the 'new elite' of the nation, that is, the communists."[42] And again, Chipman demonstrated embassy reliance on literal readings of communist propaganda to discern PCF motives: "Judging by communist material published during the past 25 years," he argued, "there are ample grounds for believing that the French Communist Party is a powerful 'Trojan Horse' which is harnessed to Moscow."[43] In this context, subsequent intelligence analysis provided concrete details that seemed to support department assertions about communist intentions. Just ten days before the election, the War Department's new Strategic Services Unit (SSU) forwarded intelligence to the State Department conveying an Army Counterintelligence Corps (CIC) report that a communist arms cache had been found in Nîmes. The arms were allegedly confirmed to belong to communists when they tried to recover them. Moreover, instructions accompanying the arms indicated that they were to be used "between October 25 and 30 in the event that the elections were unfavorable to the party."[44] As we will see, alarmist reports like this became more common over the next two years as the Cold War deepened.

And yet Chipman's analysis contained an inherent contradiction. If the PCF was then directly controlled by Moscow – a point of intense debate among historians even today – then the Soviets should have been a powerful brake on any revolutionary tendencies because they still desired good relations with the West in 1945. Moreover, it is not clear why the PCF would pursue nationwide strikes while they retained preponderance in the assembly and a legal path to power. Furthermore, intelligence analysts failed to consider other explanations for alleged arms caches. France was awash in weapons after the war. At the same time, there was mounting evidence that rightist groups were engaged in stowing and moving weapons; moreover, arms smuggling to aid political causes outside of France was also widespread.

There was, of course, no communist coup after the French elections in October 1945. But administration officials could still point to the "boring from within" thesis. Caffery suggested that PCF demands for one of the big three ministries – Interior, Foreign Affairs, and War – was proof. Furthermore, all but one of the party's proposed ministers were veteran Stalinists and Comintern operatives.[45] And despite the PCF's support for de Gaulle's election as the president of the Provisional Government in November, Caffery viewed communist leader Jacques Duclos' statement reserving the party's right "to express their opinion on subject of composition of cabinet and program of government," as further proof of a communist attempt to dictate terms to the government, rather than a powerful political party hoping to wield its influence in proportion to its electoral following.[46]

That winter, battle lines were drawn, and a political crisis over the composition of the next government ensued. However, French sources let the Americans know that the government was aware of communist plans and working to thwart them. De Gaulle, for one, accused the PCF of domination by Moscow and refused their entreaties for one of the big three ministries. The general, Caffery said, was well aware of communist hostility to him and would resist efforts to replace him through appeals to the French people and the support of those opposed to communism.[47] On December 29, the Information Group reported that a former French deputy had notified them about communist front organizations in France operating as centers in the "clandestine and propaganda network of the French Communist Party and the Communist International." The French secret services, this source said, had responded aggressively to stop these activities.[48] The same former French deputy also told the Information Group that Gaullist secret services had informed him that they had provided the general with a plan for a political attack on the PCF in the event of their break with the government. They had damning evidence of collusion and special favors granted to certain PCF leaders by the Vichy regime, especially in securing their releases from prison. The source felt that this information, if released at an opportune time, "would greatly influence opinion among the labor classes."[49]

A PARTY OF GOVERNMENT

Assessments of the French situation and the threat posed by the PCF were not uniformly pessimistic. In fact, the OSS and the military attaché in Paris hewed closely to a more liberal, pro-Gaullist perspective and suggested a much more hopeful image of French affairs. While they acknowledged the economic and political difficulties facing de Gaulle, these observers argued that he was still firmly in control from the outset of 1945. Nor was he to blame for communist strength in France; that was, instead, a product of legitimate working class grievances, misery brought on by the war, and the communist role in the Resistance. OSS analysts continued to view the PCF as a legitimate political party. Military Attaché Ralph Smith thought it embodied revolutionary potential, but none of them believed that the PCF possessed the strength or the intent to seize power in France in the near term. At the same time, these analysts argued that pro-American sentiment prevailed in France. Perhaps even more importantly, they suggested ways in which the perception of a communist threat was shaping Franco-American relations by providing French officials an avenue by which they could encourage American support that might otherwise have not been forthcoming. Indeed, just days after Roosevelt's death, OSS analyst Ramon Guthrie, now in Paris, offered critical insight into French political behavior that went unnoticed by Truman and his advisers. Of great significance, Guthrie's sources – influential Socialists – suggested the efficacy of using the threat of communism as a political and diplomatic tactic: "At San Francisco or at a peace conference, a France that threaten[s] to become the standard-bearer of a socialized Europe, unless her needs are attended to," they argued, "would have more bargaining power than a France trying to court Anglo-American favor and allay misgivings by an excessive display of moderation."[50] In other words, it was clear to French officials that they would get more out of the Americans by playing up the threat posed by communism than they would by convincing them of their competence and skill.

Differences in analysis were related to French sources. But in 1945, the analysts themselves assumed even more importance. As noted in the previous chapter, OSS analysts tended to come from academic circles with depth of knowledge and experience in French affairs. Military Attaché General Ralph Smith had commanded an army division at Saipan. However, he understood more than island battlefields in the Pacific. Known for his calm and stoic demeanor, he was also an intellectual who spoke fluent French, had studied at the Sorbonne and the École de Guerre, and whom General George Marshall recognized as an expert on the French military.[51]

These observers roundly denied claims of French government weakness and communist collusion. After conversations with members of the French government and various political parties, Smith's assistant military attaché, David Rockefeller, reported in July that de Gaulle was in a stronger position and had displayed political acumen. Rockefeller, an economist and the grandson of John D. Rockefeller, also spoke fluent French. He argued that de Gaulle had successfully forced the hand of the left over upcoming elections, having presented them with a fait accompli – in the form of his plan for elections and the referendum in October – before they had a chance to meet in a planned gathering of the Estates General on July 14. This course of action was, Rockefeller argued, "bold and showed a considerable understanding on his part of political maneuvers."[52]

The newly formed State Department IRIS also refuted persistent claims of de Gaulle's lack of adaptability and weakness in the face of the revolutionary movement. Days before the October elections, IRIS distributed "The Political Ideas of Charles de Gaulle," an unvarnished recounting of de Gaulle's prewar rightist, semi-fascist tendencies in his approaches to foreign policy and his traditional imperialist views. During the war, they argued, he was forced into an alliance with the leftist-dominated Resistance movement, and he began to emphasize interdependence between France and its allies as a means to restore France's power and to recognize the necessity for reform in the empire. Since Liberation, they said, he had assumed the role of arbiter between divergent elements of the national community; he defended conservative interests threatened by revolutionary tendencies but refused to identify with the status quo. The report asserted that, despite his shift leftward during the war, de Gaulle actually played a counterrevolutionary role in the post-Liberation period by diluting the embryonic revolution emerging from the Resistance and by subordinating resistance elements to the regular army and committees of Liberation to the central government. His recent conflict with the Resistance had necessitated strengthening the authority of the state. Moreover, his advocacy of reform was not an end but rather a means to restore French power. Thus, any changes in de Gaulle's thought pattern, they argued, were not due to changes in fundamental principles (or communist collusion) but rather an adaptation to different circumstances.[53]

In a conversation with new Assistant Military Attaché Thomas Hammond in late November, André Dewavrin, the infamous head of de Gaulle's foreign intelligence service, also denied charges of government weakness. A young man at thirty-four, Dewavrin was tall with thinning blond hair and piercing blue eyes "whose constant scanning unnerved those who dealt with him." Known by his nom de guerre "Colonel Passy," he had joined the Free French and built up Gaullist intelligence networks during the war; in the process, he also acquired a formidable list of enemies who accused him of operating a Gestapo-like office and associating with far-right associations like La Cagoule.[54] Passy argued that de Gaulle was firmly in command of the situation and positioned to play the three major parties against each other. The PCF, he said, would not support de Gaulle's foreign policy because they were loyal only to Moscow, but the SFIO and MRP would likely support the general's initiatives. Generally speaking, one-third of the French population was probably leaning communist, he argued, with the other two-thirds non-communist supporting de Gaulle. The PCF, he said, would not get one of the big three ministries; they would instead likely be offered National Economy or Agriculture, ministries that have serious problems no matter who is in charge; these are also posts, Passy said, in which de Gaulle thinks he can observe and control the activity of communists.[55]

OSS analysis also contrasted with other administration reporting on PCF capabilities and intent to seize power in France in the near term. Guthrie's Socialist sources in April placed PCF actions within a postwar context in which most parties agreed that the French system required major restructuring. They argued that progress was immediately vital for war-torn France; the PCF desired unity, they said, but felt obligated to ensure the implementation of critical reforms. Once the PCF determined that deference was not getting results in the best interest of France, that political apathy akin to reaction was hurting French prestige in international affairs, or that it was not solving food and economic problems and could stall "the bloodless revolution that France must have in order to get in step with the rest of the world," the sources argued, "the communists will emerge as an active opposition once more and other leftist parties will be obliged to follow their example."[56]

While State Department (and embassy) analysts attributed much of the tumult in France to communist agitation, OSS analysts gave legitimacy to working class grievances and reported that discontent among workers was related to quality of life concerns rather than a particular ideology. The cost of living was rising while wages remained frozen; this meant that most workers earned only one-third of what they needed for subsistence. The OSS further reported that the CGT had tried to be a moderate force and prevent strikes but that it had been overwhelmed and some groups had taken direct action on their own.[57] One-day strikes by coal miners in the Rhône over food shortages and low wages would continue, they said, as long as living conditions failed to improve; they were not a precursor to insurrection.[58] Under these conditions, it was hardly surprising that the left used elections results to press economic and political reforms. Far from fomenting a coup, the PCF on May 20 called for greater participation in the government and immediate action on reforms.[59] OSS Paris further noted PCF leaders' continued insistence on the French basis of communist ideas, warnings against "opportunism" and "ultraleftism," and reaffirmations of their willingness to support the government and their desire take a more active role in governing the nation.[60]

Even though General Smith viewed the PCF with some suspicion, he too continued to dismiss arguments that communist action was imminent. He accepted Interior Ministry claims about communist arms caches throughout the country, but he also noted that French officials believed that a communist coup was presently unlikely unless the international situation were to dramatically change in the next few months.[61] In July, Assistant Attaché David Rockefeller noted that two communist ministers had voted with the cabinet in announcing elections before the Estates General could convene, despite this plan being at odds with PCF desires, and he concluded that this demonstrated that PCF leaders did not believe they had the strength to take over the government at the present time. "Radical change in the government," he said, is "unlikely before the elections."[62]

Subsequent OSS reporting confirmed that the communists had no intention of passing into opposition. On July 12, 1945, OSS Paris detailed the PCF's 10th Party Congress held in Paris the last week in June. The PCF, much like the PCI in Italy, was the largest organized party in France, though not necessarily in popularity. While the PCF claimed 900,000 members, OSS experts believed the number was closer to 600,000, but noted the party's dramatic growth. More than four-fifths of current members, they pointed out, joined since September 1944. This was a crucial distinction. Most party members were not hardened militants but people who recognized the role of the party in the Resistance and yearned for a change from the prewar status quo. OSS analysts further suggested that the PCF would focus on production and democratization. Communists planned to push for early elections and direct popular vote for a Constituent Assembly with full powers, which they believed would increase the party's influence.[63] Most importantly, PCF leaders wanted to avoid isolation of their party and seek alliances with all groups. OSS analysts also directly challenged the "boring within" and "coup" theses. The PCF, they argued, sought open political contest – through elections – because they believed this was the best way to check the "uncontrolled maneuvers of their enemies in the government."[64] As Smith had argued, OSS analysts believed that the communists would remain in the government, without admitting that it was fully representative of the people as then constituted, until they could achieve a greater popular mandate from national elections that would allow for a shift to the left.[65]

OSS assessments and analysis out of Smith's office also doubted the depths of anti-American and pro-Russian sentiment in France. In mid-May 1945, OSS analysts and Military Attaché General Smith noted that news of the German collapse was greeted with great celebration in Paris. In contrast to other military sources, Smith detected no anti-Americanism, reporting that the press and crowds he had encountered were friendly to the United States. However, he did detect growing hostility to Russia in official circles and the press due to concerns about Stalin's exclusion of the London Poles from postwar governance and other repressive Soviet behavior in Eastern Europe. This all pushed France in the direction of the United States, he said, although a spate of recent misunderstandings over de Gaulle's effort to secure a French zone of occupation in Stuttgart and French annexationist claims in the Italian region of Val d'Aosta had prevented a visible improvement in relations at the official level. But Smith warned that the continued perception of an American occupation would strain matters, as would continued shortages of food and clothing. American economic assistance, he argued, "can either be made a means of cementing Franco-American friendship, or if it is mishandled, it can prove to be an additional factor in breaking down Franco-American understanding."[66] Koren in Paris also noted widespread feelings of being let down by the Russians, especially over French efforts to restore control over the Levant. Despite US support for the British intervention to stop a French assault upon native regimes in Syria and Lebanon in May, there did not seem to be any hostility toward Americans.[67]

A PARTY IN GOVERNMENT

For their part, French officials were keenly aware of American fear that a weakened France would fall prey to the PCF. They thus sought to both increase awareness of the dangers posed by domestic communism and to dispute characterizations of weakness (like those put forward by outside groups hoping to discredit rivals in the government) to make the case for increased economic aid and support for French policy positions through their contact with American diplomats and intelligence officers. Like their American counterparts, they viewed the PCF as a grave threat to the government's authority. However, French internal memoranda indicate divergence over the PCF's immediate intentions and the nature of the threat. Gaullist officials and PCF officials alike suggested that the communists were eager to remain a part of the government, and to participate in the French political community from a position that PCF leaders believed they had earned from their role in the Resistance and their showing in French elections.

Officials in Paris knew that French recovery depended on American assistance. They remained preoccupied with American perceptions of France because these images would shape Franco-American engagement and the degree of US benevolence in the critical years to come. In August, one observer warned about the persistence of anti-Gaullism in American policy and among certain US officials, as well as the unfortunate effect of American soldiers returning from France with stories of poor treatment by the French public. He also alerted them to the continued nefarious influence of "the émigrés of 1940" – many of whom had become naturalized US citizens while maintaining a claim to speak in the name of France – and others who had come to the United States after Liberation. Many of these informants, it should be noted, continued to provide information to stateside MIS units and State Department officials. This observer believed that infighting between French factions shocked Americans and created a dreadful spectacle where "each French is the representative of a social or political clan, full of open bitterness against other French."[68]

French intelligence officials also recognized the growing concern of their American allies about the leftward drift in French political affairs. They reported that the White House had asked US intelligence services in France to list communist officers on the French military staff; it also requested biographies of individuals who may be called to lead in the event of de Gaulle's departure, analysis of the chances for the various political parties in the next elections, the means and numbers of the PCF, and, finally, the security of American lines of communication.[69] To French officials, these requests further demonstrated American preoccupation with communism in France and its potential impact on French military readiness. It also hinted at American doubts about de Gaulle's longevity and their concerns about the political complexion of France in the event of his departure.

In late August, officials in the Foreign Ministry's American Bureau reported conversations about European problems with Assistant Secretary of State James Dunn, H. Freeman Matthews, and Soviet expert

Chip Bohlen. The Americans "greatly fear the possibility of a government of the extreme left," one official wrote. French leaders, he further suggested, should take advantage of any goodwill on the part of the American government to consolidate their positions. It is likely that de Gaulle's growing anti-communist rhetoric and refusal to entertain communist demands for one of the big three cabinet posts in November was directly related to this understanding. The author further warned that there were "enemies of the French in the president's entourage." Admiral Leahy in particular, he said, exerted great influence over Truman and the military chiefs, a development certainly not favorable to France. He warned that the government should ensure that reports from American representatives in France were not hostile, because the complaints of US soldiers and businessmen in France have sympathetic ears in the US. Important Americans had warned him, "you will only discover in steps ... the consequences of this period in Franco-American relations, but you will recognize yourselves that the repercussions will be deep."[70] Other French reports indicated that the best way to argue for de Gaulle with Americans was "to insist on his anti-communism and on the communist campaign against him."[71] After the resolution of the French political crisis in November, French intelligence reinforced this assessment, reporting that American reaction to de Gaulle's refusal to entertain communist demands was positive in all circles. Americans were becoming more anti-communist, and they thus appreciated de Gaulle's actions terminating a situation viewed in Washington, DC, as extremely serious.[72] The message was clear; the best way to assert authority and shape American engagement in France was to highlight the communist threat and the government's anti-communist character.

French anti-communism was hardly manufactured for the benefit of the Americans. Despite communist participation in the government, many French officials believed that the PCF intended to infiltrate and discredit the government. In June, one of de Gaulle's advisers (likely Gaston Palewski) showed him a document allegedly from the Central Committee of the PCF, detailing a meeting of communist cell leaders in Paris. The document was reportedly obtained from a Paris factory worker, Palewski said, and it contained directives to continue "infiltration" of government ministries (especially the Ministry of War) and the police by pursuing a "Trojan Horse" policy, to discredit government ministers, continue communist agitation on pretext of insufficient supply, and to denigrate de Gaulle and the foreign policy of the government. It is likely that French intelligence shared this information with their American counterparts, as it was reflected in subsequent American assessments of the situation. However, communist directives also suggested less conspiratorial reasons for these attacks on de Gaulle; they also underscored the Soviet desire to maintain good relations with the United States, a point that Raymond Murphy and MIS analysts seemed to ignore. Such tactics were necessary, the directives said, because de Gaulle did not keep his promises and that, even if he did, he could not be trusted as a Catholic and man of the right. However, they recommended proceeding cautiously; the Soviets did not want to upset the United States.[73]

For their part, the PCF claimed that elements of the government were fomenting labor troubles as a pretext for government repression and establishment of a dictatorship of reactionary elements. The press, CGT leader Benoît Frachon argued, had exaggerated the character of one-day strikes in the railroads and coal industries, one of which was, he claimed, merely a reaction to management intentions to employ a well-known collaborator as a foreman in a coal mine. Moreover, he pointed out that he had helped to avert other strikes. This was, Frachon said, a clear attempt to divide the Resistance and to divide workers from the middle class and peasants with the specter of disorder and strikes. He warned against those in the government who sought "personal power," an obvious reference to de Gaulle.[74]

Subsequent French government reports suggested that PCF officials were pursuing a cautious policy. They believed that PCF participation in government was necessary to avoid the appearance of opposing a government with a patriotic character. Nor did they wish to provoke any trouble before the elections that could lead to a backlash in public opinion.[75] At the same time, however, other reports suggested that the PCF would continue political maneuvers against de Gaulle, hoping to discredit its rival, obtain a majority in the assembly, thus forcing the selection of a new chief of government more amenable to their program.[76] PCF officials also apparently recognized that the confluence between PCF and Soviet policy could damage their position given Soviet obstruction of French postwar designs. One government report indicated that certain PCF leaders believed "it would be prudent not to unreflectively support Moscow's foreign policy, or least not too visibly."[77]

The French Interior Ministry's analysis of the elections in October determined that PCF leaders were generally happy with the results and awaited decisions made by the next leader elected by the assembly to form a government. However, the report warned that if the party was left outside the government, it was certain that it would provoke unrest in short order, another assessment likely shared with American colleagues. But the report also suggested that if the party held sufficient numbers in the government, then party policy would be to profit from its success in order to take power during the next elections in May or June.[78] De Gaulle believed that the communists remained very eager to stay in the government and doubted that they would set out difficult conditions.[79] French government analysis, then, suggested that the PCF aimed to become the governing party through victories at the ballot box, rather than by fomenting insurrection.

For their part, PCF leaders indicated that they would demand full representation in the new government in accordance with their electoral strength. Benoît Frachon also suggested that the party would continue to emphasize production and reconstruction, and he said that they would be willing to work with MRP elements that sincerely desired social and economic reforms based on the CNR program. The communists remained opposed to a Western bloc, but still favored friendship with the United States and Britain. When asked by a member of the US embassy staff what the PCF would do if they were excluded from the government – a somewhat leading question – Frachon responded that this would lead to "unavoidable discontent and disorders would arise and France might be 'Balkanized.'"[80] This was not a call to arms but instead a warning that attempts to disenfranchise a powerful voting bloc could further destabilize and divide France.

On November 15, PCF leader Maurice Thorez wrote de Gaulle that "the French people await the formation of a government in the image of the nation in order to apply the program of the CNR." The Constituent Assembly had given the communists a mandate, and they were ready to assume a large part of the responsibility of governing. He asked thus for fair representation in the number and importance of jobs in the different ministries, and that a PCF member hold one of the big three ministries. De Gaulle again refused to give them one of the major ministries, invoking questions about the patriotism and policies of the PCF. Thorez agreed to sacrifice for the sake of national unity but said that he could not accept the reasons that de Gaulle invoked; this was, he said, "an outrage to the memory of 75,000 communists who died for France and for freedom."[81]

WHO WILL STOP ATTILA?

Franco-American relations were also shaped by genuine and growing fear of Soviet aggression. Both governments watched Soviet actions in Eastern

Europe with alarm. Many in the State Department had maligned the Franco-Soviet Pact in December 1944 and charged de Gaulle with moving France into the Soviet orbit. However, it soon became apparent that the French government was disappointed with the alliance and recognized the necessity of good relations between France and the United States. French informants thus attempted to utilize their contact with American diplomats and intelligence analysts to convince them of the common threat posed by the Soviet Union and to whitewash differences over other policy concerns. This threat again provided a powerful framework under which French officials could hope to shape US policies to their advantage. On the international level, the analysis emanating from various US agencies was largely in sync. All detected growing hostility toward the Soviets among their French counterparts and their efforts to reset Franco-American relations. OSS and Smith's office's analysis also continued to highlight pro-American tendencies within the French government and underscored the realpolitik that had driven French engagement with the Soviet Union in the first place; MIS reports provided concrete examples of Soviet subterfuge, which served to confirm more alarmist assessments. Of note, however, OSS analysts warned against loose talk of war between the United States and the Soviet Union then circulating in Paris.

In the spring of 1945, as the Soviet Union consolidated its position in Eastern Europe, French officials had repeatedly drawn American attention to the dangers of Soviet expansionism. It was a way to ensure that the United States would not retreat into isolation, leaving France vulnerable to renewed German aggression or Soviet domination. They expressed both fear and apprehension over the future of France, Foreign Minister Georges Bidault asking Caffery on April 20, "who is going to stop Attila; he is covering more territory every day."[82] In early May, Caffery reported that a number of observers had expressed fear that the PCF would blackmail the government into supporting Soviet foreign policy; French communists, these sources argued, were "a strong weapon, which Moscow will not overlook in implementing Soviet foreign policy."[83] Other influential Frenchmen, Caffery said, "fear Soviet domination of Europe, including France, and refer frequently to the 'unilateral Soviet action' in central Europe and the Balkans as a portent of things to come."[84]

French officials also routinely framed other international issues – such as the future of Germany, France's alignment in Europe, and support for French recovery – within the context of a growing Soviet threat in their discussions with American representatives. After the Stuttgart dispute over occupation zones, de Gaulle told Caffery that France's allies must recognize its right to participate in decisions that touch directly upon French interests.[85] He deftly tied this to Soviet advances in Europe, and warned that Russia was poised to take over the entire continent.[86] There would be only two poles after the war, he said. The French would, of course, prefer to work with the United States; however, if America could not meet France's needs, then he would have to work with the Soviets in order to survive, "even if in the long run they will gobble us up too."[87] Among his grievances against the United States he included the failure to supply coal and other promised supplies, lack of substantial assistance to help rebuild the French military, and the exclusion of France from the Big Three negotiations. "Your people seem to think that France is going to fall in any event," de Gaulle charged, "but she would not fall if you helped her."[88] Alarmed over the Russian arrest of Polish leaders, de Gaulle asked Caffery the next day about stopping the Soviets. "You are the only ones that can do anything about it," he argued. "You have the cards as they are hoping to obtain so many things from you."[89] Not long after, William Donovan told Harry Truman that the head of French intelligence told him that he had been with de Gaulle the day before and had never seen him so distressed over Soviet aggression in Europe.[90]

On May 17, OSS Paris reported that its government sources – local prefects, regional commissioners, and an official in the Ministry of National Economy – again tied the German settlement to the PCF and Soviet influence in France in order to bend American policy. These sources claimed they feared a backlash against the United States because they had not let the French people exploit the industrialized and coal-rich areas of the Saar and Ruhr valleys. This would, they said, play into the hands of the PCF, which would not otherwise have been so popular, and would thus draw France away from Anglo-American influence and into a "closer political and economic association with Russia."[91] Caffery wrote the same day that Bidault told him the French were very fearful of a centralized German government because they believed the Soviets would use that government to Sovietize all of Germany and reach the French frontier.[92] Two days later, Foreign Ministry official Jean Chauvel told Caffery in strict confidence that the USSR was working toward the establishment of a central German Communist government. A Soviet-controlled Germany, Caffery said, is "a nightmare to most Frenchmen."[93]

De Gaulle again brought up Germany when he traveled to Washington, DC, to meet with Harry Truman that August. He reasserted French claims to the Rhineland and demanded the internationalization of the Ruhr. He also expressed concern over the possibility of a reconstructed central authority in Germany that could be dominated by the Russians, forming a powerful Slavic bloc. When Truman insisted that the German threat should not be exaggerated, de Gaulle responded that a weak Germany made it "all the more susceptible of becoming the political instrument of other Powers."[94] In subsequent talks with Secretary of State Byrnes, Bidault again raised the specter of Soviet domination of Germany, extending Soviet influence to France's borders, concerns which Byrnes again dismissed as unfounded.[95]

Meanwhile, OSS analysts and General Smith noted French apprehensions about the international situation and their desire to align with the United States. In May, Smith noted the growing hostility toward Russia in official circles and the press. Concerns about the Polish government, the peace settlement, and Russian actions in Eastern Europe, he said, pushed the French closer to the United States even if there had been tension over French actions in Northwest Italy and Stuttgart. The French were not as friendly toward the Soviets as they had been after the Franco-Soviet Pact, he argued, and they hoped to strengthen their relationship with the United States.[96] Even State Department officials, who had routinely charged French officials with anti-Americanism, now seemed more convinced of their sincerity and worthiness as an ally. Matthews wrote to Dunn that both de Gaulle and Bidault had been disturbed by Soviet actions in Eastern Europe and by the success of the PCF in French elections. Despite recent disputes, there are indications, he said, that the French are realizing that American friendship is crucial to gaining economic assistance and in protecting their position in Europe.[97] A high Interior Ministry official, known to be both pro-American and Gaullist, told a member of Caffery's staff about Soviets meddling in French affairs; by implication, he suggested that this was related to PCF preparations to move into open opposition to the government. The source expressed the strong belief that de Gaulle was ready to move France firmly into the Anglo-American orbit. He suggested too that if the United States gave France important economic assistance "very cordial relations would ensue, and the 'Communist danger' would be largely eliminated."[98]

De Gaulle's intelligence chief André Dewavrin secretly contacted Assistant Military Attaché Colonel Thomas Hammond in another important attempt by French officials to gloss over past differences with the United States. Caffery, who sent a copy of Colonel Hammond's intelligence report to Washington, DC, in November, noted that Passy was very anti-Soviet and that Hammond's report was of interest because Passy had probably emphasized French friendship with the United States, believing that his remarks would be conveyed to American authorities and could help to ease the negative effects of French actions in Stuttgart and Val d'Aosta. Moreover, Passy was close to de Gaulle, and his comments represented the opinion of friendly French officials "who, for the past several months have been emphasizing that de Gaulle is becoming increasingly conscious of the communist menace and therefore wishes to do everything possible to cause past Franco-American misunderstanding to be forgotten."[99] Indeed, Passy told Hammond that French survival depended on close relations with the United States. The Soviet Union, a nation then of 170 million, now stood opposed to Britain and France; if they were to withstand an attack, they could only do so with the United States. De Gaulle, Passy said, knows this, and is determined to get along with his American allies. Passy indicated that he was, personally, not pro or anti-Soviet but that he recognized that the USSR, with a huge population and immense power, could be "a very dangerous instrument in the hands of a madman."[100] The only way for the British, French, and the Americans to avoid "being Russians," he said, was to stand together. The job of Americans in Paris, he argued, is to convince the American public of France's determination to be a close ally of the United States above all other considerations. When asked about Germany, Passy dismissed the question with impatience; "the fate of Germany [is] not of immediate concern as is Russia," he said, and France would not allow anything to interfere with strong relations with the United States "to ensure the survival and independence of France."[101] This was a shocking revelation, given French determination to shape the German settlement in France's favor. It was likely reflective of growing French appreciation that the Americans hoped to use German soldiers against the Soviets, and their belief that the long-term presence of US forces in Germany fulfilled some of their security concerns. The secret nature of the contact meant that Passy could hint at flexibility even when French officials could not admit it in public.

OSS analysts, however, warned that the fear of another conflict had assumed dangerous proportions in France. On May 11, John Sawyer, an economic historian who later served as the head of Williams College, reported that there was "widespread loose talk" among the French of a US–Russian war.[102] This atmosphere also worried members of Congress. On July 3, 1945, a bipartisan group of senators who had worked with Truman on a Senate Committee investigating the National Defense Program met with him about their recent trip to Europe. Above all, they believed that Roosevelt's policy of cooperation with the Soviets was in jeopardy. They reported that American representation in Europe (England excepted) was very weak, especially in France and Italy. They expressed particular concern about "uncurbed, provocative talk about the possibilities and even the desirability of hostilities with the Russians" common among the highest US officials in both nations.[103] Caffery, for one, had complained that he did not like the people running France because they "did not know anything about the business of governing a nation" and that "unfortunately the people who did know this business were all in jail as collaborators."[104] The senators reported that it was very clear that Caffery believed that the Soviet Union would be a grave threat against which France should be built up as a bulwark, whereas Eisenhower and Ambassador John Winant in England still seemed to believe that US and Russian interests could be compatible. These senators appealed to Truman to clarify American foreign policy, and also to ensure better administration and personnel in America's European embassies.[105] As Martin Weil has pointed out, however, "it was difficult to make an occasional visit carry the weight of a steady succession of official cables based on an apparent expert knowledge of European politics."[106] Although the congressmen were unable to alter Truman's course that summer, French warnings and entreaties for assistance still had an effect. Despite France's "pathological craving for prestige," State Department officials in late June recommended treating France based on her "potential" rather than her current situation because the French had valuable international experience and sway over lesser European nations,[107] another remarkable shift in policy in light of the changing international situation.

Despite improvement in Franco-American relations, the feeling of crisis only intensified in the weeks before the French elections in October. On the 8th, the Army's Information Group reported that a former French deputy told them that the center of Moscow's liaison with Western Europe was located in the Soviet Embassy in Paris. The source also reported that, as late as January, the French Interior Ministry was aware that transport planes were taking off from the Dalmatian Coast and dropping Soviet and Eastern European agitators in Haute-Savoie every night. Moreover, these planes also dropped containers filled with portable arms and explosives. The informant also asserted that de Gaulle's intelligence had found evidence of gold traffic near the Swiss border for the benefit of the Comintern. French secret services, he said, were also convinced that Thorez had returned from Moscow with two billion francs.[108]

On December 7, Caffery wrote Washington, DC, that de Gaulle told him the night before that "there are only two real forces in France today:

the communists and I [*sic*]. If the communists win, France will be a Soviet Republic; if I win, France will stay independent."[109] And when Caffery asked who would prevail, de Gaulle replied, "if I get any breaks at all, especially in the international field, I will win."[110] He again expressed great fear of Germany becoming Soviet-dominated, a grave menace for France and Europe; if France fell, he argued, Western Europe would follow, and the whole continent would fall under communist control. De Gaulle also warned that continued shortages of coal and wheat would make the winter even harder and breed discontent favoring communism. These were extraordinary circumstances, which he implied could be remediated with American help.[111]

Privately, French officials worried about Soviet meddling in French domestic affairs as relations between the two nations steadily worsened. Back in the summer, French officials had discovered that Soviet military representatives had arrested, in France, six members of the Confédération Française des Travailleurs Chrétiens (CFTC) of Ukrainian origin. On August 9, 1945, the Foreign Ministry sent a note to the Soviet embassy protesting arrests on French soil.[112] A week later, de Gaulle gave orders to arrest Soviet soldiers engaged in police operations on French soil and put them before a tribunal. The Interior Minister further authorized force to oppose any interference in French affairs by foreign authorities or citizens.[113]

As the summer had worn on, tensions between the French and Soviet governments continued to grow. On September 21, 1945, Pierre Charpentier, the French chargé d'affaires in Moscow, wrote to Bidault about Soviet press reactions to de Gaulle's statement about a "Western bloc" in the London *Times* on September 10. Just nine months after the signing of the Franco-Soviet Pact, the Russian press now claimed that the French government and de Gaulle did not represent the aspirations of the French people, and they accused de Gaulle of trying to drive a wedge between the allies.[114] In October, Soviet Ambassador Alexander Bogomolov listed a number of grievances, such the treatment of the Soviet Union in the French press, which accused it of intrigue and imperialist designs, France's failure to support the Soviet position on the administration of occupied Germany, and its alignment with the Anglo-Saxons on other issues. Bogomolov asked if French policy toward the Soviets had changed despite their common interests and Soviet support for de Gaulle in difficult times. French Ambassador to the Soviet Union General Georges Catroux responded that the French had greeted the Franco-Soviet alliance with great warmth but had become disillusioned when the Soviets failed to help France regain her strength or status and even opposed the French in their desire to be included in the peace settlement for Eastern Europe.[115]

A Foreign Ministry report in late October further listed the difficulties: Soviet reserve toward France's demands on Germany and French participation in international conferences; Soviet attacks against an occidental bloc and their attempts to tie French claims to the Rhineland to this issue; Soviet encouragement of an Arab League that emanated hostility to France; and problems with the repatriation of French POWs and with Soviet activity on French soil, including refusals to grant French access to Soviet repatriation camps and arrests of Soviet nationals who wished to remain in France.[116] A few weeks later, another report from Moscow indicated considerable interest in the French political crisis there, and especially in the letter from Thorez to de Gaulle. It also noted that de Gaulle's prestige in Russia had declined after his supposed advocacy for a Western bloc.[117]

In mid-December, Catroux wrote that the anniversary of the Franco-Soviet Pact had not been officially commemorated, as one would envisage. The French government, he said, can expect that its claims to the Rhineland and Ruhr would be viewed unfavorably. The Soviets were angry, he argued, about the French idea of a Western bloc, "which could only be hostile to Moscow and contradicts the tenets and spirit of the pact."[118] Furthermore, he noted that French attempts to maintain a freedom of action in international affairs and align with neither West nor East were viewed by the Soviets as betrayal. "The Soviet conception of the responsibilities of friendship and alliance is exclusive and unilateral," he said, "and is unable to accommodate these affirmations of independence."[119]

French officials also noted their American allies' growing concern about communism and its effect on Franco-American relations. That summer, de Gaulle's adviser Burin des Roziers had reported that French ambassador to the United States Henri Bonnet and Jean Monnet both believed that the Truman administration's desire for better relations was due to American fear of the Soviet Union.[120] Subsequent foreign ministry reports noted this link between American attitudes toward France and "the fear of seeing the Soviet enterprise spread over all of Europe."[121] These reports also suggested that the Americans needed to know more about the French situation and government positions before they could offer their full support. Americans want to like de Gaulle and to help France, the report said, but the French needed to know how to ask them for assistance in "language they understand."[122] US officials certainly understood the emotional language of danger, and French officials thus sought to heighten American appreciation of the threats facing France, while at the same time allaying their worst fears and assuring them of France's resolve in the face of these menaces.

But the French also appreciated the difficulties of France's weakened position and its efforts to regain its prewar standing. Armand Bérard, the counselor to the French Embassy in Washington, DC, wrote the Foreign Ministry that the French people still enjoy enormous sympathy, he said, but that the Stuttgart and Val d'Aosta incidents had resurrected prejudices, and many Americans felt that France was an obsolete nation that offered nothing new. The Americans, he argued, feel like a "jilted lover."[123] The Americans wanted a partner on the continent, and they awaited from France, a past wellspring of political ideas and a model of resistance and liberation for Europe, the solution to the problem of European democracy; that is, a way to adapt old democratic formulas to the new situation on the continent. This solution, they felt, would stem the spread of Soviet-inspired communist influence. "Either we appear to the US as a European democracy par excellence," he argued, "or they will lose interest in us."[124] Yet he further noted that they should also avoid the "frequent error of presenting France as the sole rampart against Soviet expansion in Europe. France does not inspire enough confidence for anti-Bolshevik elements," he said, "and the more that [US] officials fear the Soviets," the more they would incline toward an anti-communist agenda.[125]

Whatever the method for bolstering American confidence, Foreign Ministry reports at the end of the year suggested that growing American apprehension about communism had helped to improve de Gaulle's standing. On December 4, Bernard Hardion, the French minister in Spain, wrote to the Quai d'Orsay that Russian action in the Balkans and Italy greatly concerned US officials who viewed it as the pursuit of universal communism directed from Moscow. When Hardion suggested to one of his interlocutors – an American military officer attached to the American Embassy in Spain – that perhaps communism was only a means at the disposition of Russian imperialism and was not necessarily an end in itself, his interlocutor responded that this could be true; however, while the United States could accommodate itself to Russian imperialism, it could never tolerate communism with global pretensions. Hardion's informant went on to say that "the question of communism has become for US such a preoccupation that we can pinpoint when General de Gaulle became popular with Americans – the last French elections."[126] De Gaulle's position against Thorez and Duclos had won

him support in the United States, he argued, and if de Gaulle chased the
PCF from power, he will have "all of the United States behind him ...
[and] that anything he wishes we will give to him ... our aid in this case,
I can assure you, would be total."[127]

* * * * *

By the end of 1945, the range of possibility in French affairs had dramat-
ically narrowed. Hardline anti-communists gained influence in the State
Department, while many wartime intelligence agencies – including the
OSS – predicated on cooperation within the Grand Alliance, disappeared.
They left a crucial void to be filled by military intelligence and State
Department analysts. After the war, intelligence priorities also changed.
OSS analysts, with their array of analytical skills and depth of experience,
provided near-term intelligence as well as long-range assessments and
contextual studies of the issues facing France. As new conflicts emerged in
the immediate postwar period, the focus shifted to current intelligence and
crisis reporting. Relegated to relative obscurity within State Department
bureaucracy, some former OSS analysts continued to provide thoughtful
studies on important French issues, but they never again enjoyed direct
access to senior administration officials. In the process, an important source
of alternative analysis and an essential challenge to entrenched beliefs
was lost.

Although increasingly minimized, OSS analysts in 1945 were again
largely proven right, while State Department, Embassy, and MIS reporting
required constant adjustment to account for outcomes that failed to
materialize. US officials continued to deny de Gaulle's strength and grip
on power in early 1945 until it was apparent to all that he had won
significant victories in French elections that fall. Unprecedented voter
turnout further belied embassy and MIS claims of apathy among the
French public. At the same time, reports that suggested French communists
were strong enough and intent on seizing power also had to be adjusted to
account for the party's emphasis on legality and the fact that the PCF
displayed no intention to withdraw its ministers or break with the government in 1945. State Department experts in Washington, DC and Paris and
MIS analysts also struggled to reconcile their claims that the PCF was
directed by the Soviet Union and intended to foment trouble in France
with the growing recognition that the Soviet Union still desired good
relations with the West. Despite its apparent limitations, administration
views coalesced around this analysis, which foreclosed any real possibility

of cooperation with the PCF. Viewed within the construct of international communism – an image stoked by French officials in contact with American diplomats and intelligence officers – administration officials succumbed to linear thinking that denied the role of the war in French public life; that is, they assumed that the postwar PCF had merely returned to its prewar goals and habits.

This view of the PCF, coupled with fears of Soviet expansionism, was, in large part, a product of French government and émigré efforts. Their assiduous cultivation of American perceptions of crisis invited increased American interest and scrutiny of French affairs, while prescribing important points of engagement: French recovery, the German settlement, and France's role in postwar Europe. French officials did not always succeed in altering US policy in their favor, but they did triumph in many ways. They convinced the United States to treat France based on its potential, rather than its actual position.

At the same time, the American perception of threat in Europe was intimately linked with developments in France's overseas empire. French officials argued that the growth and strength of communist-inspired liberation movements in North Africa and Indochina threatened to undermine France's recovery and status as a bulwark against Soviet inroads in Europe. As we will see, they were able to use this perception of threat to reverse American resistance to French colonialism and, ultimately, to support French efforts to retain control over its prewar colonies, thus contributing to a to a quickening and deepening of a global Cold War.

3

Restoration

Even as the war came to its climax in Europe in early 1945, French officials kept a steady gaze toward France's vast empire and moved quickly to reestablish control in the wake of victorious Allied armies. Agitation in North Africa, the Levant, and Indochina threatened to undermine this enterprise. The empire was crucial not only to France's quest to regain its status as a Great Power but also, French leaders believed, was a necessary salve for domestic unrest. The empire provided raw materials and markets crucial to recovery; it gave a struggling French government a luster of strength. It also became a crucial component of the basic formula French officials used to influence American policy.

As in the metropole, French officials abroad sought to outmaneuver and delegitimize rivals who threatened their authority in a deeply contested domain. They began to explicitly the nationalist agitation in Algeria and the Levant, and in French Indochina, to local communist action and PCF activity inside France. In Algeria, Morocco, and Tunisia, they also traced an apparent evolution in local communist rhetoric from criticism of nationalist activity to collusion aiming for electoral gains, to rejection of the French theory of assimilation in favor of independence. In Indochina, French officials employed the same methods used to discredit de Gaulle's government in 1944 and 1945. They charged the Viet Minh with collusion with the Japanese and of harboring anti-French sentiment; they also argued that Ho Chi Minh's government were inept and ineffective administrators. Internally, French officials acknowledged that the PCF was a political rival rather than an existential threat to the regime; however, the same officials also began to test arguments that they would use in the years to come to convince Americans that local communists and PCF militants alike were part of a monolithic insurrectionary movement aimed at worldwide revolution. While their expressions of fear and sense of crisis were genuine, French officials in Paris made sure to highlight the confluence of domestic, colonial, and international threats posed by the growth of communism in the colonies to their American counterparts. Already in March 1945, months before Germany's surrender and the final showdown with Japan, de Gaulle warned US ambassador to France Jefferson Caffery: "If the public here comes to realize that you are against us in Indochina, there will be terrific disappointment and nobody really knows where that will lead. We do not want to become communist; we do not want to fall into the Russian orbit, but I hope that you do not push us into it."[1]

French officials faced determined anti-colonial sentiment in the United States. For most of the war, Franklin Roosevelt had strongly opposed France's return to Vietnam. However, by April 1945, events began to evolve in France's favor. The growing influence of Europeanists at the expense of the State Department's Far Eastern analysts meant that US officials were focused on France's role in Europe. Deteriorating relations with the Soviet Union amplified France's importance at the heart of Europe and thus the necessity to avoid any blows that could undermine French authority and empower the PCF. And on April 12, Roosevelt, the fiercest of critics of French colonialism, died suddenly in Warm Springs, Georgia. Preoccupied by the threat of domestic French communism, US officials in 1945 appeared less concerned with the future of overseas France, at least for a time. However, American interest would quickly refocus as discontent in France's empire soon exploded into open rebellion and warfare.

US intelligence officials in East Asia and North Africa were hamstrung by other priorities – the denouement of the war in Europe and the coming battle for Japan – and by the personnel shortages that accompanied them and events that disrupted the flow of intelligence from the distant outposts of the French empire back to Washington, DC. A Japanese coup in March 1945 wiped out the intelligence picture in Indochina; at the same time, American intelligence in North Africa assumed a lower priority once the now provisional French government departed Algiers for Paris. Whatever incomplete picture there was, though, it displayed many of the hallmarks of wartime American intelligence reporting on France. OSS liberals retained more sympathy for local peoples – a product, in part, of their contact with colonized populations – and remained less concerned about communism. Most famously, OSS operatives collaborated with Ho Chi Minh.[2] Conservative US military intelligence, while initially focused on defeating the Japanese, reflected its analysts' contact and alignment with French military and colonial elements desperate to retain France's control over its empire – at any cost. While US officials in Washington, DC, remained preoccupied with events in Europe and in the Pacific, a subtle shift was already underway as French officials and a transimperial web of sources sought to convince the Americans that Roosevelt's dream of "trusteeships" and colonial liberation had died with him that spring, another victim of the communist menace threatening the globe anew.

NORTH AFRICA AND THE LEVANT

French colonial representatives were already concerned about the growth of nationalist agitation and sensitive to any alleged connections to local communist activity and the PCF well before war's end. However, in early 1945, French reports suggested that any connection between the two groups was tenuous at best. In January 1945, French military and police intelligence in North Africa underscored some incompatibilities between nationalists and communists and the mutual suspicion and denunciations that undermined any potential collaboration. These officials also reported only limited success of local communist parties in North Africa. However, the same reports warned about eventualities yet unrealized. They suggested that colonized populations and nationalist groups drew from communist propaganda "all that is useful to them" and that a possible entente between the various militant parties could not be excluded. At the same time, the intelligence suggested that, while the "majority" of the French population in North Africa viewed the future of France under de Gaulle with confidence, there was a "pessimistic minority" that contested the solidity of de Gaulle's government in the face of communist progress, again suggesting that rival factions and machinations in the metropole threatened to undermine the authority of the French government in the empire.[3]

General Charles Mast, the resident-general in Tunisia, further underscored the damaging effects of communist political activity and propaganda on January 8, 1945. Communists had taken to criticizing government efforts to provide food and supplies to the population. Further, he argued, they made demands that could not be satisfied to incriminate the administration and turn the public against the protectorate government and, by extension, the provisional government and de Gaulle himself. The communists, Mast continued, were looking to the PCF for support. Should they find that support, he warned, "we would risk losing the confidence of Muslims of all classes who remain faithful as well as the support of local cadres without whom the protectorate can't survive." The masses, he said, view the passive attitude of the government in the face of these attacks as a sign of weakness, and he alerted metropolitan officials to an impending "crisis of authority." Mast argued for something to do be done to stem the communist push in North Africa, which "seems to be more violent here than in the metropole as the local milieu is most sensitive to its action."[4] That spring, Mast repeated his warnings about the growth of communist outreach beyond the cities and into rural areas, and noted the success of communist propaganda about the lack of supplies and aid to colonized populations. The party, he said, would stop at nothing to grow its influence, to include collusion with the nationalist "Destour" party, activity that greatly complicated the regency's task of governing.[5]

French officials were also on alert for any suggestion of active collusion between local communist parties in North Africa and the PCF in the metropole. At the end of January, the Foreign Ministry wrote to Tunis that the communist newspaper *L'Humanité* had reported that Ali Djerad, the leader of the PCT, had been spotted in Paris at a reception hosted by the political bureau of the PCF; they asked for information as to why Djerad had come to Paris. Although the report turned out to be inaccurate, the interest in Djerad's whereabouts and possible liaison with the PCF demonstrates the evident concern of the French government.[6]

French intelligence also reported alleged links between PCF and local parties, but other reports suggested a greater divide between a metropolitan party of government and local parties determined to undermine the same enterprise to which French communists were party. Early that year, the director of General Security in Algiers reported to Paris that a PCF deputy had been ordered by PCF leadership to travel to Morocco to investigate alleged "bullying" of local communists by authorities of the resident-general. The same report indicated that Djerad had complained of similar treatment.[7] Other reports, however, suggested that the PCF then maneuvered as a party of government and thus hesitated to support liberation for France's colonies. Local communists, General Mast reported, seemed to be somewhat disconcerted by this reorientation and could throw in with nationalist groups like Destour.[8]

French officials were also increasingly unnerved by apparent nationalist affinity for the Anglo-Saxon powers, especially the United States, and noted how nationalist groups downplayed any sympathy with local communist parties. In early February, one police memo from Tunisia noted that nationalist Destour members had chanted "down with Djerad"; likewise, nationalists had also spread rumors of Russian sympathy for

Jews and argued for the incompatibility between Islam and Communism. This correspondent suggested that nationalist groups were conspiring to obtain British and American support for Tunisian autonomy; one orator went so far as to claim that the party had the "complete support" of the United States. The author of the report noted that there had been some contact observed between members of Destour and "agents" of the Anglo-Saxon consulates in Tunis but offered no further details.[9]

At the same time, French colonial administrators were aware that American officials were increasingly interested in communist activity in the region. Gabriel Puaux, resident-general in Morocco, sent a telegram to the Foreign Ministry in Paris, in which he detailed the contents of an American questionnaire regarding communist activity there. The Americans, he said, want to know about communist relations with nationalists, as well as information on party members and leaders. However, Puaux also warned that the new consul general in Casablanca (a "Monsieur Lewis") could not pass for a Francophile.[10] American officials seemed to hedge their engagement in France's empire and would have to be convinced that nationalists were part of the same threat posed by communists.

By the spring of 1945, colonial officials also feared that nationalists could exploit communist propaganda designed to attract voters in order to undermine French authority. They worried that PCF rhetoric against Muslim "bosses" and "feudal lords," the same ones the administration relied upon to govern, would undermine French control. Yves Chataigneau, the governor-general of Algeria, thus pleaded with the Interior Ministry in Paris to engage the PCF Central Committee on the matter, without which "it would be impossible to avoid the recourse to force."[11] In May, French intelligence in Morocco warned that nationalists had already claimed that they would wait to act until "the communists have sufficiently weakened the French government."[12] The same report also suggested that the only French party then active was the communist party, which had undertaken a propaganda campaign through public meetings with local populations, the distribution of tracts, and publication of journals in order to attack the colonial administration by capitalizing on poor living conditions and shortages. The report went on to warn about the nefarious activity of certain elements of the French population – a reference to communists – and the fact that similar elements had publicly undermined the authority of the protectorate with obscene displays. In one such exhibition, a bishop accompanying the resident-general to commemorate the taking of Paris was loudly booed; in another the resident-general, then commemorating the fall of Berlin, was drowned out by calls for "Épuration" – purges of Nazi collaborators – then a rallying cry for the communists.[13] Subsequent reports suggested that political rivalries among French parties had effectively divided French nationals in North Africa into two camps – a reference to the extreme right and the extreme left – which greatly complicated the task of governing in North Africa.[14]

Many of the colonial administration's fears were realized when riots broke out in Setif and Guelma in Algeria, signaling a rebellion against French rule in North Africa. The disturbances started on May 8, 1945, during V-E Day celebrations, when crowds carrying nationalist banners and Algerian flags – demonstrations banned by the colonial government – took to the streets in many of the towns of the Constantine department. In Setif, the demonstration became a riot when police forces intervened; similar violence broke out in Guelma. By the end of the month, a hundred French settlers had been massacred, along with thousands among colonized populations, mostly at the hands of civilians and militias. Additionally, the French military bombarded villages in retribution for the rebellion. Although there had been ample warning about desperate shortages and the threat of famine before the violence,[15] there was no sudden introspection about French administrative failures or colonialism. Instead, charges of communist duplicity were a convenient way to obscure the real reasons for the revolt – misery and poor administration. One government report claimed "an insurrectional atmosphere was created by the publication of extremely violent political journals ... radio propaganda, and by agitation at public meetings. All of this acted like a veritable poison in the social body of Algeria."[16] The same report repeated a now familiar refrain; that is, that Algerian nationalists had only to take up the propaganda already prepared by French communists.

In the aftermath of the rebellion, colonial officials again reported to de Gaulle that the nationalist Algerian People's party (PPA) and Ferhat Abbas' Amis du Manifeste de la Liberté (AML) were behind the riots. However, again, they also suggested a dangerous role for communists. They warned that nationalist agitation could take the form of terrorism, which would be even more dangerous than open rebellion. In the presence of this danger, they argued, the "state of mind of the French population is far from satisfactory." Part of this they attributed to the activity of the communist party, which continued to attack the government and colonization, which they alleged had the effect of stirring up the population. The same officials maintained that the party did this for political ends in the hopes of drawing to them those who could not openly militate within the PPA under the cover of legality.[17] This was evident in the arrest of

PPA adherents who had been caught in anti-French activities under the umbrella of the local communist party. Once again, colonial officers asked leaders in Paris to call upon the PCF to exert pressure on the local parties to stop the activity. The PCF, they asserted, had reaffirmed a number of times its position that Algeria was an integral part of France. "We all want justice and social progress," one author wrote, "but these press campaigns compromise France's position and the security of its citizens and this cannot be tolerated." Thus, they argued, pressure on communist leaders was of capital importance.[18]

Linking communist agitation in the colonies to the PCF in the metropole was a delicate maneuver, given the PCF's position within the government, but it was another way to deflect blame from the administration, and it provided a powerful lever with which to undermine the PCF domestically and push it to support colonial policy. The May 10 report, for example, indicated that communist methods became dangerous when applied to the colonies: "What in France might only cause malaise and brawls here leads to insurrection and massacre."[19] The author, colonial official, ethnographer, and "liberal rightist"[20] Robert Montagne, further argued that it was necessary to shield Algeria from the enterprises of French political parties because it would undermine France's international position: "France cannot today," he said, "... allow a serious political crisis in Algeria without putting all of North Africa in great danger ... before foreign eyes who do not wish us well."[21] In late May, Interior Minister Adrien Tixier wrote de Gaulle that because the French government included two communist ministers and it was "infinitely possible" that the Parti Communiste Algérien (PCA) obeyed instructions from the PCF, it seemed advisable to have a discussion with PCF leaders about the situation in Algeria. Chataigneau felt that communist propaganda served only to efface the responsibility of nationalists (blaming instead old Vichyites and grands colons, protected by colonial administration, for the troubles) in the riots in Setif and Guelma; if the PCF could not be persuaded to intervene, then he recommended government action to close down communist journals and printers.[22] Subsequent reports to de Gaulle reiterated concern about the effect of communist propaganda and growing linkage between discontent in the Levant and Algeria and the possibility it could spread to other parts of North Africa.[23]

By June, French fears about the consequences of communist-nationalist collusion had evolved from damaging propaganda to communist legality offering a cover for illegal nationalist agitation. Meanwhile, Yves Chataigneau, the governor-general in Algeria, continued to discount misery as causing a spontaneous uprising, claiming that one area of unrest – Guelma – had not known famine and had fared better than the rest of Algeria. In reality, he argued, the movement was purely political with the aim of independence.[24] Subsequent reports to de Gaulle from across North Africa that summer and fall continued to highlight the premeditated, political nature of the attacks and reiterated familiar charges against local communist parties and concerns about collusion between communists in the metropole and in North Africa.[25] In one such instance of metropolitan affairs bleeding into local issues, PCF representative Jean Llante, then on a visit to Tunis, spoke of the upcoming French constitutional referendum, over which communists disagreed with de Gaulle on the sovereignty of the assembly and the power of the presidency, and blasted de Gaulle's "dictatorial government." He also denigrated the role of Gaullist "London" resistors and attacked the French government, de Gaulle, and the colonial administration for incidents between the military and Tunisians that fall. General Mast, who alerted authorities to this activity, wrote that he thought it useful to draw the Foreign Ministry's attention to "the attitude of a political delegate" in front of a native audience.[26]

Despite French efforts to keep the situation in North Africa an internal matter, colonial officials reported increased Soviet activity and nationalist attempts to situate their struggle on an international level within the context of already deteriorating relations between the Soviet Union and the West. In early February 1945, General Paul Beynet, the French delegate general to the Levant, reported that anti-French agitation also had an anti-communist tinge to it, as the principal agitators were "young men of Mohammed" who share a common hatred of communism, Christians, and France. Beynet further reported the reserve on the part of the Soviet representative in the Levant, Daniil Solod.[27] But by April 21, French Minister Plenipotentiary Stanislas Ostrorog reported that the actions of the Syrian and Lebanese communist parties seemed inseparable from those of the Soviet legation. In years past, he claimed, the PCF had directed the local parties, but now the Kremlin controlled their program. The activity of the Soviet embassy had intensified over the past weeks; Ostrorog argued that "it was no exaggeration to say that the actions of the communist parties are the principal means for expressing Soviet policy in the Levant."[28] Reports like these continued throughout the year, only increasing French concern about Soviet intrigue against France's position in the Middle East.[29] They were certainly on the minds of French officials as they intervened militarily to put down nationalist protests in May, despite a prewar promise of independence.

However, amid the Levant crisis and British intervention in Syria and Lebanon in July, and against the backdrop of the Franco-Soviet Treaty the previous December, de Gaulle attempted to use potential Soviet influence in the Near East as a lever to balance Anglo-American interests in the region, suggesting a four-power conference between the major powers to discuss the Middle East. In August, however, Quai officials told de Gaulle that the suggestion to include the Soviets in the discussion of the Middle East was met with "cold suspicion" in the United States and that if France wanted American support it would have to assure the US that it would not favor Soviet penetration of the Middle East at the expense of Anglo-Saxon influence.[30]

At the same time, nationalist activity demonstrated another way the changing international situation threatened to undermine French colonialism in North Africa. One tract circulating in Algeria raised the issue to the international plane and appealed to growing anti-communism in Anglo-American circles to plead for assistance in their liberation from France. The authors argued that this was a new era of competition between the three powers with interests in North Africa: Britain, France, and the Soviet Union. The Soviets, the tract claimed, would lean on their French ally to get a foothold in the region. Evidence of this, it continued, could be found in the PCF's success in France and "the extraordinary funds used by communists in North Africa in their anti-national and anti-British propaganda."[31] The nationalists astutely appealed to British geopolitical concerns to encourage French eviction from North Africa. British supremacy, the tract argued, could only be assured "to the degree that the French – the Soviets' valets – are ousted from their positions in the Mediterranean."[32] As Matthew Connolly has argued, these developments lent urgency to early French efforts "to define 'the West' not only against the East but also against 'Asiatics and African and colonial natives' as well,"[33] effectively globalizing the Cold War before the last war had even ended.

By late autumn, it appeared that communist agitation in North Africa had had a tangible effect. The PCF won the largest percentage of the vote in legislative elections that fall; the same results were apparent in North Africa, with communists winning and losses for socialists and other traditional parties. Subprefects in the Algerian towns of Tizi Ouzou and Blida reported that communists in recent legislative elections had exceeded political forecasts. Communists received 32 percent of the vote in cantonal elections and 56 percent of the vote in the general elections. One official attributed this success to higher numbers of nationalist/ autonomy voters, and to communist efforts to bring in undecided and new voters. He also tied these developments to the PCF, pointing out that European militants had observed the election operations.[34] Other colonial officials blamed the PCF for furnishing rhetorical weapons against French colonialism. One PCA leader, a subprefect reported, echoed Thorez's rhetoric, declaring that Algerian communists, with the French, Spanish, Jews, and Arabs together, wished to form a "strong and happy Algerian nation side by side with other nations."[35] Chataigneau also pointed out that *Liberté* had recently reprinted Thorez's 1939 report, which recommended that democratic France should help "in the development of an Algerian nation in formation," and that the PCA had adopted some of this rhetoric.[36] Discouraged, the prefect in Blida wrote, "It is evident that if the communists pursue their actions with the near and far goal of opposing assimilation and constituting an Algerian nation, they will get the provisional agreement of the nationalists."[37] One subprefect suggested that this was an electoral stunt by communists. However, the danger lay in the possibility that the communist party could attract so many nationalists that the latter could take over command of the party with all its means of action. That situation, he reported, would be "very grave."[38] Despite the obstacles to more permanent collaboration – including the PCA's lack of emphasis on race and religion – this alliance posed a threat because a great part of the Muslim population was rising up against France.

Several days later, the situation appeared more ominous. Interior Minister Tixier sent de Gaulle another letter from Chataigneau indicating plans for revolutionary action by Algerian nationalists against France in January or February 1946 and warning of potential Soviet involvement. He further detailed contact between a nationalist delegate and Amar Ouzegane, the secretary general of the PCA, including alleged discussion of the support of the communist party and the USSR for the creation of a national front and a committee of liberation in North Africa with a communist preponderance.[39]

Later that week, the prefect of Algiers noted another apparent evolution in communist policy away from assimilation, which they previously supported. In particular, some PCA representatives now refused to admit "Algérie Française" but would instead proclaim, separately, "Vive La France" and "Vive l'Algérie." Ouzegane had given a number of speeches recently without even mentioning France. There had also been a subtle shift in communist rhetoric, which now separated Algerians from the French as distinct peoples joined in friendship, instead of acknowledging "Algeria as an integral part of the French nation."[40] The prefect concluded that this fraternization between communists and nationalists showed no signs of abating as both groups viewed collusion in their interests, the communists as a tactic for gaining electoral strength, the nationalists as a means to "exploit ambiguity in order to acquire serious trump cards, all in reserve for the future."[41] Mast in Tunisia noted the rapprochement between the PCT and Neo-Destour as "a fact" but acknowledged that the PCF may not share this "purely local view" and that the collusion may not have been approved by the Central Committee.[42] In Algeria, Chataigneau again raised the danger of communist exploitation of the themes of "Algerian unity" or of "an Algerian nation in formation," but he did not believe that the PCF would jeopardize its electoral gains by "letting itself be pulled along on such an adventure."[43] He could only state "the themes it defends cause today a certain agitation in European and Muslim circles," and he regretted that "they no longer bring, as in the past, its support to the policy of the government."[44]

INDOCHINA

France's fragile hold over its colonies was also complicated by the popularity of the communist Viet Minh, a Vietnamese group that had proven indispensable in the resistance against Japan in Indochina. For years, French officials had been more occupied by other "revolutionary" groups in the region. However, by the end of 1944 and into early 1945, as the war began to shift toward the Pacific, French officials reported growing concern about Vietnamese communists. At the end of February, Jean Royère, the French consul at Kunming, wrote French ambassador to China General Zinovi Pechkoff to offer an ominous warning of preparations for an uprising among revolutionary groups in Vietnam. The information he forwarded, gleaned from French military intelligence in the region, suggested that communist and nationalist groups had intensified their anti-French propaganda and had begun recruiting among colonized soldiers; while the groups may have different political ideas, they pursued the same purpose – the total elimination of French sovereignty – through the same means: infiltration of the army. Soon, reports began to characterize revolutionary groups in Indochina as "majority communist." The Indochinese Communist Party, the reports argued, had been further buoyed by Soviet prestige, the democratic impulses of the Allied armies in Europe, and the orientation of American policy in Asia, which seemed to favor liberation.

The communists viewed the liberation of Europe in the wake of victorious Allied armies as the natural precursor to the liberation of Vietnam following the victories of the united nations in the Far East.[45] The March coup against the Vichy regime in Indochina only increased the significance of the Viet Minh to the Allies, as they resisted the occupiers and helped downed Allied airmen safely escape their grasp. A French intelligence bulletin in mid-June 1945 reported that the Viet Minh was gaining in importance every day and that there were notable tensions between the group and the French populace because of past repression. They felt more affinity for French resistors who had come from the metropole, the authors argued, but they still saw the French as an enemy they would have to fight at some point.[46] Unable to dent Soviet prestige or Allied democratic impulses, French officials recognized that the American position was perhaps the most pliant, and they soon turned their efforts toward influencing US policy in the region.

In August, Asian affairs analysts in the Quai d'Orsay offered a clear domestic and international justification for France's return to Indochina. Keeping Indochina, one report indicated, would allow the government to survive the domestic crisis, and it would help make the case for continued French influence in the region. If they lost Indochina, however, then they faced elimination from the hemisphere. As had French officials in North Africa, these analysts argued that the French government should direct its diplomatic efforts to the United States rather than other interested powers; the British did not wish to offend the Americans, and the Chinese government would wait for US reactions. American anti-colonialism, Quai officials contended, was first directed at the British in India, but the British had been able to convince the United States that the abandonment of British sovereignty would lead to chaos and make it easy prey for the USSR. It was only then, they asserted, that Roosevelt decided to prevent France from reestablishing control over Indochina despite assurances already made regarding French sovereignty there.[47] This argument suggested that a similar appeal to US officials increasingly consumed by anti-communism could be effective. Other reports suggested growing American preoccupation with the "Soviet problem" – influence and domination of Europe and world economic markets – and concern about France's alignment in the event of hostilities. One report suggested that Americans wanted to help France but that they needed to hear "language they understand," which presumably meant, given the subject of the report, assurances on France's position on the Soviet Union and communism. The same report suggested that various rival French factions in the United States were muddying the waters and that it would be better to have a unified French approach to propaganda.[48] Before long, there were already signs of Franco-American rapprochement on the issue; later that summer, a high State Department official told French representatives that no one on the American side would contest France's return.[49]

Shortly after the Japanese surrender, however, the situation grew more complicated. Vietnamese communists launched the "August Revolution," and Viet Minh forces took control of parts of Annam and Tonkin, and eventually Hanoi itself.[50] Subsequent French reports highlighted the threat from the Viet Minh, which they now claimed had collaborated with Japan – a duplicitous charge given their cooperation with the American OSS and resistance to the Japanese – and that they were anti-French and bent on seizing power in Vietnam.[51] As further proof of an emerging link between communism and colonial ferment, French intelligence services intercepted a telegram from Vietnamese officials in Hanoi to Paris several weeks later, appealing for the support of the French people in their quest for independence. The letter denied collaboration with the Japanese or anti-French sentiments; they further refuted claims that the government even represented the extreme left. These charges, the letter argued, were part of a feeble attempt to discredit the Vietnamese government because they sought independence.[52] What French intelligence failed to report is that those calls for help went unanswered.

French officials continued to levy these charges against the Vietnamese to delegitimize their movement. In the confused weeks after the August Revolution, US State Department officials asked their counterparts in the French Foreign Ministry for their government's position on this situation. On September 21, the Foreign Ministry directed its Washington, DC, embassy to inform the Americans that France followed the activities of the parties of the Indochinese resistance with great interest and would give them as many concessions as possible in recognition of their legitimate aspirations toward autonomy within the future regime in Indochina. However, they also asked their representatives to assert collusion between elements of the Viet Minh and the Japanese in the form of arms, money, and secret liaisons, and to note the incapacity of the "pretend" government in Hanoi to maintain order and deal with urgent issues of resupply. In particular, Quai instructions made it clear that its representatives should tie events in Vietnam to the communist threat when engaging American officials: "In your commentary," they directed, "you should not conceal that the preponderant influence of communist elements in the heart of the Viet Minh is a subject of lively preoccupation for the French government."[53] They must have been gratified to learn the following month that some US officials in the Far Eastern Division of the State Department expressed growing suspicion of Ho Chi Minh as a communist "formed in Russia."[54]

Colonial officials in Indochina warned of communist influence and the international dimension of the problem. At the end of September, Albert Torel, a member of the provisional government's Indochina Council and High Commissioner Admiral Thierry d'Argenlieu's legal adviser,[55] claimed that the nationalists had been too compromised with the Japanese and had passed the baton to a more extremist revolutionary organization, the Viet Minh, in the heart of which "we find our most irreconcilable enemies."[56] While local authorities might call them the communist party, he said, they were wrong because it was not a party but a revolutionary faction with an anti-French spirit as evidenced by the name of its leader – Nguyen Ai-Quoc (Nguyen the Patriot) – who was better known then as Ho Chi Minh. This group, he said, was hoping to exploit differences between France and the allies and to persuade world opinion that all nations are behind them and oppose the reestablishment of French sovereignty.[57]

Later that year, French officials also sought to rebuff apparent Soviet meddling in the region. De Gaulle rejected a Soviet request to allow eight to nine officers to travel to Indochina to coordinate the release of Soviet prisoners because there were no known prisoners there, and even if there were, there was no justification for that many Soviet officers. He did not intend, he wrote, to open the doors to Indochina to the Soviets.[58] French officials now had to fear not only colonized efforts to internationalize their struggle and appeal to the outside world but also apparent Soviet interest in historically French domains.

Meanwhile, General Philippe Leclerc, now commander of French forces in Indochina, reiterated the connection between local communists and the PCF, and the necessity to show strength in dealing with the problem. France was having trouble in Vietnam, he said, because it was seen as weak – a defeated nation in 1940 and again in March 1945. They could only dispel this conviction with a show of force. He argued that it would be an absolute error to negotiate with the Viet Minh before such a display. Leclerc believed that the Americans would protest the use of force but that they would "admire it and will accept it," their attitude having changed since France was no longer "beaten."[59] He also warned "the local communist party was asking for instructions from the PCF and will not delay in making trouble for us."[60] Other reports seemed to confirm the link. Sometime in December, officials again intercepted copies of telegrams between Hanoi and the PCF in Paris. The first, addressed to communist delegate Florimond Bonté, congratulated the PCF on its success in recent elections and especially the appointment of five communist ministers to positions in the government. The telegram further asked PCF leaders to intervene with the government against Leclerc's armed expedition and decried the pillaging, rape, and massacres of the colonized by the same people who fought heroically for liberty against German domination.[61] A subsequent telegram extolled the common history between French and Indochinese communists. It also indicated that Vietnamese communists hoped to use the influence of the PCF on the French people to "demand retreat of French troops and recognize the independence of Vietnam, the only condition that could assure the economic, political, and cultural interests of two peoples on an equal basis,"[62] a development that government officials likely viewed with great alarm.

US INTELLIGENCE

Preoccupied by the war in Europe and plans for assaulting the Japanese mainland, US interest in French Indochina centered on guerilla warfare and subversion to defeat Japanese occupiers. However, US intelligence activity in the region also had the longer-range aim of "making informed decisions on ultimate peace settlements in the Far East," which included gathering secret intelligence and analysis of economic, political, and military information.[63] American diplomatic involvement in Indochina, administered by the Vichy regime until March 1945, remained limited to debates regarding French sovereignty. And in North Africa, US officials maintained limited contact with Arab nationalists but remained focused elsewhere until concerns about Soviet penetration recommended a more active policy. Limited attention and resources also restricted American intelligence analysis of Indochina and North Africa. However, fundamental differences over the threat posed by communism in the French colonies were evident between the analysis of OSS agents and local diplomatic representatives, on one hand, and State Department and White House analysis in Washington, DC, on the other. As State Department Europeanists shifted in favor of French colonialism as a way to strengthen France's position in Europe, OSS analysts remained critical of the French imperial enterprise and dubious about the threat from communism among the colonized. Both took advantage of existing imperial networks to access intelligence from French settlers and the colonized; in turn, their sources used those circuits to transfer knowledge in the hopes of aligning American policy to their own.

As the war in the Pacific reached its climax in 1945, American intelligence on Indochina was dominated by military concerns. In particular, the US military in China utilized informants within the French colonial administration to glean valuable information on Japanese targets, air defenses, weather, and troop movements in Indochina. Earlier in the war, the US Navy had given Commodore Milton Miles (who also then happened to be the Far East director for the OSS) the mission to prepare for Allied landings on the coast of China.[64] With this in mind, Miles extended his intelligence network into Vietnam with the help of French officer Robert Meynier, a member of General Giraud's staff with pro-American credentials and contacts within the colonial administration. In turn, Meynier had recruited a number of other French officers to round out his group. However, French political differences soon threatened to undermine the effort. De Gaulle, despite his earlier rivalry with Giraud, had approved of the Meynier group and its mission. Meynier nonetheless soon found himself at odds with the Gaullist French Military Mission in Chungking, which was also collecting intelligence and conducting operations in Indochina. Once again, political rivalries and intelligence work were intertwined, and, at the request of OSS officials, the Meynier group was eventually absorbed under the French Military Mission in China.[65]

The "most reliable and widely used" source of intelligence in Indochina before the spring of 1945, however, was the "GBT Group," named after the first letter of the last names of its three leaders – Gordon-Bernard-Tan: a Canadian oilman, a British tobacco merchant, and a Chinese American businessman.[66] This group also enjoyed reliable contacts inside the colonial administration, in the French armed forces, and among the French populace of Indochina. The group had begun as a rather casual arrangement to maintain contact between the French in Indochina – then under Vichy control – and the outside world but quickly began to take on the appearance of an amateur intelligence network, which for a time collaborated with the Americans, the Free French, the British, and the Chinese. By 1945, however, the OSS – then the largest supplier of the group – envisioned its own expansion into Indochina and absorption of the organization.[67]

French officials remained concerned about American anti-colonialism and US intelligence activity in Indochina and the effect it might have on US policy. Before early 1945, OSS officials in Kunming had demanded that the French military mission share its intelligence on Indochina only with the United States. American officials hoped to combine intelligence gathered by their own "Gordon" network and push it out as quickly as possible to Allied units. In January 1945, General Zinovi Pechkoff, the French ambassador to Chungking, reported to Paris that he had had a long conversation with General Donovan, who had also recently met with Passy. Pechkoff believed that he had received assurances from Donovan and other military officials that the OSS would cease contact with the colonized and "revolutionary" elements in Indochina, and further, that American intelligence services would coordinate with French intelligence. Donovan privately derided the "Gordon" network as "sellers of intelligence" and claimed that they did not operate under the auspices of the OSS. US Army General Wedemeyer further indicated that he would oversee OSS activities in Indochina and that they would operate as his intelligence arm. While there was some movement toward a combined Franco-American intelligence system in Indochina, it was never realized. In any event, French officials continued to remind Donovan and his US intelligence officers that French and American secret services should not appear to Indochinese resistors as independent organizations but as "military instruments of a common plan of action."[68]

In early March, French officials' fears were further reinforced by a "Very Secret" French intelligence (DGER) report that suggested that the US military around Kunming had hired three Vietnamese nationalists to provide intelligence on Indochina, a development that warranted underscoring in red by the recipient of the report.[69] French officials continued to express concern about OSS engagement with the Vietnamese well into the following autumn. In late October, French officials reported that OSS officer Archimedes Patti had left Hanoi for Washington, DC, and that "he would be carrying a dossier hostile to the French position in Indochina." The same Foreign Ministry report noted Patti's participation in a ceremony with the leaders of the Viet Minh.[70] This expression of concern demonstrated French trepidation over the influence that OSS views of the Viet Minh might have on US policy in Washington, DC.

Limited as it was, the Allied intelligence picture in Indochina was erased in one stroke on the evening of March 9, 1945. After the liberation of France the previous August, French citizens in Indochina began to organize resistance to the Japanese. However, Japanese officials observed these efforts and launched a preemptive coup, assuming direct control of the colony's government, police, and armed forces. Paul E. Helliwell, the director of the OSS detachment in China, grimly noted, "the GBT Group is knocked out, the French system has been destroyed, and General Tai Li's[71] setup has been knocked out lock, stock, and barrel."[72] The Viet Minh were the only remaining viable source of information.

The Japanese coup also presented an opportunity for the OSS. Shortly after the coup, General Melvin Gross, the acting chief of staff in China, ordered the OSS to establish an intelligence network in Indochina. Notably, he also directed them to treat all resistance groups equally "irrespective of any particular governmental or political affiliations" as long as their resistance to the Japanese "accrues to the advantage of the United States and China military operations."[73] Just as OSS operatives had worked with communist elements of the French Resistance, so too did they engage the groups most capable of resisting the Japanese. In the spring of 1945, OSS special intelligence teams were inserted into Indochina, where they established at least twelve "chains" by May, thus increasing the flow of intelligence into the hands of US military planners.[74]

Some intelligence also filtered out of the OSS station in Kunming, the product of the OSS's engagement with Vietnamese nationalists. In August, Helliwell reported that Vietnamese leaders in Kunming and representatives of the Central Committee in Hanoi had expressed their desire to have Indochina placed under the United States as a protectorate – like the Philippines – to exclude Chinese and French reoccupation of the region. The same representatives warned that they would oppose any attempt to restore French sovereignty with force. Meanwhile, Jean Sainteny, then working for French intelligence, told OSS agents that France felt betrayed by lack of American support for France's return to Indochina. Eventually, Sainteny would be allowed into Vietnam but only under the auspices of a "Mercy Mission" led by Patti to ensure the well-being of prisoners of war then held by the Japanese in Indochina.[75]

Perhaps the most famous of the contacts between the OSS and the Vietnamese came between Patti himself and Ho Chi Minh in the spring and summer of 1945. Patti later recalled that French representatives in China warned him against intelligence cooperation with the Vietnamese because they were "infantile" and "communist."[76] Other French officers alerted him to the seditious activity of Russian legionnaires among the Vietnamese independence movement and the anti-white, pro-Japanese sympathies of Viet Minh. Patti also heard that the "embassy boys" did not want to deal with the Vietnamese because they were communist and anti-French, a charge dismissed by Helliwell who was in favor of using any group with proven intelligence value.[77] Patti, who shared Roosevelt's desire to prevent the French from reclaiming control in Indochina, met with Ho in April to discuss potential OSS-Viet Minh cooperation against the Japanese. He was struck by Ho's dedication and desire to work with the United States; he also noted that the political situation was "critical," and that the Viet Minh possessed both strength and an anti-French posture.[78] Other OSS operatives were similarly impressed and uncon- cerned by Ho's political philosophy: "I was told he [Ho] went to Moscow as a communist and that kind of thing, but so what?" wrote

OSS agent Ray Galecki, "The Soviet Union and we were allies."[79] Viet Minh official Vu Dinh Huynh later recalled that he "had the impression that at that moment, the Americans didn't care if we were communists or not. The only thing they cared about was fighting the Japanese."[80]

Eventually American policy beganbegan to shift away from anti-colonialism toward support for French and British retention of their empires. Some of this had to do with American desires to access overseas bases and markets in their allies' colonial domains. But much of it was related to growing concerns about the power and expansionism of the Soviet Union. Intent on winning the war against Japan and retaining a great deal of sympathy for colonized peoples, US officials early on were not as preoccupied by the political coloration of nationalist movements in North Africa and Indochina as their French counterparts, yet, but French officials worked to heighten their concerns. Not long after the Japanese coup in March, French officials again raised the issue of American policy on Indochina. The French wanted to participate in the war in the Pacific, a thinly veiled attempt to provide an avenue through which to reestablish control over their Far Eastern empire. Rebuffed in January by Roosevelt, who thought it premature to make any determination on the future of Indochina, French officials now used the Japanese coup as a pretext to revisit the issue. Fully preoccupied with defeating Japan, US officials soon realized that French officials would never agree to a trusteeship and that they would be supported by other colonial powers, notably Great Britain and the Netherlands.[81] Through "Magic" intercepts of Allied communications, US officials also became aware of French ire over American refusal to support French resistance groups in Indochina, then holding out against the Japanese. One intercept of the Dutch Ambassador (Lovink) in Chungking revealed that Pechkoff blamed this lack of aid on "the sinister efforts of an American secret organization to make contact with the revolutionary ... organizations in cooperation with China"; he also detected American neo-imperialist designs on France's Far Eastern empire.[82] Other intelligence through the US military attaché in China from a Swiss source suggested that the strained relations between the US and France in the China Theater stemmed from American uncertainty over the future of postwar French Indochina.[83]

In time, however, French officials successfully connected these movements to domestic communism and the Soviet threat. In mid-May, de Gaulle again wrote to Truman asking to participate in the fight against Japan; this would, he argued, have "very important political, moral, and military consequences."[84] US policy softened as well, as the State-War-Navy

Coordinating Committee (SWNCC, a precursor of the US National Security Council) recommended that "the United States should neither oppose the restoration of Indo-China to France . . . nor take any action which is it is not prepared to take or suggest with regard to the colonial possessions of our other Allies."[85] By June, it was clear that Truman had abandoned Roosevelt's Indochina policy.[86]

There was a significant divide between OSS experts working to fulfill their anti-colonial, anti-Japanese mandate, and State Department and military officials who were growing increasingly concerned about the Soviet Union. On April 30, the State Department recommended a reevaluation of US policy on Indochina. There was a schism between the European Division analysts more concerned about PCF influence and rebuilding France as a bulwark against Soviet expansion than opposing a French return to Indochina, and more anti-colonial Asia specialists.[87] By May the Europeanists prevailed, and Secretary of State Stettinius reassured Georges Bidault that the United States would not prevent the restoration of French sovereignty over Indochina. Meanwhile, department officials continued to subsume French concerns about Indochina within larger fears about the Soviet threat.[88] This concern was misplaced. As David Marr has demonstrated, in 1945, Vietnamese communists expected Soviet support for their liberation but were bitterly disappointed when they did not get it.[89] Nevertheless, anti-communism increasingly shaded American judgments about Indochina, and other avenues of inquiry were shut down. Despite the quality of intelligence provided by Patti's liaison with the Viet Minh, embassy experts in China maintained that he had been taken in by "communist fanatics" and was wasting his time.[90]

While OSS operatives geared up for their first forays into Indochina, the OSS in Southeast Asia remained a "bastion of Rooseveltian sentiment."[91] Immersed in local politics and culture, R&A analysts seemed "almost oblivious to the growing military concerns about the Soviets and the early phases of the Cold War."[92] At first glance, this seems to suggest a complete lack of geopolitical awareness on the part of OSS officials in Asia. While much has been made of covert support for the Viet Minh through Deer Team missions[93] and Patti's liaison with Ho Chi Minh, OSS R&A personnel played a lesser role. Because of the emphasis on guerilla warfare and subversion, and in support of defeating the Japanese in the Pacific, OSS R&A analysts often found themselves assigned in support of other missions. Several were assigned to support Claire Chennault's Fourteenth Air Force with target studies; others were assigned to prepare strategic surveys of North China and Korea. High-level analysis was also handicapped by the lack of personnel. Shortages of political analysts meant that little information of strategic value flowed to Washington, DC.[94]

After the war, William Langer, head of OSS R&A, wrote that R&A had "no important role in the war in the Pacific." This was due in large part to General Douglas MacArthur's[95] refusal to allow any intelligence activity outside of his control. MacArthur's subordinates did attempt to enroll R&A personnel, but it was always with the condition that they sever all ties to the OSS and integrate into his intelligence units, a demand to which Donovan would never accede.[96]

Despite their marginalization, OSS analysts certainly already understood that Southeast Asia, including Indochina, would hold major importance in the postwar world. Anthropologist Cora Du Bois, the head of the R&A branch of OSS/Southeast Asia Command, wrote to Washington, DC, to decry the shortage of analysts and research materials, which were required in light of OSS operations in Thailand, Sumatra, and southern Indochina; she further indicated that they felt a "very heavy responsibility to American foreign policy" and that "this area is the largest unexploited colonial region of the Far East and therefore, a potential bone of contention in the future."[97] At the same time, OSS experts believed that their views were in line with the administration's anti-colonialism. In May 1945, sensing a shift within the State Department, US ambassador to China Patrick Hurley asked Truman if there had been any change in American policy on Indochina, which Truman denied. This information – that Roosevelt's policy remained in effect – was shared with OSS representatives in China.[98] Furthermore, OSS officials in Indochina received their instructions before Roosevelt's death, and they continued to implement his policy, laboring under the assumption that they had one overarching goal, to help defeat the Japanese.[99] They did not yet know that they were increasingly out of step with US policy.

Despite Patti's complaint that "strong Francophile elements in our Research and Analysis Branch [in Kunming] ... took exception to my assessment of the French position as too severe" and that "it was the consensus in R&A that the French were being deprived of their rightful claim to Indochina and that we Americans should be more understanding in that regard,"[100] the reality was that OSS analysts and operatives were largely anti-colonial even while they retained some sympathy for the French. In 1943, Ralph Bunche and other R&A officials had suggested the international trusteeship formula for colonies in Southeast Asia.[101] And there were a number of French-American OSS officers who sympathized with the French predicament in Indochina, especially with those French forces who had fought a desperate retreat to Kunming after the Japanese coup and with local French populations whom they feared would be massacred by the Viet Minh. However, many of them also agreed with the thrust of American anti-colonialism; some came to believe that Ho Chi Minh was a "great statesman whose nationalism transcended his communist background."[102]

Viet Minh leaders knew that OSS agents would be more receptive to their drive for liberation. Shortly after the Japanese coup, one letter directed to the OSS (likely from Ho Chi Minh himself) extolled the "national front" character of the Viet Minh and proposed a partnership with the United States, based upon American democratic ideals and the example the United States had set in the Philippines.[103] This was certainly reflected in a July 6 report from Kunming, in which OSS analysts argued that the Viet Minh was a nationalist group and the core of the resistance in Indochina whose success had alarmed French authorities.[104] This was also reflected in Cora Du Bois's *Social Forces in Southeast Asia*, written just four years after the war, at a time when it was even less popular to extol Ho Chi Minh's nationalism. While she did not deny Ho's communism, she did highlight the "wide gap between the presence of nationalists of Marxian persuasion and the presence of active conspiratorial groups of Soviet communists."[105] She further noted that any Soviet attempt to make a lasting impact on Southeast Asia would have to go beyond a few disciplined leaders and an ideology but also offer practical programs for mass education, industrial development, and modernization, none of which had been proposed by the USSR thus far.[106]

OSS R&A experts also developed comprehensive studies of France's Far East empire that did make it to the White House and the highest echelons of the US government. One study, "Indochina's War-Time Government and Main Aspects of French Rule," written to inform evolving policy in the Pacific, offered some nuance in explaining French political parties' relations with Indochina, explaining that "French home points of view influence the grouping of French cliques in France's outposts of empire as well." French socialists and communists, for example, who had been focused on strengthening labor and social welfare services, anti-clericalism, and fighting big business in France, denounced big banks and business, press censorship, harsh use of police force, and racial discrimination in the colonies. Communists and socialists called for greater political responsibility for the colonized, along with better education, economic opportunities, and public health. Yet none supported complete independence; all seemed to support France's continuation as a colonial power and its influence in the Far East. Instead, they envisioned something like a "dominion status" akin to the British Commonwealth. At the same time, French settlers and colonial administrators, the report indicated, viewed any devolution of power with suspicion and as likely to undermine their future prospects.[107] This dynamic proved an important factor in efforts to influence American policy in the Far East.

As it had in Indochina, American intelligence on nationalist agitation in North Africa remained sparse, the result of preoccupation with the war in Europe and the Pacific. Although the OSS had provided extensive reporting from North Africa in the form of "Airgrams," these reports were more focused on understanding the nascent French provisional government, then installed in Algiers. US intelligence officials noted that they were "almost exclusively dependent" on the Airgrams in the months after Liberation because "the flow of SI [special intelligence] and British documents [had] been reduced to a trickle and other sources are not very fruitful."[108] However, once the GPRF moved on to Paris in the months after Liberation, so too did many OSS and military analysts. At the same time, French officials took interest in American intelligence activity in North Africa, noting on numerous occasions the work of OSS analyst Walter Cline, a Harvard-trained anthropologist who circulated freely among the colonized populations of Morocco, and much to French officials' chagrin, nationalist circles in Marrakech. Cline seemed interested in local conditions, America's position in the region after the war, and Moroccan nationalism. One report indicated that this activity was indicative of continuing American interest in the region and their desire to increase US influence there. At the same time, the French report indicated that Moroccan nationalists continued to cultivate American friendship, despite recent pro-Zionist declarations of a number of political figures in Washington, DC.[109]

This was, of course, an area of intense interest for the French government, especially after riots broke out in the Algerian towns of Setif and Guelma in May 1945. And again, there seemed to be a divide over the sources and nature of nationalist agitation between remaining OSS analysts on one hand, and US military intelligence and French officials on the other. Military intelligence on the situation in North Africa filtered in that spring from Joint Intelligence Collection Agency – North Africa (JICANA) analysts remaining in Algiers and through military attachés in the region. JICANA, which was staffed by Army and Navy officers and enlisted personnel, had close contacts with French military officers, who often supplied information on the situation in the region, and their appreciation of a communist threat. In early February, the chief of French Naval Counterintelligence and Security Service for North and West Africa, Capitaine de Corvette Hemmerich, told JICANA officers that the French Naval Counterintelligence was "greatly concerned" about the "future effects" of communist penetration of the enlisted and non-commission officer ranks in the French navy stationed there. He reported that there were now "many communists" among these men. They did not pose an immediate threat because the Soviets and PCF supported anti-Axis war efforts; however, Hemmerich claimed, their loyalties were "dictated from Russia" and driven by considerations of Russian and not French national interests. Should those interests diverge, this would pose a grave problem for the military.[110]

Intelligence also passed through military attachés in other capitals. In particular, Spanish military officers, who also had colonial interests in North Africa, passed information to the US military attaché in Madrid. In April, Assistant Military Attaché Albert Ebright reported that a Spanish officer told him about considerable discontent among religious leaders in Algeria over communist influence among Muslims. The Grand Mufti, the source said, called for action against them before it was too late and suggested pressuring de Gaulle to outlaw Muslim membership in local communist parties.[111] Subsequent reports from Spain (which Military Attaché Wendell Johnson acknowledged were likely colored by anti-communism rampant in Spanish military circles and had been willingly handed over) claimed that communism was prevailing in North Africa and warned about a developing bond between communism and revolutionary fervor in nationalist circles in French Morocco. "The Soviet program," one report argued, "encouraged local communist parties to adapt to the situation in the colonies, and, if necessary to take a nationalist or separatist line that would bring about the collapse of the imperial powers and, ultimately, social revolution."[112] These reports echoed French colonial authorities' beliefs that local communist parties, at least, were actively inciting "Arab masses." Communists were making inroads within Moroccan labor upon which the entire economy of French Morocco rested. While the relationship was purely opportunistic, nationalist leaders, the Spanish officers argued, accepted communist support because they had the same goal – to fight European repression.[113] At the same time, the reports also displayed the concern of the Spanish Army, whose leaders, Johnson explained, seemed to be eager to convince him of "the communist threats on all sides of Spain."[114]

Earlier that year, however, OSS analysts in Algiers had reported the contrary; far from collusion between nationalists and communists, they noted PCA attacks on Algerian nationalists for "selling out" to Vichy and now selling out to the United States; they also highlighted nationalist newspaper attacks on communists, arguing that nationalism should come first.[115] At the same time, OSS analysts, capitalizing on a number of Arab sources in Algeria and Morocco, reported bitter opposition to the French in North Africa and positive feelings about the United States. One Arab source noted that anti-French sentiment was the product of recent requisitioning of grain and the scarcity of clothing. "Many persons in Algeria," the source indicated, "have nothing to wear but old sacks."[116] This assertion belied later French assertions that tumult in North Africa was purely the product of political activity among militant groups, including local communist parties. Similar OSS reports suggested that violent anti-communists could be found among nationalists, and that while nationalist parties in Algeria sported hundreds of thousands of members and rapidly rising numbers, the local communists numbered barely over ten thousand and was just as rapidly shrinking.[117]

Regarding links to the PCF, OSS analysts further noted a positive role for French communists in the colonies. PCF official Auguste Gillot, for example, was slated to head an investigating committee that was to travel to North Africa and remove the sources of unrest in Algeria, Tunisia, and Morocco; de Gaulle, however, had abruptly canceled the committee's trip. OSS analysts believed the cancellation would cause "considerable repercussions" among the left parties in Algeria.[118] At the same time, OSS analysts recognized that right-wing groups – including the *grands colons* and banking interests – did see the PCF's hand in nationalist fervor in the region, and that some had even suggested that Algerian independence might be a "good answer to the threat of Communism in France." Whenever the PCF was relatively quiescent, these interests argued, so too was the PPA.[119]

As the spring wore on, there was further alignment between JICANA and US military analyst views and that of French colonial administrators. And again, this seemed to be the product of JICANA contact with sources among French military officers and French colonial authorities. In mid-April, JICANA reporting relayed French concerns that Arab nationalist movements had been "stimulated" by contact with Americans. The author did not question the legitimacy of these concerns; at the same time, he dismissed both the idea that Americans might be sympathetic to Arab nationalism and adopted paternalistic language more common in

French reports. "In some elements of the Moslem population, which is for the most part ignorant of politics and of international diplomacy," one report noted, "there remains a sort of idealistic and vaguely defined belief in America as a supporter of all oppressed peoples, and some of these still cling childishly to the hopes of American support."[120]

Riots in Setif and Guelma in May highlighted the unstable situation prevailing in French North Africa and further alignment of colonial French-JICANA views. After initially concluding in mid-May that the riots were caused by food shortages (a fact admitted by some local officials), by the end of the month, JICANA analysts seemed more closely aligned with official French views of the uprising.[121] They met in late May with Yves Chataigneau, who repeated his belief that the riots could not be due to food shortages since this was the best-fed area in North Africa. The agitation was purely political, and French authorities had it under control. Major Rice, the JICANA chief, acknowledged that his previous report had indicated famine as a major cause of unrest, but he now expressed agreement with Chataigneau's assessment and noted French displays of strength admiringly; the Arabs were terrified of French airpower and wanted no more of it.[122]

However, an OSS Paris report written before the Arab uprising in May, but distributed during the riots, indicated that there was a very real threat of famine in Algeria as they had almost completely run out of flour. Furthermore, there were no textiles and people walked around in rags. North African delegates in the Consultative Assembly, according to one source, likely Yves Dechezelles, a former resistor and leftist political figure, had warned that government inertia and the food crisis would lead to violence and uprisings.[123] This was in line with a British General Staff report that placed blame for the "disorder" squarely on the shoulders of French police in Setif – who fired the first shots – and on food and clothing shortages. They denied that the revolt was "political" or premeditated.[124] In the aftermath of the riot, OSS officials reported the cleavage between left and right in France and its empire on the sources of the unrest. Communists and other leftist parties blamed famine and fascist colons for precipitating trouble. The right, however blamed the PPA and Ferhat Abbas's Amis du Manifeste for the insurrection.[125]

In June, OSS Paris – represented by John Sawyer – reported similar developments in French areas of the Levant, noting a growing linkage between these areas and North Africa. As violence erupted in Algeria in early May, similar demonstrations took place in Syria and Lebanon, with serious rioting breaking out toward the end of the month. The events led

to a showdown between British and French forces that gravely endangered the relations between wartime allies and left the French administration in the Levant, and de Gaulle's government in Paris, humiliated. As
they had claimed elsewhere, French officials maintained that the
Levantine disorders were political and had been "prepared long in
advance."[126] Far from active support of attacks against the colonial
administration, Sawyer and fellow OSS analyst William Koren noted
French communists' "restraint" in the matter in the metropole. Rather
than blaming the government, they blamed Vichy policy and a fascist fifth
column for French troubles in the Levant.[127]

OSS analysts in Paris also remarked on efforts by right-wing anti-
communists to invoke the specter of Soviet inroads in the French empire
to gain American attention. One source, a "rightist French journalist ...
strongly anti-Russian" reported to Sawyer in Paris that there were "secret
clauses" in the Franco-Soviet pact that had to do with France's empire.
One held that France would take necessary measures to prevent Anglo-
American dominance and oil rights in the Levant to allow for Russian
influence in the region; the other allegedly offered full Soviet backing of
French claims to Indochina in return for French efforts to facilitate
Russian propaganda in Burma and India. OSS analysts, however, were
skeptical. They maintained that this source's reliability was "completely
unknown" and that the information was "unconfirmed"; however, they
reported it because it was circulating among rightist groups in Paris.[128]
Reports like these also fueled attacks on de Gaulle's government, suggesting some complicity among government officials in allowing Soviet
inroads in the empire.

For its part, the State Department paid scant attention to developments
in French North Africa in early 1945. After the Arab uprising in Algeria,
US officials waited two months to engage the French government on the
situation, close to five weeks after the secretary general of the League of
Arab States approached the US minister in Egypt to ask for American
assistance in softening French repression after recent disorders. In the
wake of the Levant Crisis, US officials did note French efforts to balance
the United States and Britain with Soviet influence. The US Embassy in
Paris further noted that the Soviets were likely delighted to now have a
foot in the "Near Eastern door"; at the same time, they noted that the
French Communist newspaper *L'Humanité* had applauded de Gaulle's
proposal for four-power talks.[129] Ambassador Caffery reported talks
with de Gaulle soon after, in which de Gaulle lamented the lack of
American support on the Levant issue, and warned that the affair and

"constant humiliations" severely undermined France's independence. And he issued a dark warning: "The outcome of all of this may be that Stalin will take over. I shall not remain here to see him take over because I don't like the communists, and you will probably have Thorez in power to welcome the Russians." Caffery indicated that de Gaulle was "in a highly emotional state," fixated on humiliations, and he was "in no mood to reason."[130] The same day, Acting Secretary of State Joseph Grew reported that Georges Bidault had been "enraged" by British ultimatums and that he would advise de Gaulle to pursue the four-power conference. As de Gaulle had before, Bidault expressed hope that the affair would not end with "the French more dependent on the Russians than before."[131]

Finally, on July 30, the department directed Ambassador Caffery to engage Georges Bidault and express American concern over the Algerian situation. However, the dispatch also instructed Caffery to tell Bidault that the United States was actuated by motives "of the most friendly character as well as our anxiety lest there should arise a situation in North Africa which would have the most serious consequences not only to the French but to relations between the Arab world and all the Western powers."[132] In other words, they did not want France to encourage the spread of Soviet influence by overplaying its hand.

Fear of Soviet inroads, bolstered by intelligence reports, became an important factor in growing American interest in the region. That summer, Loy Henderson's Near Eastern Division warned that the Middle East had become a "dangerous trouble-spot." It drew attention to French and British failures to look after colonized peoples, who remained "ignorant" in abject poverty. But the real logic behind the intervention lay not in concerns for the colonized but in the developing Cold War context, particularly in perceived French and British weakness – a product of the two world wars – and the perception of Soviet interest and efforts to engage in the region. There was a danger, State Department officials said, that if the United States did not assume an active role there, that colonized peoples would look to the USSR to cure their ills.[133] On November 10, 1945, Henderson and several American ministers to Middle Eastern nations met with Truman at the White House. Henderson, in a preparatory note, noted ferment in this area and his hope that its people would move in the direction of western democracies rather than toward "some form of totalitarianism or autocracy which would render sympathetic understanding and cooperation between that part of the world and the United States more difficult."[134] During the meeting with Truman, George Wadsworth, the US minister to Syria-Lebanon, said that the countries of the Arab world argued for more emphasis on the area in American policy. He further noted that the area was roiling with nationalist sentiment and that the colonized looked to the United States to play a leading role. "If the United States fails them," he argued, "they will turn to Russia and will be lost to our civilization; of that we feel certain."[135]

*****

In a few short months over the course of 1945, US policy seemed to shift away from an anti-colonial tradition toward acceptance of the restoration of France's empire. This was no accident; it was tied up in growing American concerns about the threat of communism. US–Soviet relations began to sour that year as the Soviets swiftly extended control into Eastern Europe. In France, the linchpin for American recovery efforts in postwar Europe, the PCF became the most powerful political party. And in the empire, where those events seemed distant, local communists seized the initiative to throw off the imperial past in the wake of the Allies' sweeping victories. For a time, US officials seemed to keep these threads separate. As we have seen, they were already concerned about the domestic strength of the PCF in 1944, but they had been less concerned about communist strength in the colonies. Internally, French officials recognized the political role of communists in post-Liberation France. Over time, and with remarkable subtlety, French officials and a transimperial web of intelligence sources, in their contacts with US officials, increasingly tied communist political aspirations to more nefarious, revolutionary aims, thus setting the stage for more overt anti-communism in the years to come.

The American OSS largely disputed this link, and the threat posed by communism, but French officials found sympathy among some US military intelligence officers and within the State Department European Division. The OSS urged US officials to examine the root sources of discontent – poverty and scarcity, and legitimate aspirations for self-governance – rather than be distracted by French authorities' focus on communism. Other US intelligence officials and their sources – many of whom had vested interests in the empire – rejected accusations of misery and poor administration and argued instead that communists had stirred up nationalists hoping to coopt a more popular movement toward their own political ends, a dangerous game that could expose the region – the soft underbelly of the West – to Soviet influence. With the end of the war and the disbandment of the OSS, the latter narrative prevailed, with consequences for France and the United States in the decades to come. Both nations would fight bloody wars in Vietnam, and France would fight again in Algeria until 1962, hastening the end of the empire many already understood to be doomed in 1945.[136]

4

March to Power

On January 20, 1946, Charles de Gaulle strode into a hastily assembled cabinet meeting on the Rue Saint-Domingue in Paris. Appearing "stiff and drawn" in his uniform, de Gaulle announced his resignation as head of the French provisional government.[1] Speaking but briefly, he denounced the return to the "regime of parties" and internecine political squabbles that threatened to bring further misfortune upon the French people. As his cabinet watched in silence, de Gaulle declared his mission complete and exited the room crisply, "as always, in a gust of wind."[2] To many of the officials present, Charles de Gaulle's departure felt like betrayal given France's precarious state of affairs. Others, including communist ministers, sensed the opportunity posed by the departure of their greatest adversary. PCF leader Maurice Thorez, for one, remarked soon after that the political experiment that had failed with de Gaulle would certainly not succeed without him. He pushed for union between the two working class parties of France and a decided shift to the left in French political affairs.[3]

The threat of communism loomed over the French domestic and international scene that winter like low gathering clouds. Ambassador Caffery, who had learned of de Gaulle's plans two days before, reported that the general believed the PCF hoped to eliminate him through efforts to weaken the presidency and by blaming him for rising prices and shortages.[4] De Gaulle's resignation meant that MRP leaders now had to reconsider their participation in a tripartite coalition with communists and socialists. However, French Army Assistant Chief of Staff General Pierre Billotte reminded them that their departure would only favor the communists. The Army would not accept a government led by Maurice

Thorez, a communist France would lose its empire, and, he warned, it would provoke an intolerable response in Washington, DC.[5]

The New Year in France thus began as the last had ended, in crisis. An uneasy calm prevailed as the French public witnessed the sudden departure of the man of June 18 and the growing strength of the PCF. Just as Foreign Minister Georges Bidault both condemned de Gaulle's act and declared it "the best day of my life,"[6] American leaders might have harbored similar feelings about the man whom they had alternately accused of communist sympathies, anti-Americanism, weakness, and dictatorial tendencies over the past two years. However, by 1946, American images of France were shaped less by de Gaulle's obstinacy and resistance than by growing anti-communism and continued perceptions of French weakness within US diplomatic and intelligence communities. Analysts in the newly created but impotent Central Intelligence Group (CIG) sometimes challenged more hysterical assessments about communist intrigue in France. But the bulk of the current intelligence then provided to the president from War Department units and the CIG buttressed and lent specificity and urgency to alarmist State Department assessments. The intelligence did not have to challenge prevailing wisdom to be relevant; intelligence that seemed to legitimize State Department policy made it easier for those on the fence to side with a hardening line.[7]

Those OSS analysts who had transitioned to the State Department's Interim Research and Intelligence Service (IRIS) in late 1945 now felt like "outcasts."[8] Analyst Cora Dubois lamented that most officials believed "the State Department *is* an intelligence office" and that IRIS experts were therefore "constantly rebuffed, with no access to anything."[9] H. Stuart Hughes reported that his time in IRIS was "the most leisurely" of his life. Others viewed it as a sort of prison sentence, where they were cut off from the policymaking apparatus and their academic lives. In any event, they rightfully sensed that their work had little impact. As subscribers to a minority view that recognized the reality of superpower rivalry but sought to lessen its dangers by ameliorating international tensions, they also felt increasingly out of step with diplomatic and military intelligence officials.[10]

Growing friction between Harry Truman and Secretary of State James Byrnes also affected the intelligence picture. By January 1946, their relationship was visibly strained, a product of Byrnes' penchant for unilateral decision-making, Admiral William Leahy's influence, and Truman's desire to stop "babying the Soviets."[11] Truman increasingly felt that Byrnes was not keeping him informed, and so he requested a Daily Summary of important dispatches affecting foreign policy and sought information from outside the department. Recognizing that rising tensions between the West and the Soviet Union required a more robust and centralized foreign intelligence capacity, Truman created the National Intelligence Authority to coordinate intelligence related to national security and nominated Leahy to be his personal representative. Not long after, he established the CIG to furnish national intelligence. According to its first director, Rear Admiral Sidney Souers, he and Leahy became the president's "chief constables," whom Truman charged with "knowing what those birds, the dumb-bells in the various departments, were thinking."[12]

At the same time, the War Department's Strategic Services Unit (SSU) and MID expanded their analysis beyond military matters into social, political, and economic intelligence. Beginning in mid-February, the CIG and the MID began to deliver summary products – the Daily Intelligence Summary and the Intelligence Review respectively – to Leahy and Truman.[13] Leahy routinely marked items for discussion with the president when they met each morning. These summaries, along with SSU current intelligence, military attaché reports, and embassy analysis, shaped the administration's understanding of French crises and the threat posed by communism in domestic and overseas France.

These agencies agreed about the nature of the communist threat and the PCF's connection to Moscow, which seemed more apparent in 1946, and their view hardened into a basic narrative. Most also agreed on PCF and Soviet intentions – that is, that French communists intended to use any available means to "seize power" and create a "people's democracy" in France, while the Soviets would pursue worldwide revolution through expansion and subversion with the help of European communist parties – even if there were subtle differences over the timing and the capability to carry out these revolutionary objectives. As Melvyn Leffler has argued, the increasing focus on a Soviet threat in 1946 diverted attention from recovery efforts and the indigenous sources of civil strife;[14] it also denied the "Frenchness" of the PCF. However, US officials – especially President Harry Truman – welcomed resolution of the ambiguity of the previous two years.

Positions hardened in the the Cold War, and factions in France (the wartime "les américains" and "les nationaux") solidified into "anti-communists" and "communists" as the ranks of the former grew to include a wide range of parties – to include Gaullists and elements of the non-communist left – who were divided over the desired degree of US intervention in France but united in their determination that France should not be run by communists. As they had during the war, anti-communists now leveraged clandestine encounters to reassure their American partners; they were also, in some cases, able to obviate the weakness narrative and demonstrate strength, assert French agency, outmaneuver rivals, and gain US support for French policies.

BORING FROM WITHIN

In the aftermath of de Gaulle's resignation, the PCF claimed six of nineteen ministries, making their "march to power" seem more likely.[15] Concerned about American images of France, French officials closely followed American responses to the crisis.[16] French Ambassador to the United States Henri Bonnet wrote Bidault that de Gaulle's resignation was met with shock and emotion. Many observers feared that the general's departure would lead to instability and a weak government; they assumed that continued privations would further contribute to the PCF's popularity. Some believed that communists provoked the crisis, and that Thorez was attempting to transition from a coalition to a communist-dominated government, a development that could lead to other communist regimes in Western Europe.[17]

French officials hoped to carefully manage American perceptions of the crisis because they desperately needed a loan to aid recovery efforts and bolster the new government. After de Gaulle's resignation, the mood was hardly propitious. French intelligence in early February reported that State Department officials approved of Socialist Felix Gouin's economic plans but complained that French policy was too vague on Soviet matters.[18] Bombarded with reports of communist intrigue, however, Caffery wrote the department on February 9 urging a loan. He warned that the situation had "seriously deteriorated," and that to refuse the loan would undermine those "who want to see France remain an independent and democratic country."[19]

Meanwhile, international developments signaled a growing divide among wartime allies. On February 9, Josef Stalin publicly declared the inevitability of conflict between capitalist and socialist systems and the need to build an instrument of war to allow the USSR to meet any danger. To Western officials already prone to fear the worst, this suggested that the Soviet Union had embarked upon ideologically driven expansion.[20] Moscow chargé George Kennan's February 22 "Long Telegram," in which he suggested that the Soviets would respond only to American "manifestations of force," further foreclosed any conciliation between the powers.[21] French officials noted a distinct hardening of American policy after former British Prime Minister Winston Churchill's March 5th "Iron Curtain" speech, which had also warned of Soviet expansion. In Washington, DC, Bonnet reported that US officials now questioned the honor of Soviet leaders and their intention to meet international obligations. Military authorities had begun to think that conflict was inevitable. Truman and Leahy both, Bonnet said, now paid more attention to military opinion on these matters.[22]

As the international situation deteriorated, War Department intelligence retooled for the new threat posed by communism and began to expand its focus beyond military matters.[23] On February 14, the MID released the first "Intelligence Review," designed to provide worldwide coverage and timely intelligence to meet military needs. Unlike attaché and other intelligence reporting, the review offered no comment on the provenance of its information. MID directives did, however, list US military attachés, the FBI, Counterintelligence Corps, State Department, and the Office of Naval Intelligence as its sources, which suggests that the review was not the product of independent collection and analysis but an example of circular reporting – the reproduction of another agency's work clothed as original. Instead of injecting scrutiny into the analytic process, it only reinforced the apparent credibility of previous assessments. Truman's military aides read the review each week, often reporting to the president on its contents. Truman himself, on occasion, marked his copy of the report.

The new CIG also began producing a Daily Summary for President Truman and his senior advisers. This was a summary of dispatches from various departments relative to US foreign policy. Even if CIG officials claimed that a modest evaluative function existed in the selection of material included in summary, there was no assessment of the content. Journalist Arthur Krock may have declared that this "new intelligence system" allowed the president "to put himself abreast of what is happening in the world and ... have a daily key that unlocks what to most others are mysteries,"[24] but the reality was that the CIG was a small organization hamstrung from the start by the lack of independent collection capability and hostility from other agencies. As a result, for most of 1946, the Daily Summary largely reproduced Caffery's dispatches and policy recommendations from Paris in a succinct format – another example of circular reporting – rather than collecting data or offering all-source analysis. Despite its grave limitations, Truman read the Daily Summary each morning and professed approval of the product.

As before, US area experts and intelligence analysts closely monitored communist activity, and their French sources representing various factions continued to influence their assessments. Two tacks were apparent. The first – meant to raise alarm – suggested that without intervention France would go communist; the other – meant to reassure the United States and advance political agendas – decried government ineffectiveness and drew American attention to anti-communist French groups as alternatives.

In late February, for example, an "important ex-Communist"[25] explained the "dual nature" hypothesis of communist methods to embassy officials in Paris; that is, that PCF strategy since Liberation had been to attain power through legal means, but that the party had never fully abandoned preparations for illegal or armed conflict, more extreme means to be employed if other methods failed. Specifically, the source claimed that the PCF continued to "bore from within" the French military even as it organized "shock troops" and received considerable quantities of arms dropped over the French countryside.[26] European Division Chief Matthews thought it significant enough to forward the memo to Byrnes.

When asked about rumors of Soviet arms drops to PCF militants on March 5, Marc Berge, the chief of the Interior Ministry's intelligence directorate, told embassy analyst Norris Chipman "in the greatest secrecy" that while he had been unable to uncover any concrete evidence of this action, his ministry had discovered that communist militants were seeking heavy arms, including a secret order for armed trains, now more easily procured with a communist minister of armaments. Berge assured Chipman that he would obtain and share further details.[27]

Berge found an eager partner in Norris Chipman. In addition to working for Caffery, Chipman was one of a few "loyal" Foreign Service Officers who also worked for Raymond Murphy's embryonic intelligence service inside the department's European Division dedicated to rooting out worldwide communist subversion. A few years later, when Murphy asked Elbridge Durbrow[28] why Chipman was unable to find a position "doing political work" in some embassy, Durbrow told him that CIA officers in Rome (Chipman's posting after Paris) had complained that he had tried to run his own intelligence operation. Durbrow described Chipman in emotional terms, explaining how his private views influenced his public duties: "Norris is so hepped up on the subject of Communism that it affects his work."[29]

At the same time, French anti-communist sources, positioning themselves as better collaborators for the Americans, underscored the continuing importance of efforts to form an anti-communist resistance. Some lamented government weakness and beseeched allies for weapons; others suggested that there were those close to the government and military willing to organize with allied support. Using intelligence circuits, they were able to bypass normal official exchanges to get their message through. On February 12, a rightist source told the SSU that a "serious effort" was underway in France to create centralized control of various anti-communist organizations ranging from the political center to the extreme right. The informant indicated that several high-level French officials, including André Malraux, the celebrated novelist and de Gaulle's minister of information and several military leaders were willing to participate. De Gaulle was not currently affiliated with the group, but the source believed he might assume leadership in the future.[30] Following up, an informant very close to André Malraux reported de Gaulle's belief that war between the United States and the Soviet Union was inevitable and imminent, and that he would be called to head the French Army – created with Anglo-American help – in this eventuality.[31] Another conservative source indicated that an anti-communist grouping of the center-left had been assured financial backing from important industrialists in Lyon. Furthermore, the new amalgamation, designed to counterbalance communist strength in the May elections, had the support of Interior Minister André Le Troquer, Radical leader Edouard Herriot, and anti-communist Socialist Léon Blum; it also seemed to have the support of key generals: de Lattre, Juin, Bethouard, and Koenig.[32]

Despite this apparent progress, the specter of communist action persisted. On March 11, the CIG reported the first of several warnings that year of an imminent communist coup in France. Military Attaché General Smith and Ambassador Caffery believed that a coup was possible but improbable in April unless Moscow ordered it.[33] French intelligence sources in contact with the assistant military attaché maintained that the danger persisted and provided copies of recent daily bulletins. The attaché's summary of these reports detailed incidents of political violence and sabotage, and PCF instructions to prepare for their exclusion from the government by alerting paramilitary forces and preparing for strikes and disruption of administrative services after the elections.[34]

Other intelligence seemed to illustrate communist efforts to bore within and undermine French institutions. On March 19, the editor of the *Tribune of Nations*, Jean Desbois, informed SSU agents that his own paper was under communist influence as were at least half of the French dailies and periodicals.[35] Desbois' views, the officers noted, represented those widely held in conservative circles.[36] Similar reports warned that communist strength in the CGT was growing and that it had become an "instrument of the Kremlin."[37] Yet others reported growing leftist influence in the Army with the incorporation on March 1 of 3,000 members of the FFI. This development had, one report argued, "reduced considerably the conservative domination for which the French Army has long been noted,"[38] an ironic assessment since incorporation of the FFI into the regular Army was a critical step in disbanding communist militias after the war. Another report (questionably) extrapolated general election results to underscore the alleged leftward trend in the Army. "Obviously," it asserted, "since 35 percent of the votes in the October elections were cast for the Communist Party, extreme left-wing sympathies must be prevalent in ... the rank and file of the French Army."[39] More ominously, "anti-Soviet émigré" informants told SSU agents that Soviet repatriation officials in France were rounding up Soviet citizens and forcing them into repatriation camps or liquidating those who resisted, charges likely based in some truth.[40] However, Soviet arrests on French soil were not the only concern. These squads could also, the SSU report asserted, "easily act as the nuclei of a pro-Soviet militia if there were a communist uprising in France."[41] Reports like these, exaggerated and not easily disproved because they were rooted in ideological assumptions and the ethereal realm of possibilities, greatly contributed to the belief that measures must be taken to counter the communist threat before the upcoming elections.

Against this backdrop, French leaders pressured American officials to approve a sizable loan. In late March, just as Léon Blum prepared to return to the United States to resume negotiations, Foreign Minister Georges Bidault warned of a possible "reorientation" of French foreign policy if France did not receive substantial financial assistance, a statement that assumed even more importance once splashed on the front page of the *New York Times*. Miffed State Department officials cabled Caffery on March 22 and directed him to discuss the matter with Bidault.[42] When Caffery visited him that evening, Bidault expressed surprise at the affair, stating that he was merely pointing out that his government would face many difficulties applying its economic policies if financial assistance failed to materialize. France would not tilt toward the Soviet Union, he said, unless the PCF takes over the government.[43] The message could not have been clearer. Failure to provide a loan would weaken the government and strengthen the communists, who would pivot toward the Soviet Union once they took power.

By April, growing fears of Soviet expansionism and influence over the PCF began to reverberate in American policy. On April 1, 1946, George Kennan, now back in Washington, DC, commented on a draft policy statement on France, questioning whether it gave sufficient attention to "the implications of Soviet power in French internal affairs." The PCF's electoral support put it on par with other major political parties, he argued, but communist discipline and organization gave them greater influence as "the strongest single force in French political life." The PCF, in turn, he argued, was influenced and directed by Soviet leaders.[44] Kennan warned that the PCF program was hostile to American objectives and that "Russian influence in French affairs must be considered a major impediment in the path of American policies toward France."[45]

Through the FBI, French intelligence sources offered further confirmation of Soviet direction of the PCF. On April 3, FBI Director J. Edgar Hoover wrote the State Department and military intelligence agencies that "French intelligence has unquestionable proof showing that the Communist Party led by Thorez in France is taking orders directly from Moscow," a grossly exaggerated claim for which he provided no evidence.[46] The sources offered a familiar refrain: if the French could survive current economic conditions, then communism would lose its attraction, but if the PCF gained enough power within the government, they would attempt to create a false incident or national emergency in order to call in the Red Army and "effectively strangle all political opposition to the Party within France."[47] Embassy reports seemed to bear out this view. On April 4, Caffery wrote that the PCF was increasing pressure on the Foreign Ministry to align its policies with those of the Soviet Union.[48] Again, he recommended a loan to France to strengthen moderate elements in coming elections. We do not, Caffery wrote, want to give the impression to friendly Frenchmen that they are being abandoned to the communists.[49]

INTERNATIONALIZING EMPIRE

While American officials remained preoccupied by the ministerial crisis and upcoming elections in France, French leaders also kept a close watch on ferment in the colonies. Events there directly impacted the government's position in Paris; maintenance of the French empire was critical not only for domestic and economic health but also as a demonstration of strength to France's allies. In early 1946, they had reason to be anxious. US officials still viewed nationalist movements with sympathy and urged their French counterparts to concede to the aspirations of the colonized. However, the communist complexion of the Viet Minh and the North African communist parties' support for a nationalist agenda provided an avenue by which French officials could hope to change American perceptions of the situation and French colonial policy.

In 1946, the principal sources of American intelligence on Indochina were SSU reports, local press, and War Department telegrams, much of which followed transimperial routes and flowed from local French authorities. Early on, however, American observers held positive views of Ho Chi Minh and the government in Hanoi. In late January, American military adviser General Philip Gallagher told State Department experts that he detected little "Comintern" influence in Vietnam and that the Viet Minh were not "full-fledged doctrinaire communists."[50] American and French observers alike noted with satisfaction the March 6 Accords between Ho and French representative Jean Sainteny, which recognized Vietnam as a free state within an Indochinese Federation and French Union. The Vietnamese declared themselves ready to receive French troops relieving Chinese occupation forces; all sides also agreed to cease hostilities and create a positive climate for future negotiations.[51] MID analysts reported similar developments; they argued that the Indochinese communists' program "was nationalistic and not communistic" and described Ho as a democrat and capable leader willing to cooperate with the French.[52]

Meanwhile, anti-communist elements quietly worked to reshape American perceptions of the situation in Indochina and to tie it to events in France. General Yuan-Tse-Kien, political adviser to General Lu Han, leader of nationalist Chinese occupation forces in Tonkin, told SSU agents that his government suspected Ho had "sold out" to the French because he believed their government would "go communist" shortly.[53] French colonial authorities were also largely conservative and anti-communist. As Mark Lawrence has noted, these men had "risen to positions of influence under a prewar system that eschewed federalism and emphasized the assimilation of colonial peoples into a unified French empire"[54] that they had a stake in maintaining. In late May, the SSU reported that a member of High Commissioner Thierry d'Argenlieu's cabinet had wondered aloud to a US official if Thorez's determination to maintain the empire was "in order to hand it over intact to Moscow at the proper moment."[55] America's key allies in the region – France and China – thus warned that strategic concerns about communist influence should outweigh anti-colonialism.

As relations between the West and Moscow worsened, French officials in North Africa also found it increasingly difficult to stave off outside interference, for both sides realized the strategic value of France's territories on the Mediterranean. As they had for the previous two years, colonial authorities warned of growing collusion between local nationalist and communist parties, including new efforts to form national fronts.[56]

By early 1946, French officials also increasingly expressed concern over American and Soviet interest in the region. A report in late January indicated that Tunisia and Algeria were again on the brink of serious disturbances brought on by the meddling of the Anglo-Americans who encouraged agitation to prevent Russian inroads in the Mediterranean. It further warned that serious trouble could lead local leaders to call for Anglo-American intervention, a development that would have disastrous political consequences in France. The "Anglo-Saxons" would not let communism be established in North Africa, the report argued; therefore, the French must monitor the situation carefully.[57]

French officials recognized that tension in Europe had assumed a global aspect when coupled with imperial rivalry. The Foreign Ministry believed the Soviets had employed an "offensive policy" and that their attacks on the British and French were part of a concerted plan to hinder any grouping or alliance of Western powers against the USSR in the case of armed conflict.[58] In early March, General Paul Beynet wrote to Bidault about American policy in the Levant. In particular, US officials were increasingly concerned that their support for independence of the Levant states was playing into the hands of the Soviets.[59] Beynet further reported that the Soviet legation had expressed their disapproval of Anglo-French efforts to make the area a strategic zone; at the same time, communist journals continued to attack British and French imperialism.[60] As further evidence of the internationalizing of the situation in North Africa, Mast in Tunisia wrote in mid-March that the PCT hoped to exploit the March 6 Accords between the French government and Ho Chi Minh.[61]

In Washington, DC, US officials began to press French representatives about Soviet activity in North Africa. Ambassador Bonnet wrote that department experts raised concerns about reports of Soviet meetings in Tunisia, but he had assured them that this was not an important matter.[62] Meanwhile, an Egyptian official told the French minister in Egypt that he had discussed the communist threat at length with his American counterpart in Syria, who told him that the US had been "studying the Communist movement in Syria and its relationship with the Soviet legation for the past year." The Americans believed that Moscow was giving instructions to local parties but did not yet have proof of direct Soviet support.[63]

On March 18, 1946, just as political temperatures were rising in Paris over the possibility of a communist government after the spring elections, the SSU warned that communist propaganda was "rapidly making progress" in native Algerian circles and was accompanied by "marked diminution in pro-American sentiment." They attributed this to a recent change of policy in Moscow, which held that newly liberated colonies were not yet ready (by lack of ideological indoctrination) for immediate incorporation into the USSR; communists should thus work for the partial liberation through dominion status followed eventually by complete liberation. During these stages, the report continued, local militants would prepare the colonized for an eventual Soviet government. They also realized that they faced arrest if they expressed their views as nationalists but could freely espouse the same views under the "hammer and sickle." One source explained: "the French ... have driven us to Communism by not allowing us to become anything else."[64]

A "DUAL NATURE" THREAT

While attempting to stave off outside interference in their colonies, French officials continued to raise alarm about Soviet activity and potential coups in the metropole. This was a well-timed and calculated move; rumors of an armed coup were noticeably absent in internal reporting, but a constitutional referendum[65] and French elections approached. French sources played a key role in linking threats posed by the Soviets and the PCF, thus contributing to American overestimation of the threat posed by French communism and encouraging intervention.

There were a number of important streams of information feeding American understanding of the potential consequences of the political drama unfolding in Paris during the election campaigns. On May 1, Foreign Minister Bidault spoke privately with Secretary Byrnes, then in Paris for a Foreign Ministers Conference. An agitated Bidault twice mentioned the possibility of "Cossacks on the Place de la Concorde." With France's present military weakness and the danger of Soviet occupation, he warned, he should not be expected to adopt a strong position. When asked about the French loan and its bearing on the upcoming elections, Bidault said it would be helpful and should be announced early. He also asked for food aid; reduced rations could have a bad effect on the vote.[66] At the same time, Norris Chipman underscored Soviet activity in France. He suggested that Matthews review recent embassy telegrams on Soviet purchases of buildings and port facilities and communist control of customs and dockworker unions, important developments in connection with "the discharge of Soviet steamers loaded with arms, literature, agents, gold and other cargo of a special character," and Soviet economic aid, which would allegedly increase after the elections if the PCF demonstrated strength to form a new government. Chipman also obliquely referred to a potential communist "changement d'orientation" as wheat and coal arrived from the east.[67]

Meanwhile, anti-communist sources again fed rumors of communist coups. On May 2 rightist circles claimed the PCF would attempt to seize power prior to the June elections through some form of illegal action if the constitution failed to pass. Caffery and General Smith discounted this possibility since the communists hoped to improve their position through legal methods in the elections.[68] It is likely, however, that the same rightist sources, through their webs of intelligence contacts, reached the US military. In early morning hours of May 3, military intelligence reported the PCF would wait until the June 2 National Assembly elections to consider a coup if the constitutional referendum passed on May 5. However, should the constitution be rejected, the PCF would "definitely attempt" to seize power on May 6, immobilizing the US Army in the process by destroying its transport and fuel supplies. The estimate further claimed that 300,000 communists were now armed in France.

With this scenario in mind, General Joseph McNarney, commander of US Forces in the European Theater, requested the authority to move American troops into France for the "protection of critical installations."[69] State Department officials did not doubt communist aims but did question the timing and proposed response. Deputy Director of European Affairs John Hickerson, Acting Secretary of State Dean Acheson, and Assistant Chief of Western European Affairs James Bonbright did not believe the PCF was ready to abandon the legal path to power. The movement of US troops into France could make the situation worse, and "might even cause the communists to appeal to the Soviet Union for help on the grounds that the United States had intervened." Shortly thereafter, they wrote an alternate draft of the message for President Truman. Admiral Leahy, who had long ago embraced the weakness and revolution narrative, took both drafts to the president that afternoon; Truman preferred the War Department instructions, which were then sent,[70] a surprising development given the State Department's traditional role assessing internal political conditions in foreign countries. As Leahy described it later that day, it was he who had secured Truman's approval.[71]

In a subsequent dispatch, Caffery demonstrated once more that the State Department's position only differed from the military view on issues of method and timing; the dual nature thesis could explain any eventuality. On one hand, the PCF believed the constitutional referendum would pass, and this would bolster their position in the June 2 elections and allow them to introduce Soviet-style communism in gradual stages through disintegration of the "bourgeois state apparatus." On the other, PCF leaders were anxious about the campaign against the constitution and obstacles in their legal path to power and thus contemplated a military coup. Caffery claimed that the PCF Politburo believed they would eventually have to resort to force to conquer power and therefore devoted considerable attention to paramilitary matters. While he did not believe this likely for now, Caffery did not discount the possibility that "party police and military organizations could ... decide the political fate of France." Armed groups acting in concert with the Paris police and supported by the CGT had the capability to both seize and hold power.[72]

On May 5, the French public narrowly defeated the draft referendum, a major blow for the PCF. Caffery thought that the specter of Thorez as prime minister had aroused normally apathetic voters sensing danger; in this way, the referendum was less about the constitution than about communism.[73] He failed to note that the result was achieved without any of the US aid he had recommended so urgently, giving lie to the notion that France would go communist if its needs were not immediately satisfied. There were also no communist-inspired disturbances as feared. But US officials did not conclude that they had overestimated the danger; instead, they feared that the referendum results would hasten communist efforts to seize power before or immediately after upcoming elections in June.

De Gaulle himself took advantage of US uncertainty and used intelligence circuits to suggest that dark times lay ahead for France. A rightist military source told the SSU that de Gaulle believed that the present system of political parties would be destroyed in what he called "L'événement" – the financial collapse of France and ensuing debacle – "during which the Communists would assume leadership, and, finally, the war between the Western Allies and the USSR." The same source reported de Gaulle's intense interest in the upcoming elections.[74] And so, Caffery again urged a loan to be announced in mid-May to derive the maximum political benefit. Likely thinking about reports of Soviet wheat and Polish coal deliveries, he also recommended that ships carrying US food and products should also arrive just before the June elections. This would, he argued, "hearten French elements which look to the west."[75]

On May 7, Colonel Robert Solberg, now the US military attaché in Brussels, reported the PCF would attempt to seize power on May 12 in light of the defeat of the draft constitution; agitation would begin immediately with strikes in nationalized factories. He further estimated that the

PCF "are capable of seizing and remaining in power and will do so if Moscow directs."[76] Leahy noted Solberg's telegram the following day, remarking in his diary that a "reliable source" had reported the possibility of an "extensive" communist uprising in France.[77] The next day, SSU intelligence indicated other communist preparations to seize power.[78] A rightist source close to the French General Staff told the SSU that large groups of communists from Central Europe and Holland were then gathering in southern France and alleged parachuting of arms all over France (but especially near Paris) by Soviet and Yugoslav planes and considerable arms traffic into the interior of France from the Belgian border; the source also reiterated the belief that Soviet cargo ships carrying wheat were also loaded with arms. This activity, they believed, suggested an "important revolutionary international chain" forming in Western Europe around all PCF organizations, controlled ultimately by a Soviet General Staff.[79] Despite these indications, the coup failed to materialize. Solberg later suggested that it had been "postponed."[80]

Chipman sought to explain why there had been no coup after all, warning that electoral setbacks and communist moderation did not mean that the PCF had abandoned its quest for power or conspiratorial methods. Many observers, he claimed, had erroneously assumed that French communists were only revolutionary when their propaganda and slogans reflected pure Marxism or Leninism. Communist leaders justified present moderation and participation in bourgeois governments, he said, because they believe that the masses will be radicalized once they are put in motion.[81] The purpose of French communism was, above all, "to favor under all circumstances the Kremlin's policies." Through the French fifth column, Chipman claimed, the Soviets hoped to force profound economic, social, and political transformations with the eventual goal of "the disappearance of France as an independent nation" and its incorporation into a "multinational Soviet state system."[82] Chipman maintained that an armed coup in France had not yet occurred because the internal climate and international situation had not matured. He returned to the dual nature thesis put forward by anti-communist sources: the communists would conceal their real program through moderate policies but would continue to undermine the state by "boring from within" and engaging in "parallel operations" – to prepare their militias for "the assurance of ultimate victory."[83]

In Washington, DC, Ambassador Bonnet noted the effects of this analysis: "alarmist pronouncements continue to circulate."[84] René Massigli, the French ambassador to Britain, reported that the Soviet problem continued to haunt the Anglo-Americans. "They feel that communist infiltration is everywhere," he said; "they even ask to what measure French policy is still autonomous."[85] The urgency of the situation overcame the hesitation of the preceding months; the United States signed a $650 million loan agreement with France just four days before the elections.

Despite alarmist pronouncements and fears to the contrary, the PCF did not gain substantially in the June 2 elections. The MRP's success meant that the PCF would no longer be the single largest party, nor would there be a communist-Socialist majority.[86] Caffery noted the difficulties facing Bidault – then working to form a government – but believed the PCF would cooperate to avoid a chaotic situation that could return de Gaulle to power. "The communists are not afraid of Bidault," he wrote, "but [they] are very much afraid of de Gaulle."[87] MID analysts attributed the results to anti-communist opposition in the Catholic Church and the effects of the US loan, which many saw as American commitment to help French recovery.[88] Bonnet reported that the results – seen as the most important in the history of postwar Europe – had both increased French prestige and demonstrated France's leading role in Europe.[89]

On June 16, 1946, Charles de Gaulle reentered the political scene. He spoke in Bayeux, the first town liberated by the allies during the Normandy landings. He weighed in on the future form of the constitution, warning against dictatorship and factional politics, and calling for a bicameral legislature and a strong executive standing above the parties. MID noted the speech with interest as indicating de Gaulle's wish to return to power.[90] A few days later, a group of 100 young men vandalized the PCF headquarters in Paris after a day commemorating the anniversary of de Gaulle's famous June 18, 1940, call to resistance. Soon after, the PCF mounted a massive counterdemonstration against these "fascists" and called for a 25 percent wage increase. For three hours, hundreds of thousands "bearing red flags and singing the 'Internationale' and 'Marseillaise'" paraded through Paris.[91] The MID warned that these events represented "the most serious civil disturbances in France since the end of the war" and could presage violence as battlelines between communists and anti-communists "[had] never been more sharply drawn."[92] Subsequent CIG reports reinforced the importance of de Gaulle's return to active politics.[93] Privately, de Gaulle maintained clandestine contact with US intelligence through anti-communist sources who reiterated his firm alignment with the Anglo-Americans and his belief that "l'événement" in France and an impending showdown between the West and the Soviet Union would bring him back to power.[94]

Norris Chipman viewed the communist march of June 20 as a "dress rehearsal designed to prepare the mob of the proletariat of the Red Belt encircling Paris." One of his contacts, an ex-communist, told him that PCF strategy to seize power would mirror the Bolsheviks in 1917, but instead of soldiers from barracks, workers from factories would act in concert with communist militias. The PCF remained in the government, Chipman argued, because Moscow wanted to pressure French officials on matters affecting Soviet interests and because they did not want to alienate the petty bourgeoisie or peasants yet by threatening violence or a general strike with another important election slated for the fall. It was obvious, he maintained, that communist policy in France conflicted with the US aim of helping French recovery, and he warned that there could be a grave social crisis if the financial situation did not improve; in this event, the PCF could launch a coup de force the Soviets would have to support because the PCF was their most important fifth column abroad.[95] Again Chipman did not explain why, if the PCF was a sacrificial pawn, the Soviets would intervene to support an ill-conceived power grab that could lead to American intervention and raise the potential for a war for which they were not ready.

SOVIET STRONGHOLDS

The situation in Paris was further complicated by the sense that French government did not have full authority over its territory, that it had moved from one occupation to the next. Attention was particularly focused on historically communist areas in southern France. The SSU reported in detail and specificity about Soviet inroads there, largely based upon information gleaned from anti-Soviet Russian émigrés, but also Italian, Spanish, and Swiss intelligence services whose networks ran through the region. The substance of the reports remained the same: covert communist activity in southern France threatened the state, but there was an underfunded anti-communist resistance willing to act once it received assistance. While much of this alleged activity was related to efforts against the Franco regime, the presence of communist agitators and a robust arms traffic into France only fed fears of a communist coup against the French government in the aftermath of two major electoral disappointments for the PCF.

The French press began to report the discovery of numerous arms caches, some of which allegedly had their origin in mysterious parachutages, in the summer of 1946, publicly lending credence to many of the reports already circulating in American and French intelligence circles.[96] In mid-June, French police discovered forty tons of arms and munitions at the Château de Cambes in southwestern France. While US intelligence officials assumed the caches were connected to Soviet intrigue, the destination for these arms remained unclear.[97] French authorities and a British Embassy source soon linked the discovery at the Château de Cambes to a Zionist arms-trafficking ring, which had smuggled enormous quantities of guns out of the Low Countries through France en route to Palestine.[98]

Ominous reports about communist activity continued to flow in that summer. On June 10, the SSU reported a "well-placed member of the Italian Military Intelligence Service" told them that 2,000–3,000 pro-communist agitators of Yugoslav, Italian, Spanish, and Hungarian nationalities had recently passed from the Italian border into France with the help of local PCF members.[99] A source with contacts in Swiss intelligence told the SSU they had discovered arms traffic entering France from the Swiss border, including machine guns and other heavy weaponry.[100] Another "anti-communist" informant told SSU agents that the party was conducting extensive training in street fighting for local militants.[101] In early July, one report suggested that parts of southeastern France had become "Soviet strongholds," with Grenoble as the seat of the "extreme-left-wing activities of the Russian emigration in France," and alleged that these activities could serve as the nuclei for future military operations.[102] Spanish officials in Madrid decried alleged French weakness in the face of the communist threat, claiming that Spanish communists, and not the French government, were the "real masters of the South of France," where they were allegedly organizing 10,000 men into detachments and international brigades for an invasion of Spain with the help of the Red Army.[103] Despite the obvious motivations of these anti-communist, pro-Franco sources, Caffery wrote Byrnes that he agreed with their substance.[104]

French military sources also sought to capitalize on American concerns about French weakness. One report from the French General Staff warned that the Soviets would move a huge land army of 250 divisions into France in the event of war. The report repeated claims that the Soviets were creating a "vast military-revolutionary organization" in France "with the knowledge and perhaps even complicity of the French government." Echoing previous claims that the French military and police forces would be no match for this invasion, the sources suggested that the Soviets hoped to marshal their forces in France for full-scale invasions of Spain and the British Isles. The report concluded with a dire warning: "there is not a minute to lose if Russian strategic maneuvers in southern France are to be effectively counteracted," and it recommended French government action to thwart fifth column activity and the reestablishment of US and British air bases throughout southern France.[105] Reports like these – that Soviets were attempting "to cover all of Europe with a network of secret organizations whose centers of control lie behind the Iron Curtain," for use in the event of civil wars or an anti-Soviet war – continued to circulate into the fall, only heightening the American sense of danger.[106]

On July 18, growing tension with the USSR and the looming Paris Peace Conference led President Truman to direct the CIG to prepare special estimates of Soviet foreign policy. ORE 1, "Soviet Foreign and Military Policy," touched on many of the issues raised by current intelligence reporting but also contradicted SSU and embassy reports of secret communist preparations for an armed insurrection. The Soviets, CIG analysts concluded, may seek "world domination," but they were not ready for war and hoped to avoid any conflict for the foreseeable future. In Western Europe, the Soviets would try to prevent the formation of regional blocs and to influence national policies through the activities of local communist parties. Specifically, the estimate concluded that Soviet policy earlier that year had been designed to support the PCF in a bid to gain control of France through "democratic political processes" and shape French policy in the Soviet Union's favor. The estimate indicated that a resort to force was "unlikely" due to the possibility of provoking a major international conflict.[107] Despite the apparent brake on more sensational claims in the estimate, US officials continued to view these reports as evidence of communist preparations for an eventual war, whenever it might come.

On July 28, de Gaulle gave the second of his major speeches at Bar-le-duc. Informants close to de Gaulle alerted Caffery to the important speech two weeks before.[108] This time, the general spoke of international issues and France's place in the world, which he argued was tied to decisions on Germany. Again, anti-communism provided a common language to explain the issues of the day. American observers were clearly struck by the general's implicit message: Germany was weakened by the war, but danger still existed in the possibility that it might link its ambition to that of another great power, a clear reference to the USSR. De Gaulle recognized that the world was now dominated by the United States and the Soviet Union. He called for an Anglo-French alliance, and for Old Europe to unite in a "Western bloc" to reestablish equilibrium on the continent and exert influence in world affairs. De Gaulle himself told an embassy representative afterward that he hoped his speech would be "useful."[109]

This was, politically, "one of de Gaulle's best speeches," Wallner wrote; intended for domestic audiences, it was also likely an attempt to rally a western-oriented anti-communist majority around de Gaulle in France.[110]

Franco-Soviet relations continued to deteriorate in the aftermath of de Gaulle's speech. General Georges Catroux, the French ambassador in Moscow, reported that Soviet Foreign Minister Vyacheslav Molotov had accused France of failing to support the Soviet Union. Catroux remarked that perhaps he was basing this opinion on recent comments made by "someone outside of government" – a reference to de Gaulle – and reminded him that only Bidault and the Quai made policy.[111] Bidault later remarked that there now appeared two camps where the middle powers were no longer grouped against the great powers but aligned behind one of them based on their "tendencies."[112] Similarly, the CIG noted a change in French objectives. A "very close" associate of Bidault told Caffery that Bidault no longer believed France could act as a mediator between the East and the West. He also relayed an important message: if Bidault continues in the new government, he plans to "eliminate communist participation within five or six months."[113] The SSU further reported that recent speeches of Thorez and Duclos and the emerging struggle in the CGT between communist Benoit Frachon and Socialist Léon Jouhaux suggested that the communists were shifting to opposition.[114]

With an eye to changing circumstances, the State Department issued a new policy statement in mid-September. "France today," it said, "is the scene of an internal political battle, the outcome of which is of the greatest importance to the United States, and whose ramifications will extend to all the countries of Western Europe." Echoing intelligence appraisals of the situation, the statement asserted that Soviet expansion "is being played in miniature on the stage of France." The PCF, directed by Moscow and with anti-American policies, has attained "a position in the political ... and economic life of France which give it for the moment a virtual veto on the domestic and foreign policies of the Government." The United States needed a strong and stable France and should help her regain former strength and influence and prevent it from becoming "the western bastion of an inherently hostile continental system."[115]

The statement mentioned two specific problems worthy of consideration. First, the statement suggested that French obsession with the German problem meant they were often "blinded to newer and possibly greater dangers." Because France's importance to the German settlement and Western Europe could not be overlooked, it was vital to include them in decisions and avoid faits accomplis, which the PCF could exploit.[116] As we have seen, however, French leaders had already expressed grave concerns about Soviet aggression but adeptly tied it to popular desire to gain the most from the German settlement and the threat posed by domestic communism.[117] The statement further warned of the PCF's anti-Americanism and the "inferentially anti-American" chauvinism of the right and their support for de Gaulle's "inflexible attitude." However, the United States still had friends within the majority of the French people who recognize the common historical and ideological bonds of the two nations, and French financial and industrial circles, "who see in the US the salvation of their particular interests and values." The statement, though, warned that American officials should be wary of the last group because many have ulterior motives; affiliation with them could make the US "a reactionary factor in French internal politics" and turn the mass of Frenchmen against us,[118] a prescient concern given the actual influence of reactionary French elements within US diplomatic and intelligence circles.

Not long after, the CIG, now tentatively engaging in analysis, prepared a Special Study on Soviet Military Intentions for President Truman, a follow-up to their earlier ORE-1 and in response to recent intelligence – including the French General Staff report – suggesting the imminence of Soviet military aggression. CIG analysts noted recent claims that Soviet intelligence chiefs in Western European countries had been ordered in late August to disrupt industrial activity through sabotage, strikes, and disorders, "in preparation for military action in the months to come" and that Stalin had ordered a halt to Soviet demobilization. Again, they suggested that the more sensational reports should be taken with caution; each of the reports "may be explained on other grounds than the imminence of aggressive Soviet military operations," and they noted a clear distinction between Soviet capabilities and intentions. The alleged orders referred to a future operation; the fact that there had been no strikes or disorders suggested that the action was, at the very least, not imminent. Furthermore, this intelligence came from an "unsure" source, and it was possible that the alarmist element was introduced in the report's transmission. These analysts considered it "unlikely that the Soviet Union would resort to overt military aggression in the near future."[119]

That fall, another constitutional referendum narrowly passed. This draft presented two major differences from the one rejected by voters in May, namely that it proposed a bicameral legislature and enlarged the functions of the presidency. De Gaulle had, however, opposed the draft. A reliable source with "important connections in high rightist and Jesuit circles" told SSU agents that de Gaulle had likely called for rejection of the draft constitution in order to enable Popular Republicans to force the PCF and SFIO to concede to expansion of presidential powers as outlined in his Bayeux speech, powers he hoped to deploy himself.[120] War Department Intelligence suggested that high abstention rates (31.9 percent), de Gaulle's opposition, and voter dissatisfaction with the "inefficiencies and halfway measures of tripartite government" foreshadowed a bitter struggle between communists and anti-communists during the campaigning season.[121]

Fully consumed by Cold War imperatives, the War Department further refined SSU objectives the day after the referendum in France. The first priority of the unit was "the collection of secret information on the internal organization and covert or semi-covert activities of the major communist parties throughout the world." Intelligence on communist parties who are "national political groups" would come, the memo said, from "public sources of information" and "satisfactory general estimates of the activities, plans and potential power of the party." Intelligence on internal party matters – purges, funding, paramilitary activities, etc. – would come from secret sources. This information, it stated, would come from "informants not members of the CP." Indeed, the memo contained an important revelation – "the great preponderance" of reports on communists in the past had come from "the large number of anti-communist groups and individuals currently active in almost every country, ranging from ... Socialist[s] and right-wing parties, government officials, and business and clerical figures to anti-Soviet émigrés and professional informants" – without acknowledging the fundamental problems posed by this array of sources. Moreover, it anticipated no attempts to penetrate communist organizations and gather their own intelligence.[122] The lack of insight into communist organizations meant, of course, that War Department intelligence was viewed only through the lens of its anti-communist informants, many of whom had a stake in delegitimizing their communist rivals.

While the summer had brought positive developments – the May constitutional referendum and June elections, warmer weather, and more abundant food – the situation that fall was deteriorating in the face of another cold winter and rising prices. There were widespread feelings that the government could not cope with France's economic problems; all parties were seen as horse-trading in their own interests. Caffery described the mood in emotional terms; the situation in France had led to "profound malaise" and "deep psychosis" among the electorate, which could impact the November elections. "Mental confusion" was leading some to believe that some form of authoritarian government either under the PCF or de Gaulle was needed.[123] As the elections approached, War Department intelligence, borrowing from similar reports the previous month, reported that Soviet anti-American propaganda was in full swing. French anti-communists recognized the success of these efforts, they said, and had been "begging the American officials in France to take counter-measures."[124] Leahy read the report, marking it for the president's interest.

SECRET ALLIANCES

While all eyes remained fixed upon France during the election period, American and French leaders also continued to carefully observe the situation in France's overseas possessions. French authorities prepared for upcoming negotiations with Vietnamese representatives at Fontainebleau in July, and focus turned toward events in North Africa, where US officials were now concerned about reports of growing Soviet influence.

That spring, American authorities increasingly drew connections between French Indochina and elections in the metropole, echoing similar language used by their French contacts. On May 4, US chargé d'affaires in Moscow Horace Smith wrote to Byrnes that Soviet criticism of French colonialism in Indochina had disappeared, and he offered two possible explanations. First, the Soviets wished to avoid embarrassing the PCF before the elections by forcing them to adhere to a Soviet policy that was bound to alienate a sizable number of followers. Second, in the event of a communist-dominated France, French Indochina within a French Union could be more valuable to the Soviet Union than an independent Vietnam. In this case, Smith said, Indochina would constitute a base for communist activity in Southeast Asia.[125] In mid-June, the CIG reported Smith's belief that the Soviets were employing "more dangerous" indirect methods of influence there and contrasting Soviet anti-colonialism with the imperial policies of the United States and Great Britain. They were also, he claimed, working to manipulate and control native fifth columns.[126]

When Byrnes asked Bidault in early May about the colonies, Bidault cited the "tranquility" of French North Africa, and France's dependence upon the region's manpower and resources, comments that clearly reflected French desire to keep the colonies an internal matter.[127] Nevertheless, there were growing indications that geopolitics were increasingly shaping dynamics there. The CIG reported intense anti-American feeling in the Levant, and the Syrian prime minister told the

US minister there that Soviet influence was gaining daily ground at the US's expense.[128] In his May 10 report, Norris Chipman highlighted the importance of the French colonies in Soviet international calculations. The French strategic position in the Near East and Africa was especially crucial because these were areas where the Kremlin was beginning to assert itself.[129] Bonnet himself noted that Soviet interest in Libya and Tunisia had drawn American attention to France's possessions in North Africa.[130] That same month, the State Department recognized the sovereignty of France over its nonmetropolitan possessions,[131] indicating that US policy for the French colonies was based primarily on its relations with the mother country and the developing situation in Europe.

Despite Bidault's pronouncements about the tranquility of French North Africa and the Levant, colonial officials privately remained concerned about communist activity. On June 11, Beynet wrote that a Syrian union leader and editor of a communist journal had recently traveled to Moscow for an international trade union conference. His sources, however, told him that the journey was a cover to report to Soviet leaders. Beynet said that he had obtained a copy of his report; in addition to the internal situation, it discussed communist penetration and the possibility for expansion, as well as American inroads.[132] US intelligence also highlighted Soviet interest in the region. On May 21, the SSU reported that an anti-Soviet émigré source had told them that UPS members in France had received secret orders from the Soviets to reestablish contact with friends in the French colonies to persuade them to form pro-Soviet cells in their adopted countries.[133]

That summer, French talks with Vietnamese officials at Fontainebleau broke down over Vietnam's position in the French Union and the unification of the three historic "kys" of Vietnam.[134] Caffery reported that Vietnamese representatives had bitterly accused the French of violating the March 6 accord. Leftist French press, notably the communist *L'Humanité*, sided with Vietnam, while conservative papers unleashed an "explosion of wrath" against the Vietnamese delegation.[135]

Intelligence reporting reflected growing suspicion of communist intentions in Vietnam and the narrative that local communism could not be considered independent of French communism and Soviet intrigue. Citing no specific evidence, a reliable Socialist source told the SSU that the Soviets "attach primary importance" to Ho's success because they believed he could cause the nationalist Chinese government maximum annoyance in the event of a US–Soviet war in which China engages on the side of the Americans.[136] The Soviets had allegedly ordered the PCF to "fully support Viet Nam claims in the press and in the government and to present Ho Chi Minh as the liberator of Indo China," to provide Vietnamese negotiators at Fontainebleau with advisers and to dispatch loyal Army officers to Indochina to help organize cadres for a future Vietnamese Army.[137]

In Saigon, High Commissioner Thierry d'Argenlieu continued to sabotage negotiations.[138] Determined to avoid a complete breakdown, Ho stayed behind in Paris in a last attempt to reach an agreement. To an American journalist there, he called upon the United States to exert influence upon France in order "to swing the balance toward peace and independence before it is too late for all of us," and he implored Americans to "not be blinded by this issue of communism." Instead of a lasting agreement, however, both sides signed a modus vivendi, which put off major points of contention until later negotiations slated for early 1947. Ho likely signed the agreement in the hopes that the November elections might bring a more sympathetic government to power in Paris.[139] Like US intelligence, he may have overestimated the possibility of substantial support from the PCF.

By September, the Foreign Ministry could report that Franco-American relations had improved on the Vietnamese issue. The termination of the Patti mission – an OSS intelligence-operation viewed as pro-Vietnamese and anti-French by French officials – in late 1945 had removed one thorn in the relationship. Moreover, they noted, there had since been "a readjustment in US policy in the face of Chinese and Russian imperialism." This, plus the Americans' increasing acceptance of French orientalist arguments that the Vietnamese government had not demonstrated the political and economic capacity to govern, had led to more reserve toward Ho and a hands-off attitude on the part of the American administration.[140]

US officials continued to watch developments in Indochina closely. On September 9, the State Department referenced the August 29 SSU intelligence about PCF support of Ho Chi Minh, and asked the US Consul to report "indications subservience to Party line by Ho and other leaders, relative strength communist and non-communist elements Viet Nam, and contacts with communists other countries."[141] Soon after, Caffery received Ho Chi Minh at the embassy. Ho confirmed that Fontainebleau talks had broken down over the status of Cochin China, which the French wanted to be independent within the French Union but the Vietnamese insisted should be part of Vietnam under one government. Ho indicated that he would welcome US assistance, and, Caffery said, "took [the] occasion to say that he was not a communist."[142] American skepticism, however, was growing.

In Saigon, US Consul Charles Reed reported that d'Argenlieu adviser Pierre Clarac and the Chief of the French Sureté had approached him about increased communist activity in Indochina, a "disquieting" trend. Chinese communists were active in Saigon and Haiphong, with Vietnamese communists most active in Tonkin and Annam, and even in Cochin China. Deftly linking metropole and empire, Clarac added that it was difficult to address this problem when the strength of the PCF in France precluded any possibility of using the word "communist" in connection with any unfavorable trends in the empire. Nevertheless, "[t]he communists are in Indochina," he said; "close watch ... must be maintained as agencies outside French Indochina are undoubtedly supplying propaganda."[143] While US Consul James O'Sullivan urged some skepticism of this revelation,[144] French military intelligence reports were unequivocal. They claimed that Chinese communists had intensified their activity in Vietnam in collaboration with Vietnamese communists. They hoped to use Vietnam as a sanctuary and propaganda base, while the Vietnamese hoped to gain support from a China eventually aided by the USSR.[145]

American concern about communism in North Africa also grew that summer, as officials feared that Soviet propaganda undermined historic affinity for the United States among the colonized. One episode demonstrates how overriding concerns shaped intelligence. In mid-July, the SSU reported growing anti-American sentiment in the region, blaming both pro-Axis and Vichy groups who had lost much after the American intervention in North Africa and communists working against the United States. Together, the report claimed, these extremes exercised majority control in the colonial administration.[146] American consul general in Algiers Harold D. Finley disagreed. He had not observed an anti-American trend in Algeria, and he maintained that official cooperation with the French continued.[147] Interest in this reporting did not stop there. On July 29, the State Department asked the SSU to resend the original report.[148] A month later, despite Finley's evidence to the contrary, the Intelligence Review repeated the claims. Borrowing language directly from the SSU memo, this version omitted the role of pro-Axis and Vichy groups, placing blame solely upon an "open anti-American campaign of the communists in Algeria" as "part of their penetration program for Africa." This activity, they argued, posed "a serious threat to the influence and prestige of the Western Allies in that area."[149]

The dangers of a communist-nationalist alliance and the pernicious influence of communists on the local political scene consumed French colonial authorities. In August, the resident general in Morocco Eirik Labonne wrote the Foreign Ministry about communist attempts to form a National Front for independence and espousal of nationalist themes. This coalition had not been yet realized due to nationalist hesitations. Any alliance, Labonne said, would likely be a matter of tactics than of any real sympathy.[150] Understanding the "sensitivity of North Africa to all political influences," French officials asked for periodic updates on the situation.[151] General Charles Mast in Tunisia likewise reported that Tunisian communists, despite having attacked nationalists in the past, now posed as champions of Tunisian liberties and sovereignty. It was crucial, he argued, that the Quai "appreciate the danger that would come from nationalist access to the communists' entire political arsenal and the means of expression that come with an authorized journal and political meetings."[152] Offers of collusion, he said, "almost always" come from the communists; as in Morocco, communists in Tunisia now hoped to organize a National Front. The PCT, as a legal party, now found itself at the head of a movement with claims as far as independence. Rather than a local section of the French Communist Party, the PCT was now dominated by Tunisians, a development that Mast claimed made the party illegal (native parties had been outlawed by a 1943 CFLN decree); their violation of statutes requiring respect for French sovereignty was also problematic. Mast thus requested that "the French government in the heart of which the communist party is represented," give him instructions regarding his approach to the communist group in Tunisia, now autonomous from the PCF and passing into illegality.[153]

PCF officials in Paris defended their record in support of the oppressed but stopped short of supporting independence. In September, Raymond Barbé responded to a letter from a PCT leader requesting their intervention against colonial repression in Tunisia. Somewhat defensively, he assured the writer that French communists had always supported native peoples, citing PCF intervention in the Chamber of Deputies against repressive measures and arrests in Tunisia. Barbé further argued that the PCF would not hesitate to support "the legitimate aspirations of the Tunisian people." This endeavor would represent a "common effort by the peoples of Tunisia and France against their common enemy."[154] However, far from signaling support for complete independence, the PCF letter's careful use of "legitimate" aspirations suggested, as French colonial authorities had, that there were some aspirations they would not countenance. Further, the call for continued union of the French and Tunisian peoples suggested preference for a solution short of independence.

French officials were certainly aware of growing American interest in the region, and they sought to exploit it. The CIG reported governor-general of

Algeria Yves Chataigneau's statement to the US consul general in Algiers that "he [was] working to prevent the formation ... of a communist-nationalist Alliance," but that "he [was] not too sanguine of success." It is likely that these warnings influenced American policy there, for the CIG also noted Ambassador Caffery's recommendation to postpone US–French negotiations over bases in North Africa until after the French elections in the fall.[155] Days later, Chataigneau "confirmed" an intelligence report that the communists "with Soviet inspiration" were offering an alliance to the nationalists, which he believed they would accept,[156] after which the CIG noted Caffery's suggestion that the USS *Franklin D. Roosevelt* aircraft carrier visit Algiers and Bone.[157] General Mast wrote Bidault that the US consul general in Rabat had asked about PCT influence on the Muslim masses and its relations with local nationalists; he suggested he had intelligence that local communists had received sizable funds for propaganda from France through Algiers. Despite the debate earlier in the summer about anti-Americanism in North Africa, this consul believed North African communists were increasingly hostile to the United States, and he saw the hand of Moscow – recently opposed to US views on other points – as the guiding force. Mast believed that the focused nature of the diplomat's inquiry demonstrated that he was obeying precise instructions from the US government on the matter.[158]

On September 12, the Intelligence Review reiterated the substance of French reports on the situation in North Africa: that communist parties in Algeria and Tunisia, acting on orders from Moscow, had reversed their policy of support for greater autonomy within the French Union and now demanded complete independence from France. They had also worked to effect an alliance between nationalists and communists, which would, by broadening Muslim suffrage, endanger French hegemony in North Africa and Anglo-American security in the Western Mediterranean.[159] This report, reviewed by Naval Aide Captain James Foskett at the White House, was marked for Truman's interest.

Just as fears of a communist coup circulated in the metropole during that summer and fall electoral campaign, similar chatter about an insurrection in North Africa began to circulate as French officials adopted a similar line. In July the CIG reported that a French colonial officer told the US consul general in Tangier that the French did not expect an uprising soon, but they did not discount the possibility of trouble ahead. This source gave the impression that he was more concerned by "communist-inspired activities" than nationalist agitation.[160] In September, the CIG reported that the US military attaché in Paris had spoken with "responsible French authorities" who expressed fear that "communist-inspired nationalists in North Africa may stage an open revolt and that existing French forces there may not be able to cope with it."[161] Interestingly, the US diplomatic agent in Tangier suspected recent disturbances "were not unwelcome to the French who hoped to justify intervention."[162]

US officials were indeed taking notice. The State Department policy statement in mid-September noted open PCF support for "the nationalist aspirations of the native North African populations," who, despite their skepticism toward communism, were unlikely "to discard the support offered for the first time by a major French political party."[163] And in the coming weeks, the African and Near Eastern Divisions in the State Department worked to align their implementation of department policy on North Africa. African Division experts argued that the policy for North Africa should be to "prevent [it] from falling into unfriendly hands," to favor the evolution of peoples toward self-government, and to maintain the open-door principle in Morocco. This policy, they wrote, was based on North Africa's strategic importance and the sense that American interests would be endangered if the Soviets controlled the area. Communists had, they wrote, been supporting the more extreme demands of the nationalists and urging an alliance. There was "a very real danger that, without radical change in the political setup of North Africa, the nationalists will not long resist the tempting assistance proffered them by the communists."[164] Nationalist leaders themselves warned this would happen if the Anglo-Saxon powers failed to support their objectives.[165] State Department analysts concluded that the United States should warn nationalists against joining the communists. Adopting French orientalist discourse, they also argued that the United States should "make it clear that in our opinion they are not ready for independence" but should anticipate gradual political and social evolution. At the same time, US officials should pressure the French government for a more liberal policy and work to persuade French colonial authorities and the Arab population that the communists were their common enemy.[166]

This posed a dilemma: the United States could not expect to develop a friendly, noncommunist France if they openly encouraged nationalists to work against it, nor could they afford to completely ignore the aspirations of the North African peoples. These policy recommendations were based upon the assumption that elements "friendly to the United States" would continue to control the French government. However, they argued that a communist government in the metropole would necessitate a shift in policy to "encourage and assist North African peoples" to gain independence from France and lean instead toward the United States. American goals in North Africa would require "interference in the internal affairs of another state, but the heavy responsibilities of leadership ... make such interference inescapable."[167] Communism, not nationalism, now guided American responses to France's crisis of power in North Africa. Not only were US officials moving away from anti-colonialism, many adopted French orientalist attitudes. Of significance, they were moving toward a more interventionist policy to prevent Soviet domination of this strategic region.

POLARIZATION

The French public voted in general elections on November 10, 1946. US officials reported gains for the PCF, making it again the largest political party in France. The MRP and Socialists lost ground, while rightist parties made substantial gains. State Department experts attributed this decline in the moderate parties to the PCF monopoly of Marxist ideology and to de Gaulle's attacks on the MRP and repudiation of the constitution. The PCF's political position gave them claim to leading cabinet posts if not the premiership; moreover, the possibility of governing France without the communists was no longer possible.[168]

Military intelligence bolstered the belief that France was torn between two extremes, either anti- or pro-communist. An Intelligence Review – marked for the president's attention – warned that the weakening of moderate groups in France and strengthening of the extremes was not conducive to political stability.[169] Soon after, another noted that prospects for a "strong, effective, democratic government in France ... are even dimmer than in the past."[170] Embassy officials maintained that the communists were contributing to the "decomposition" of the existing regime. They viewed Thorez's reference to a "French path to Socialism" in his November 18 London *Times* interview as a sign that the PCF still hoped to exploit "liberties enjoyed in a bourgeois democracy in their attempt to install gradually and legally a 'Soviet' dictatorship in France." There appeared "no force in France ... capable of arresting the advance of this 'Soviet Trojan Horse.'"[171]

French officials, however, sought to reassure their American counterparts that France remained friendly to the United States and that anti-communists were poised to challenge the PCF. On November 18, General Pierre Billotte, a "close collaborator" with General de Gaulle, told

General Matthew Ridgway[172] that the French elections actually showed that 75–80 percent of the French people inclined toward Anglo-American policies. While the PCF was the strongest numerically, they were not able to take power legally. However, there were signs that the communists might attempt "an illegal and forcible assumption of power." Only de Gaulle could prevent this, he argued, as "he is absolutely uncompromising in his opposition to the Communists." However, he warned that de Gaulle would need some assurance that he would have "the morale [*sic*] and political support of the United States," including material and financial assistance. Billotte hoped to see several powerful US senators and receive some guarantees that might overcome de Gaulle's reluctance to seek the presidency.[173]

The problem of determining PCF capabilities and intentions remained acute. As the CIG began to assume some of the SSU's collection capabilities and analytical functions, subtle disagreements over the PCF continued. On November 26, new CIG director, General Hoyt Vandenberg, disputed Caffery's mid-November claim that "the communists now have sufficient strength to seize power in France whenever they deem it desirable to do so." As evidence, Caffery had pointed to communist infiltration of key positions in government ministries and the Air Force; the ease with which workers could seize arsenals; communist maintenance of FTP cadres and international brigades; and the absorption of 2,000 "communistic officers" from the FFI into the French Army. Echoing Chipman's analysis and sensational claims about arms caches, international brigades, and an impending civil war, Caffery had argued that the PCF had not attempted to seize power because they believed it was better obtained legally and because it was contrary to current Soviet policy. Vandenberg, however, argued that there was reason to doubt that the communists were now able to seize power through a coup d'état. Any attempt would be opposed by the Army, which remained loyal to regularly constituted French authorities. He also denied that the FFI officers were all communists and maintained that the Army officer corps was largely anti-communist. Moreover, critical supply dumps remained under the Army, not the workers' control. Vandenberg also noted that PCF militants would have to contend with an armed and organized anti-communist resistance. "Although the communists have an undoubted capacity to precipitate civil war," he argued, "it is unlikely that they could at present succeed in a coup d'état."[174]

On December 16, Léon Blum became prime minister of France, head of a Socialist caretaker government before the election of a new president.

Ambassador Bonnet reported American satisfaction with Blum and their hope that the interim period would demonstrate the regular and parliamentary nature of the French government.[175] The next day, Caffery indicated that the overwhelming vote of confidence for Blum was in recognition of the weakness of French democracy and that a failure to do so could result in an attempt at an extreme solution – a reference to a communist government or de Gaulle's return. Some officials expressed relief but also fear that the basic issues of which parties will constitute the government and obtain ministerial portfolios had not been resolved. If these issues are not solved by January, Caffery said, then "France will ... be faced with the gravest of political crises."[176] Caffery maintained that present communist tactics were to continue "to attempt to 'colonize' France in gradual stages."[177]

WAR

While uncertainty prevailed in France, the situation in Indochina worsened, as both French and American views hardened. Two days after the elections in France, State Department Southeast Asia expert Abbot Low Moffat told his British counterpart Richard Allen that Vietnam was "susceptible to Communist influence." D'Argenlieu, he said, had become "bitterly anti-Vietnam, which he considers strongly communistic." Moffat illustrated the dilemma for American officials. He was very concerned that a continuation of present French policies would lead not only to anti-French sentiment in Vietnam but bitterness toward the Western democracies, which could lead to strong communist influence in the region.[178] At the same time, French intelligence and colonial officials continued to tie Ho's government to Moscow and claimed that it pursued ideological and territorial expansion;[179] they also warned of Soviet inroads in the region.[180]

On November 20, 1946, simmering tension between the French and the Vietnamese boiled over as French forces clashed with Vietnamese nationalists in Haiphong. Likely thinking about recent French intelligence reports, a high Foreign Ministry official told Caffery that they had "positive proof that Ho Chi Minh is in direct contact with Moscow and is receiving advice and instructions from the Soviets,"[181] a claim since discredited by lack of credible evidence. Ho was not in direct contact with Moscow – he did not have a good relationship with Stalin – nor was he receiving instructions from the Kremlin.[182] For his part, Admiral d'Argenlieu placed responsibility for the skirmishes directly on the government in Hanoi. The attitude of Vietnamese officials, coupled with documents seized from Vietnamese communists, he claimed, offered clear proof that they had launched a premeditated attack.[183]

Based upon the information shared with them by French officials, but lacking definitive proof, the United States was increasingly concerned about the Hanoi government's ties to Moscow. The State Department asked its representatives in Vietnam about the possibility that Ho had been in contact with the Soviets. Vice consul in Hanoi James O'Sullivan thought it possible that Ho had some contact with Moscow but that he would maintain relations with the French. But O'Sullivan also saw developments in Vietnam tied to the political situation in France. If communists controlled the French government, then the Vietnamese would likely progressively apply Marxist principles. However, he thought it curious that the French only now expressed their concern about these ties since they knew that Ho had been an important Comintern official and had strongly suspected he had received instructions from Moscow for the past year. He also thought it "peculiar" that the French should raise these concerns at the very time when they could be preparing to force the Vietnamese to accept their terms or establish a puppet government. "French concern over communism," he wrote, "may well be devised to divert [the department's] attention from French policy in Indochina."[184]

In Paris, French officials continued to view Indochina through a metropolitan lens. Philippe Baudet, the head of the French Foreign Ministry Asian Bureau, told Caffery that French decisions on Indochina were only temporary due to the "uncertain political situation in France." He admitted that d'Argenlieu might have to be relieved because of his intransigence and disdain for Vietnamese representatives. But he also claimed that the deteriorating situation in Indochina was part of a deliberate plan by the Vietnamese to exploit the French political situation in the metropole to gain concessions and that they were going to great lengths to obtain PCF support. This was embarrassing for PCF leaders, Baudet said, because they were trying to convince the French people that they would safeguard French international interests.[185] The next day, d'Argenlieu told Caffery that the situation was not as bad as reported in the press; unless Thorez headed the government, he would be able to restore normality without a campaign of reconquest. However, he remarked, "We must face the fact that all the members of the Ho Chi Minh government are communists and use communist methods."[186]

On December 5, Acheson wrote to Moffat, then in Vietnam to investigate the situation, with a summary of US thinking for his use when he met with Ho. Acheson asked him to "keep in mind Ho's clear record as agent of international communism, absence evidence recantation Moscow affiliations, confused political situation France and support Ho receiving French Communist Party [sic]." The least desirable outcome of current troubles, he wrote, would be a "communist-dominated, Moscow-oriented state [in] Indochina."[187] French officials were aware of the importance of Moffat's visit. The Quai had sent instructions to colonial officials in Indochina to "grant every assistance and complete information to Moffat since it is felt that his visit may be of great assistance."[188]

On December 17, Byrnes reported to US missions abroad that Moffat had concluded "the Vietnam Government is in control of a small communist group probably in indirect touch with Moscow and direct touch with [Chinese communists]." However, he also reported that some leaders, including Ho, desired cooperation with the French. In a remarkable shift from the American wartime position, Moffat now suggested that French influence was important as an "antidote to Soviet influence" and "to protect Vietnam and SEA from future Chinese imperialism."[189]

Analysts in the State Department Office of Intelligence Research (OIR, formerly known as IRIS), however, disputed these conclusions. They squarely blamed French officials for the hostilities in late November, which they argued marked the end of any French commitment to the March 6 Accords and modus vivendi. The current French policy of postponing a referendum on Cochin China, retaining control over foreign trade and currency, continuing military control over the region, and their determination to eliminate undesirable personnel in the present Vietnamese government by force, if necessary, were each, OIR argued, violations of the March 6 agreement. They accused French authorities of duplicity: While they had publicly claimed these actions necessary to enforce the modus vivendi, safeguard the interests of local populations, and protect Chinese interests, "to American officials they stress, confidentially, the communist character and the incompetence of the Vietnam government." The reality, according to OIR analysts, was that French authorities denied the Viet Minh's popular following and viewed the Vietnamese as weak, politically immature, and not amenable to the concessions they required. This position represented the orientalist attitudes of the French in Indochina – including d'Argenlieu and colonial administrators – "reactionary and military elements whose reasons for suppressing the Vietnam regime mutually reinforce one another." These same officials sought definitive action in Vietnam before the establishment of any leftist government in Paris could undermine those efforts.[190]

Finally, OIR analysts further noted French government efforts to gain support for their current policy. "Since September 1946," they said, "numerous French officials have called the attention of American representatives to communist influences in the Vietnam regime." This "sudden concern," they said, was likely an attempt to forestall negative American reactions to the new French policy to progressively pressure Hanoi into acquiescence. This policy, OIR analysts warned, gave the Vietnamese only two choices – surrender or war; the Vietnamese would likely choose war unless a new leftist government in France reversed current policy. OIR analysts also pointed out the error of French officials who seemed to think that pressure on the Vietnamese government would lead to the elimination of small anti-French elements and would only require limited police action. There had already been heavy loss of life, they warned, and present French policy would lead to "an indefinite period of large-scale guerilla warfare."[191] Just two days later, OIR warnings came to pass. On the evening of December 20, Vietnamese forces attacked French installations in Tonkin.[192] Calling for unity regardless of religion or party, Ho called upon the Vietnamese to use all means to chase French imperialists from their land.[193]

War in Vietnam weighed heavily in the metropole. Caffery reported that French policy in Indochina was an important factor in the domestic political crisis. Left-wing parties demanded a more liberal policy and accused d'Argenlieu, colonial officials, and the French military of sabotaging the March 6 agreement and modus vivendi. Right-wing groups, Radical-Socialists, and the MRP demanded a firmer attitude toward Ho Chi Minh and Vietnam. The communists, Caffery said, did not want to oppose public opinion at a time when most were very anxious over the possibility of losing Indochina.[194] John Carter Vincent, the director of the Office of Far Eastern Affairs, also noted the role of domestic politics in the international situation affecting Vietnam. He expressed concern that the French, with "inadequate forces, with public opinion sharply at odds, with a government rendered largely ineffective through internal division … have tried to accomplish what a strong and united Britain has found it unwise to attempt in Burma."[195] Despite these warnings, American officials demurred when Chinese representatives suggested a joint offer of good offices; they did not want to make difficulties for the present French government, especially if the communists used it as proof that the government allowed foreign intervention in French affairs.[196]

Thousands of miles away, over lunch with State Department officials, Alexis Léger fortified his collaborators; the revolt was clearly a communist-instigated insurrection, directed by Moscow to create disorder in Indochina. The only way to solve the dispute in Vietnam, he argued, was the "use of power."[197] As Mark Lawrence has noted, French officials had successfully "recast the Vietnam problem in a way that would over-come disagreements over colonial questions and permit common military and political action to suppress the Vietnamese revolution."[198] In other words, the Cold War was playing out in Vietnam.

While the French government faced a determined communist-inspired independence movement in Indochina, officials concerned with African affairs warned that North Africa was becoming another flashpoint in the emerging Cold War. The region's strategic importance and perceptions of French weakness meant that the Soviets and Anglo-American powers were maneuvering to assure their positions in the event of a showdown. On December 2, 1946, Foreign Ministry officials warned that the French position in North Africa was increasingly tenuous. Local communist agi-tation had assumed greater importance when tied with PCF policy in the metropole and Soviet designs on the region, more apparent since the summer. They argued that the Soviets had bypassed PCF leaders and directly intervened in North Africa. Proof lay in the fact that PCF deputies did not adopt an attitude in line with North African communists until the Soviets took a position. Thus, the memo continued, "the PCF has been compelled to align itself with a position taken, without its consultation, by Soviet officials." The Americans, Quai officials reported, repeatedly expressed concern and asked French authorities in North Africa and Paris about the connection between nationalists and communists. French officials believed that North African nationalists continued to view local communist parties with suspicion but would take help from any quarter.[199]

The major issue, the report continued, was that "the same Communist label covers North African movements that are overtly anti-French and in Paris a large party which participates in the government."[200] At the same time, reports from the region suggested that local parties were benefiting from PCF success in the recent elections. In Tunisia, for example, the strength the PCT drew from PCF success now meant that some nationalists were rethinking relations with the PCT; nationalist leader Saleh ben Youssef had suggested that communist "cover" was indispens-able because they held 170 plus seats in the National Assembly.[201] Government policy assumes, the Foreign Ministry memo asserted, that the PCF will adopt a national line and conform with efforts to maintain the French Union. However, the PCF was not likely to oppose orders from Moscow to the local parties, and it may thus attempt to keep them in their orbit by constituting something like a "French Union of Soviet Socialist Republics," a move that would bring upheaval and Anglo-American intervention. Quai officials argued that there was only one solution. "As long as France is strong and shows without equivocation its desire to maintain its preponderance in North Africa, its position will not be seriously contested." If, however, France does not seem able to maintain its position, they warned, then North Africa will become a key battleground between the two blocs, one helping nationalists, the other the communists, a catastrophic situation since both ideologies anticipate France's eviction from the region.[202]

*****

Transimperial webs of sources thus painted a dark picture of communism on the march in France and its empire. Despite Soviet discouragement of insurrection in Western Europe[203] and PCF commitment to a legal assumption of power, French officials – including Charles de Gaulle, now out of office – used the communist threat to encourage American financial and military assistance and support for French demands on Germany, and to demonstrate their resolve to work with their American partners against a common threat to Western civilization. And even though the Soviets had offered no assistance to Ho Chi Minh and communists in Indochina and failed to exploit growing ferment in North Africa,[204] and despite the PCF's determination to maintain the empire, French colonial authorities also began to successfully subsume anti-colonial movements in the French colonies into a larger communist threat. Other factions used the threat to decry government incapacity and inaction, and to encourage support for anti-communist groups. In most cases, these groups maligned the PCF as anti-American and anti-French, a foreign "other" beholden to Soviet interests; in doing so, they further foreclosed the possibility of accommodation with the largest political party in France who also happened to be their most capable political rival.

5

L'Événement

If France seemed to teeter on the edge of communist revolution in the immediate postwar period, events in 1947 appeared to many Americans and Europeans to suggest that French communists and Soviet officials had decided that the time for action had come. Years of ominous warnings about communist intrigue now coincided with accelerating international tensions. Fears of communist revolution and military weakness in Europe prompted American announcement of the Truman Doctrine in March and the Marshall Plan in July. In France, yet another government crisis erupted over funding for the French war in Indochina and domestic wage freezes, leading to the expulsion of the PCF from the ruling coalition in May. And in October, representatives of nine communist parties – including France and Italy – met at an old hunting lodge in Poland to form a new Communist Information Bureau (Cominform) to better coordinate the activities of Eastern and Western European communist parties and ensure their alignment with Soviet interests and policy objectives. No one doubted that the Cold War, growing in intensity for some years, had become a global phenomenon.

However darkly uniform the analysis of the preceding year had been, some analysts expressed growing concern about the type and quality of intelligence produced on France that likely impacted its accuracy and effect. Ludwell Montague, a former historian who had served in military intelligence during the war, was now a senior officer in the CIA's ORE. Even as violence broke out in Marseille and general unrest threatened, he complained that the only coverage of France had been in the form of current intelligence: "no thorough analysis of the French situation has ever been attempted or projected." Yet, he wrote, "France is the key to the situation in Western Europe."[1] More generally, new Secretary of State George Marshall expressed reservations about the quality of intelligence emanating from overseas military missions. "There are too many people who like to be 'gum shoe artists.'" he said. "You get in trouble over the work of the amateur." He further argued that members of expanding military missions "should not be expected to be professional intelligence officers. Intelligence can be overdone very, very easily."[2]

Meanwhile, the State Department's OIR routinely dissented from CIA estimates. By March 1947, these addendums to CIA analysis provided one of OIR's few remaining avenues to the president after Chief of Staff Admiral William Leahy asked OIR to discontinue sending its reports to him.[3] At the same time, US consular officials in Vietnam and North Africa resisted alarmist claims emanating from Washington, DC, and Paris about Soviet and PCF support and encouragement of communist revolution in the French colonies.

For their part, French officials astutely noted that Ambassador Caffery routinely met with French political personalities, but not with communists,[4] the same source dynamic apparent in secret War Department instructions the year prior. They also observed that US intelligence had employed former French intelligence agents who had been jailed after the war for collaboration to inform them about French domestic politics.[5] This was a disparate group of factions, but they all shared an anti-communist outlook and agenda.

TROJAN HORSE

As the Cold War deepened in Europe, France too appeared divided along pro- and anti-communist lines, and the potential for civil war or a wider East–West conflict deeply concerned authorities in Washington, DC, and Paris. Two key issues preoccupied diplomatic and intelligence officials: the potential for a PCF-led insurrection or Moscow-directed subversion, and the state of French military readiness should communists rise up or a larger war break out. Embassy officials and intelligence analysts struggled to make sense of communist activity and to offer coherent assessments of PCF capabilities and intentions.

For their part, embassy and CIG analysts sensed a shift in communist tactics in the new year. On January 6, 1947, the CIG Daily Summary reported Caffery's belief that the PCF would participate in the next Cabinet rather than oppose it because the Soviets wanted them to hold as many high posts as possible in order to influence French domestic and colonial policy in their favor.[6] At the same time, CIG ORE analysts reported that the Soviets would employ more "subtle" tactics due to the Western powers' firmness and their realization that further expansion in Europe would risk war. But the more subtle methods they described offered no real departure from previous estimates: Communists would militate toward a communist-controlled government through legal or revolutionary means in nations like France; the Soviets would pursue political and economic penetration of key strategic areas in the Middle and Far East, and they would continue to develop their war potential.[7]

Internally, French analysis suggested that PCF leadership was pursuing a "prudent attentisme." While these analysts believed militants had hoped for a seizure of power – or at least a guiding role in French affairs – at several points since Liberation, they argued that communist officials knew that any power grab would paint them as the aggressor and justify repression that would eliminate them from the political scene entirely. They also appreciated the international situation and Soviet interest in avoiding war. Instead, PCF officials felt it was better to strengthen communist cadres and groups to be able to respond in the event of an emergency; the CGT remained the trump card, both as a source of mass maneuver and the core of potential militants in the event of trouble.[8]

Publicly, though, senior French officials expressed pessimism about communist intentions. Foreign Minister Georges Bidault warned Caffery that the new government might not last long because the PCF was fighting it every step of the way. He was convinced, he said, "that the communists are out to eradicate western civilization as we know it." Bidault also drew upon American concerns about French military reliability when he expressed particular concern about communist François Billoux, an "extremely able, very likeable, and an extremely dangerous communist militant" whose position as minister of National Defense did not bode well for the French military.[9]

While debates about communist intentions continued, US intelligence analysts and French officials continued to report specific activity that suggested communist preparations for civil war in France or a more general Soviet offensive from sources in French far-right circles.[10] As they had in years past, that winter and spring they described "international brigades" gathering in France to be used in several scenarios: against General Franco's government in Spain or the French government in southern France, or, increasingly, for action in the Greek civil war.[11] In February, French internal reporting claimed as many as 120,000–150,000 men of various nationalities were concentrated in southwestern France, charged with a double objective.

In the event of a republican uprising in Spain, they would cross the border to help depose Franco; in the case of troubles in France, they would engage the Army and other anti-communist elements suspected of supporting de Gaulle's return to power.[12] Despite the fact that much of this activity – including large concentrations of militants – should have been readily observable, there was never independent confirmation of its existence.

Likewise, reports of hidden arms caches again circulated as relations between the East and the West deteriorated. In early March, French intelligence services reported to President Vincent Auriol the discovery of arms caches in the region around Paris, which French officials duly reported to their American counterparts.[13] Press coverage and public statements by the French Interior Ministry shed further light on the activity. PCF officials, aware of rumors that they had stores of hidden arms and maintained armed military formations in southern France, publicly denied the claims. Instead, they accused Gaullists of stockpiling weapons.[14] Auriol nonetheless assumed the caches were of communist origin.[15]

Other signs suggested the revival of the prewar Communist International. In fact, any gathering of communist officials seemed like a resurrection of the Comintern to those deeply suspicious of communist motives. In mid-February, Caffery noted ominously that "[t]he long hand of the Kremlin is increasingly exercising power, or at least influence, in all European countries"; in France, this was largely through the PCF and "its fortress the CGT." According to Caffery, this Soviet Trojan Horse was "so well-camouflaged that millions of communist militants, sympathizers, and opportunists have been brought to believe that the best way to defend France is to identify French national interests with the aims of the Soviet Union." Paris, he said, had become a center of this activity and now resembled a veritable "hive of Comintern agents with their swarm of followers and dupes."[16]

In the event of such a crisis, the strength of the French military was of signal importance. Embassy analyst Dick Byrd had reported communist infiltration of the French Army in Alsace and the French occupation zone in Germany. Ernest Mayer, a former political officer in Brussels now serving in Baden-Baden asked to review these findings, found Byrd's report "unduly alarming" and noted that he had "neither seen nor heard anything which would indicate that the French Army has been penetrated to the extent the report suggests," but the Paris embassy refused to relent.[17] When Western European Affairs chief Woodie Wallner sent them the conflicting assessments for comment, they pointed to information Norris Chipman had unearthed; the communists were aggressively indoctrinating soldiers prior to their departure for Indochina. While the embassy did not believe that communists represented a substantial portion of the French armed forces, it did maintain that the PCF – "even if communist penetration amounted to no more than 15 percent" – had the ability to neutralize the French Army. The Army was "woefully weak" and "hopelessly inadequate" to fulfill its traditional role in defense of the metropole; moreover, there were questions about whether it could maintain order in the rest of the empire.[18]

Beyond exposing latent communist sympathies, US intelligence also suggested active communist attempts to undermine the military. In late February, the CIG reported the possible removal of key Army officers. If this happened, analysts wrote, "[t]he communists will have gone far in neutralizing the effectiveness of the Army in putting down any communist attempt to take control of the government by force."[19] Soon after, the Intelligence Division reinforced Bidault's warnings about François Billoux. The communist minister of National Defense had replaced French Air Force Chief of Staff General Paul Jacques Henri Gerardot with General Jean-Ludy Piollet, about whom little was known, but there was "little doubt of his left-wing sympathies." Billoux also replaced Air Force Inspector General P. A. Jacquin, a pro-American conservative, with Martial Henri Valin, "a left-wing political-type officer of reputedly communist tendencies."[20] Such arguments only furthered American perceptions of French weakness in the face of grave danger.

Caffery and Chipman continued to contest assessments of PCF capabilities, namely the argument that French communists were too weak to take over the government by force unless they received foreign assistance. Instead, they asserted that "the combined clandestine and legal apparatus of the communist movement is still probably strong enough to permit them initially to seize power in France." The question should have been what Caffery meant by "seize power," and whether the PCF was intending on doing so and to what end. Instead, he dismissed the PCF's pursuit of parliamentary tactics as less due to weakness than the fact that it served Kremlin and Comintern interests. Caffery also challenged the claim that the PCF was too weak to align France with the Soviets against the West in the event of a war. This was probably true, he said, but the embassy also believed that "under existing circumstances ... France would be at least neutralized immediately and its historic role of serving as a bridge for an offensive on the continent of Europe would be 'denied' us." Furthermore, "communist armed action combined with paralyzing strikes, sabotage, and other subversive activities would certainly prepare the way for Soviet intervention on a scale larger even ... than the Spanish Civil War."[21]

Several days later, immediately following President Truman's declaration of American aid for Greece and Turkey and determination to resist aggressive communism, *New York Times* Paris Bureau Chief Harold Callender reported that the connection between the speech and the internal political situation in France had been the topic of lively discussion in French government circles. The PCF criticized the speech and pointed to discoveries of secret arms caches as signs of the mobilization of reaction "to destroy the republic." At the same time, French Prime Minister Paul Ramadier and Interior Minister Edouard Depreux issued the first public confirmation of reports of hidden arms in France.[22] Depreux said that this development was "intolerable," and the government would apply "the full rigor of the law" to prevent another February 6, an allusion to violent riots between the extreme left and right in 1934. Despite lack of clear indications about intended recipients of the caches, Depreux declared that most of the arms were in "leftist hands." Furthermore, he denied claims that the weapons were intended for Spanish Republicans as "too often a pretext,"[23] suggesting his suspicion that the arms were designated for communist use inside France.

EXPULSION

At the end of March, another crisis, this time over communist opposition to military credits to implement government policy in Indochina, was temporarily averted. On March 19, communist deputies abstained from a 421–0 vote of confidence in the government, which led to violent exchanges between communists and rightists. Prime Minister Ramadier had threatened to resign unless he received the support of all parties. Noncommunist officials privately concluded that a government crisis was imminent and that the communists would be excluded from the next government coalition.[24] Eventually, a compromise allowed communist ministers to vote for the government while communist deputies abstained. Intelligence Division analysts noted the danger of allowing a party to be "both for and against the government." Tension lingered, as evidenced by the military governor of Paris's request for more troops. This development, they argued, plus "the discovery of arms caches all over the country" – a claim for which they again provided no evidence – was a sign that "many Frenchmen in both the communist and opposition camps feel that the rift cannot be solved by parliamentary procedure."[25]

In the aftermath of the episode, Caffery reported "new courage" in noncommunist labor and more serious efforts to organize noncommunists to oppose communist groups in the event of unrest. A year before, he had been "discouraged about the possibility of preventing the communists from eventually taking over this country"; now, he said, "I have come to believe that they will not take it over."[26] OIR analysts, however, were less sanguine about the Assembly debate over Indochina. The extreme right, they argued, had chosen the Indochina policy debate to accuse the communists of not being good Frenchmen; this had touched off a near-crisis that had almost resulted in the fall of the Ramadier government. At the same time, French political life had been further polarized by the announcement of the Truman Doctrine and Moscow's response. OIR warned that French disappointments on the German settlement and failure on issues like access to German coal – without which living standards would fall – could have a serious effect on political stability in France. A growing cleavage between the East and the West could diminish hopes of not being a battleground in the event of war. These developments could lead, they argued, to communist withdrawal from the government or attempts by bourgeois parties to force them out. This could then result in "unpromising prospects of a cabinet based on the bourgeois majority in National Assembly attempting to govern a country in which the workers look to communist leadership of their trade unions."[27]

French officials noted the distinct hardening in American policy and attitudes, attributable in part to personalities with influence over French affairs. Former US ambassador to France William Bullitt warned the House Un-American Activities Committee that France was in "serious danger" of being taken over by communists and recommended application of the Truman Doctrine and US assistance to anti-communist groups there, a point marked for emphasis by Foreign Ministry officials.[28] Bonnet would remark later that Bullitt's "anti-communist preoccupation" caused him to present a "slightly deformed image of the French situation."[29] Similarly, Bonnet noted Admiral Leahy's influence. His informants at Foggy Bottom told him that Leahy had played a key role in the crafting of the Truman Doctrine speech. Truman relied heavily on him, and Leahy's influence had only grown since the departure of former Secretary of State Byrnes. Driven by his aversion to communism, Leahy had been very critical of Byrnes' attempts at conciliation with the Soviets.[30] This same preoccupation, Bonnet noted, had led him to defend US maintenance of representation in Vichy and negotiations with Darlan in spite of all that militated against it.[31] Within the State Department, Samuel Reber – notable for his role crafting a Cordell Hull speech referring to the "so-called Free French" – had been chosen as the new director of the Western Europe Bureau. Most critically, Bonnet concluded, "State Department officials who deal with French affairs are far from having advanced ideas ... their dominant preoccupation is more and more of bringing an active fight against communism to the entire world."[32]

As uncertainty in France continued, Charles de Gaulle again asserted himself, delivering three speeches that spring commemorating the Resistance and Allied aid to France, attacking the new constitution, and declaring a pro-American attitude. He also announced his new movement, the Rally of the French People (RPF). Bonnet reported that de Gaulle's speeches had heightened his prestige in the United States, and that he understood that the moment was coming when it would be decided which faction – anti-communist or communist – would control France; most US observers believed he had clearly thrown in with the former.[33] Two weeks later, FBI Director J. Edgar Hoover circulated a report on de Gaulle's activity obtained from French intelligence, which indicated some concern over de Gaulle's dictatorial tendencies but acknowledged his anti-communism. In fact, the RPF was an attempt to gather political minorities together and to break the PCF's influence on political factions and remove the communists entirely from the government. De Gaulle's objective was to maintain France – grouped with other Western European nations – between the US and the USSR and to act as a stabilizing force on the continent. However, if war came, de Gaulle believed that France must stand with the West.[34]

On May 2, another political crisis burst into the open when PCF officials declared their opposition to the Cabinet's policy of maintaining existing wage ceilings.[35] A strike at the Renault plant had spread rapidly, now supported by the CGT. It was an opportune time for the PCF to emphasize the party's domestic agenda. With the communists now opposing the government, Prime Minister Ramadier revoked the portfolios of the communist ministers on May 4. There has been much speculation about the American role in the expulsion of the PCF, but, as Irwin Wall argued, this "myth" should be put to rest, as French officials hardly needed prodding to oust the PCF.[36] Indeed, Bidault had indicated the year before his plans to do the same given the opportunity. Ramadier likely acted independently for several reasons, not least of which was the impossibility of government officials refusing to support government policy and remaining in their posts. Beyond American pressure to confront the PCF, French officials also hoped to further their case for aid, stave off a resurgent de Gaulle, and clarify colonial matters. Nevertheless, this was a moment of great consequence. To the United States it appeared that anti-communists were gaining the upper hand; for France, the expulsion signaled the end of national unity governments.

Not surprisingly, the Intelligence Division viewed ouster of the communists as a positive development, a demonstration of the strength of anti-communism, which could be attributed in part to the Truman Doctrine.[37] Caffery reinforced the importance of this development. It was in the American interest that Ramadier succeed, he argued, but he could not do so without US assistance. France still faced food and coal shortages and low standards of living for the average worker. While PCF statements had remained moderate in tone, Caffery believed that they would do everything to undercut the Ramadier government so they could force their reentry, this time with more influence. He also pointed out the consequences if the Ramadier government were to fall. In France, the Socialist left wing would take over direction of the party, and a bitter struggle between communists and Gaullists could ensue. Outside of France, a communist victory would lead to Soviet penetration not only of Western Europe but also Africa, the Mediterranean, and the Middle East. Caffery even suggested that the United States should be prepared to support "French elements which represent infinitely less in terms of democracy and public backing" in the event of a showdown with communists.[38] Perhaps he was thinking of French anti-communists who had taken pains to describe significant forces at their disposal to US intelligence, in one case even offering up collaborationist "miliciens" notorious for their wartime brutality.[39] The Intelligence Division also warned that the communist appearance of continued moderation and cooperation should be discounted: "The real communist play, which is bound to come, has not been made yet."[40]

However, French intelligence suggested that the PCF had been caught off guard by their ostracism and wished to return to the government as soon as possible in order to forestall the growth of reactionary elements in the Cabinet.[41] They had not resigned, the communists argued; the people had designated them and they alone had the right to withdraw their mandate. One communist leader commented that "the PCF is a party of the government," and that it would continue to take on the same responsibilities outside of the government.[42] Furthermore, influential members of the rightist coalition Rassemblement des Gauches Républicaines (RGR) privately reported that Soviet Foreign Minister Vyacheslav Molotov had reproached PCF representative Laurent Casanova for the party's blunders in the latest ministerial reorganization and ordered him to do everything possible to return to the government. RGR sources also noted that this criticism was given several weeks after the episode and suggested that "contacts between the PCF and the USSR are less frequent than in the past."[43]

Rumors about the international brigades continued in the aftermath of the Truman Doctrine speech and the expulsion of communist ministers from the French government in early May. That same month, Secretary of State George Marshall sent an intelligence report to the Paris embassy for comment. The memo claimed that Romanian communists trained in guerilla fighting were bound for France to join the international brigades preparing for civil war in Spain.[44] Not long after, new Director of Central Intelligence Roscoe Hillenkoetter, a Leahy ally who had served as a naval attaché to Vichy during the war, briefed President Truman that the announcement of the Truman Doctrine had led the Soviets to support Greek communist activities and an acceleration of guerilla operations and sabotage. The French Interior Ministry had confirmed, he said, the recruitment of cadres from the brigades in southern France to serve in an international brigade in Greece.[45] Truman and his aides largely accepted these claims, but nagging questions lingered. The spokesman of the Greek General Staff denied that Greek troops had encountered the brigade. Other experts cautioned that formation of such brigades would only internationalize the conflict in Greece and were thus not likely to help the cause of the Greek leftists.[46]

Ambassador Caffery in Paris, however, took statements by a Greek communist leader at the PCF's Strasbourg Congress – thanking "the friends of Greek democracy throughout the world for what they have performed for it" – as confirmation of French Interior Ministry and private observer reports that the international communist movement was involved in arms trafficking to Greece and that French communists were recruiting international brigades.[47] In Washington, DC, journalists Joseph and Stewart Alsop reported that "intelligence reports so detailed they can no longer be disregarded have reached Washington ... that an international brigade, under Comintern auspices, is being organized to fight in Greece." PCF leader Jacques Duclos, they claimed, was "sponsoring" the training of the brigade in southern France.[48] It is notable, however, that the British Foreign Office and a contemporary UN investigation all denied the existence of the brigades.[49]

French officials privately noted reports about the new brigades. An intelligence memo in mid-July recounted rumors circulating in communist circles about the formation of brigades to fight in Greece.[50] Publicly, however, authorities suggested that much of the talk about the brigades was the product of "superheated imaginations," further underscoring divisions within the French government on these issues. These sources said that the government had neither the resources nor the inclination to prevent individuals with proper papers from leaving France to fight whomever they pleased. Rumors of mass training of communist partisans for action in Greece were rampant in Spanish refugee settlements near Toulouse. It was, they said, "highly improbable that any large group of volunteers destined for Greek or other fighting could have left ... without official knowledge." It was "more likely" that young Spanish refugees and youth from the Greek colony in Marseille were leaving in small numbers to fight in Greece; these numbers were complicated by a considerable number of Jews leaving southern France for Palestine.[51]

The Soviets were shaken by the expulsions and claimed that Ramadier revoked the portfolios only after American pressure and a $250 million loan from the International Bank for Reconstruction.[52] However, as Irwin Wall has pointed out, the loan actually seemed like a paltry amount compared to the original promise of $500 million and with regard to the enormity of French needs. Prime Minister Ramadier went so far as to accuse the United States of not living up to its obligations.[53] Rather than US aid driving the expulsion, the loan was instead a reflection of French officials driving US policy through careful exploitation of American threat perceptions.

Clearly concerned by turmoil and instability in the nation upon which Americans plans for Europe hinged, Secretary of State George Marshall announced a European Recovery Program (ERP) that would help rebuild the economies of war-torn Europe and foster political stability in the region. Caffery reported that the PCF viewed the "Marshall Plan" as a tactical application of the Truman Doctrine[54] and intended to intensify efforts to rejoin the government in order to exercise pressure and influence upon domestic affairs and foreign policy.[55] Meanwhile, Hillenkoetter wrote President Truman that the announcement of US aid to Greece had precipitated Soviet efforts to forestall or defeat the program. Hillenkoetter also tied this determined plan to reports "confirmed in general by the French Ministry of the Interior" that communists were recruiting cadres from the international brigades in France to serve in Greece.[56]

Foreign Ministry officials continued to monitor American reactions to the simmering social conflict in France. US representatives in Paris paid close attention to strikes in key sectors of French industry, with particular significance to the railroad strike and its political and economic effects, especially those bearing upon Franco-American relations. These lingering uncertainties, and the questions US officials posed, French officials said, were a valuable indicator of their concerns, indeed, their preoccupation with the communist threat. The Americans believed that the PCF sought a show of force and ordered the strike that would bring them to power. They therefore posed two questions: Do communists in France possess enough force to paralyze the economic life of the country, and does the PCF have enough working class support to place the government in a position of either submission or resignation if the strikes drag out? Americans were also preoccupied with the strategic consequences of the railroad strike, wondering if the PCF's goal was to show that, in the case of war, the Soviets have means at their disposal – the control of transportation – beyond purely economic measures.[57]

By late June, State Department officials feared that the Ramadier government, which had weathered multiple crises, now appeared to crack. Communist efforts to prove that France could not be governed without them had enjoyed some success; some in other political parties seemed to accept the communist thesis that their inclusion in the government would mean an end to strikes and return to stability. However, Doc Matthews wrote, they also know that the return of the PCF would exact a high price as the chances of significant American economic aid would diminish. "We should do nothing," he said, "to discourage this belief."[58] A subsequent French Desk memo reiterated these concerns and predicted that the communists would "almost certainly" be in the next government with increased powers, and they would demand portfolios with significant influence on national and foreign affairs. The Marshall Plan, it argued, had made the situation more urgent. The Soviets desperately wanted PCF influence in the French government, but nothing would be more damaging to their interests than a successful reconstruction program led by the United States. Outside of government, the PCF had been powerful enough to cause economic chaos in France; once back in the government, they would have a "virtual veto on the conduct of France's foreign affairs" putting the Marshall Plan in grave jeopardy.[59]

State Department adviser Chip Bohlen raised these concerns the next day with Marshall, warning him of the looming political crisis and reiterating the consequences of communist participation in the government, especially for the viability of the ERP. Because this was an internal French matter, Bohlen did not think it advisable to engage a vigorous course of action, which could raise cries of American intervention in French affairs. It was not possible or desirable to create their own anti-communist fifth column. Instead, he recommended financial support for existing anti-communist organizations and suggested that the Secretary of State should have a secret fund to be used at his discretion in the interests of the security of the United States.[60] Foreshadowing future interventions, the fund was established, and it was used to support State Department and American Federation of Labor (AFL) efforts to split noncommunist "Force Ouvrière" elements from the communist-dominated CGT. Some of these funds were channeled through Raymond Murphy's secretive division in the State Department and later, the CIA.[61]

CONFLUENCE

As the PCF passed into opposition, its position on the French empire also evolved. Disagreements over the war in Indochina nearly led to the party's expulsion in March. When they did depart in May, American and French officials grew increasingly concerned about PCF (and by extension, Soviet) interest in the colonies, and the implications that domestic turmoil and the possibility of a communist regime in France held for its empire. Once out of government, PCF officials were "free to criticize the government without restraint" on colonial matters.[62]

For resident US officials, many of whom resisted efforts by colonial authorities to tie Vietnamese and North African liberation movements directly to worldwide communist revolution, the danger in the French colonies was not communism itself but the fact that continued French repression and lack of accommodation of nationalist aspirations would lead to the growth of communist influence in local affairs. Paul Alling in Tangier realized that US security depended on a strong republican France, but he questioned its ability to become and remain strong through use of military force in the face of determined opposition in North Africa and Indochina. The situation would not remain static, he believed, and it was in US and French interests, as long as France remained a republican government, to reform and move toward self-government. He warned that France could not continue to govern these areas for much longer unless the government came under outright communist control, and he noted the dilemma: "North Africa may [then] also go in that direction, or more likely French officials here, both civilian and Army, might break with the metropole and set up a separate regime."[63] Later that month, Alling further noted that the Soviets appeared to "do little" in the region. The Arabs are friendly to the United States, he said, but he could not discount the possibility that French repression could lead them to "reluctantly accept aid from communist sources in [the] mistaken idea that it would give them real freedom."[64] Similarly, US consul in Saigon Charles Reed reported his belief that "Annamite communism is perhaps over emphasized as a present danger." Communists had taken control of the nationalist movement by advocating independence from France; however, if communist leaders were removed, the nationalist movement would remain.[65]

CIG current intelligence reports however, alleged PCF support for the Vietnamese cause. The connection drawn between Vietnamese and French Communists implied that communism in the colonies was less the result of an indigenous rebellion against oppressive colonial rule than adherence to a larger Soviet line against the Western powers. In mid-January, CIG analysts reported that the PCF was particularly active among Indochinese now in France, especially in the Marseille area. In May, Secretary Marshall asked Cecil Gray for information substantiating or contradicting this report.[66] The claim was tenuous if not overblown. Even French authorities in Saigon, who asserted outside ties between Ho's government in Hanoi and Chinese and Soviet communists, observed that Vietnamese leaders had lost faith in the PCF which argued that the rights of the metropole must be respected.[67]

French officials also continued to note American concern about the link between political developments in the metropole and US strategic interests in North Africa. In late January, Ambassador Bonnet wrote Bidault that one of his associates had gone disguised to a conference in which State Department officials met with Tunisian nationalist Habib Bourguiba. One US official stressed the strategic cost of communist control of the French government: "A communist France, imposing a similar regime in North Africa, would be able to cut lines of communication passing through the Mediterranean and to menace links with the Near East." Bourguiba, after blasting French colonialism, had told the assembled group that there were no close relations between Tunisian nationalists and the PCF; however, he warned that American apathy and their despair could throw them into the arms of the USSR.[68]

Nonetheless, as with Indochina, French internal reports continued to link communist parties in North Africa to the metropole. In April, governor-general of Algeria Yves Chataigneau wrote that French officials should not accept PCA expressions of independence from the PCF without reserve. He claimed that the PCF directed the PCA and that the PCA mirrored PCF stances on all colonial matters. Moreover, Chataigneau claimed, "under the cover of a fight for the independence of colonized peoples, it is certain that the communists hope to set up a Soviet republic like the Muslim republics of the USSR."[69] These comments represented a major escalation of Chataigneau's anti-communist rhetoric from just a few years before, when he worried most that communist propaganda provided a dangerous tool for nationalist movements. Now, the communists were themselves the enemy.

At the same time, French officials cultivated American perceptions of the situation in the colonies. In February, colonial authorities in Indochina wrote the Quai d'Orsay detailing American activity in the region, decrying the influence of American intelligence agents, and criticizing American propaganda as well as vice-consul in Hanoi James O'Sullivan's apparent pro-Vietnamese views. The report acknowledged that they could not ask for the removal of diplomatic personnel acting on official instructions from their governments, nor could they take official measures against American intelligence agents in the region. Instead, they advocated counterpropaganda and other efforts to counteract the information these agents transmitted to the US government and concluded that the Quai should intervene to orient US policy on Indochina.[70] Those interventions certainly included passing intelligence to sympathetic US officials.

In France, Caffery fueled, rather than minimized, concern about the French colonies. Just prior to the May expulsions, he reported that ex-communists increasingly believed that the Soviets had directed the PCF to accelerate their agitation in the French colonies to the extent that they may not be able to remain in the government.[71] In response, Secretary Marshall asked Caffery to approach the French government to suggest accelerating progress toward a settlement for Indochina. "The Western democratic system is on the defensive," he wrote. It had become identified with denial of the colonized's rights and was thus "particularly vulnerable to attacks by demagogic leaders [and] political movements of either ultra-nationalist or communist nature." Caffery's report of PCF acceleration of agitation in the French colonies, Marshall argued, lent urgency to the situation because it "may be an indication Kremlin prepared to sacrifice temporary gains with 40 million French to long-range colonial strategy with 600 million dependent people."[72] Marshall offered a similar line of argument the following month when he asked Caffery to approach Ramadier and Bidault about North Africa. "If French do not regain faith and cooperation of Arabs, we believe the situation will continue to deteriorate to benefit of no one except communists."[73]

As questions circulated about the apparent conflict between commun-
ist policy in the colonies and communist interests in France, Francis
B. Stevens of the Eastern European Division – who had served with
Kennan, Henderson, and Chipman[74] – sent Matthews a report on
the PCF's colonial policy, which he believed offered clarification. The
Comintern may have been dissolved, he argued, but there was "little
doubt" that its directives and principles guided PCF colonial policies.
Stevens noted Lenin's 1920 "Theses on the National and Colonial
Questions," which postulated "the breaking up of the colonial empire,
together with proletarian revolution in the home country, will overthrow
the capitalist system in Europe" and that "communist parties of the
different imperialistic countries must work in conjunction with these
proletarian parties of the colonies." He also pointed to the Comintern's
1928 "Struggle for the World Dictatorship of the Proletariat and Colonial
Revolution," which declared that European communist parties must
"openly recognize the right of the colonies to separation and ... their
right of armed defense against imperialism ... and advocate and give
active support to this defense by all means in their power."[75] Once again,
State Department analysts looked past the absence of evidence of actual
PCF activity to Soviet ideology for proof of plotting, even to older official
statements that had been officially superseded.

Despite no real evidence of Soviet interest in Indochina at the time, US
intelligence maintained Ho's collusion with Moscow. A CIG report from
"reliable sources" claimed that the Soviets had supported the communist
movement in Vietnam since its inception. French military intelligence had
indicated the intensity of this activity. For proof, they claimed that Ho
received two Soviet intelligence agents when he was in Paris and that Vo
Nguyen Giap, the vice president of the Cabinet and minister of defense in
Hanoi, had been treating openly with the Russians.[76] This reporting
interested Marshall, who transmitted the report to Paris and his consulates in Vietnam.[77] In fact, this was a common refrain for French intelligence. The Chief of the French Sûreté in Saigon told US Consul Charles
Reed "the communist complexion of the Viet Minh ... is becoming more
and more apparent, even though Ho Chi Minh endeavors to show that
he is a nationalist and not a communist."[78] Although there was ample
evidence of Ho's nationalism and independence from the Soviet Union,
French and American intelligence reports no longer appreciated critical
distinctions between local and Soviet communism.

THE BLACK MAQUIS

While US and French officials remained focused on communist activity that summer, there was, in fact, other subversive activity on the extreme right.[79] On June 30, Interior Minister Edouard Depreux announced that French police had thwarted a plot by a secret right-wing organization calling itself the "Black Maquis," made up of "right-wing resistance leaders, monarchists, and Vichy collaborators." The group aimed to precipitate civil war between the right and the PCF, and to overthrow the government and establish a military dictatorship.[80] Caffery reported that the rightist plot, codenamed "Plan Bleu," intended to exploit hostility between old members of the communist and anti-communist maquis and the international situation in the hopes of igniting the powder keg that they believed France had become. Rightists in Brittany planned to seize local arms depots and US surplus army stocks to equip their formations, while other tactical groups advanced on Paris.[81] During the investigation, French police discovered a sizable arms cache in Brittany at the chateau of one of the plotters, the Count de Vulpian.[82] The forty-seven-year-old count was a friend of Marshal Pétain and chairman of a war veterans' league. Arrested with him were General Guillodit, inspector general of the Gendarmerie, and Georges Loustaunau-Lacau,[83] a former military officer of the extreme far right and an alleged member of the Cagoule.[84] Meanwhile, the French Interior Ministry continued to report seizures of communist and rightist arms caches.[85]

Some historians argue that the threat posed by these right-wing plotters was overblown; their "operations" had less to do with concrete actions against the French government than "a phase of intense psychological preparation" – of believing that communists were preparing for action in order to justify defense of the state. While this particular plot may not have been serious, the fear of communism shared by a large portion of the French right was, and it was supported by a number of indicators, particularly the discovery of arms caches.[86] For French military officials, the idea of a "fifth column" parachuting arms and sowing domestic unrest served as an emotional bridge between the lessons of the last war (and the defeat of 1940) and the new Cold War.[87] On both sides, fears of secret plots – the product of propaganda and rumor – had been nourished for a long time; in the Cold War, they had become a tool of political strategy.[88]

PCF leaders seized upon these and other revelations of rightist plots, accusing the government of secret plots to undermine the party. Central Committee member Etienne Fajon angrily declared, "If Ramadier wishes to know the leader of the secret orchestra,[89] he need only look in the mirror." Fajon also asserted, "if the communists let themselves be excluded from the government, it is in order to not betray the French Worker in associating with a reactionary policy." And again he signaled communist opposition to the war in Indochina and the belief that the United States was trying to make France a colony.[90] Soviet attacks on French leaders also intensified. One Soviet broadcast violently attacked de Gaulle as a "deserter surrounded by delinquents, valets of banks and trusts who in London created the BCRA [Gaullist intelligence] to deliver the real patriots to the Gestapo."[91]

In Washington, DC, Doc Matthews again reminded Marshall of the consequences of communist reentry into the French government and recommended two measures in support of noncommunist forces in France: the second installment of a World Bank loan and increased coal from the Saar. The situation was desperate enough that Matthews believed that they should not preclude arms or military assistance to a noncommunist government if requested. Echoing the arguments of Gaullists and other anti-communist groups in their private exchanges with US officials, Matthews also suggested support to noncommunist elements under de Gaulle if they should attack a communist-controlled government.[92]

This reflection upon US policy occurred against a backdrop of threatened strikes directed by the communist-led CGT and rumors of communist military action. In mid-July, just as ERP negotiations were underway in Paris, government workers threatened to strike; the CIG reported that an able political observer believed the threatened strike was "a communist attempt to torpedo the conference."[93] At the same time, the CIG warned that disagreements over German coal production could compel the French government to withdraw from the Marshall Plan,[94] which would jeopardize the entire program. By August, though, the CIG could report that the Marshall Plan had strengthened the Ramadier government by widening the gap between left-wing Socialists and the PCF.[95] French representatives still expressed concern that this stability could be undermined if US assistance was not forthcoming before March 1948.[96] US officials took these concerns seriously – they understood that upholding France and Italy were key to the overall success of the Marshall Plan – and recommended some satisfaction of the French position on Germany and earlier disbursement of US aid.[97]

That summer, Marshall again wrote to the Paris embassy asking for their comment on intelligence about Soviet activity in Paris and other French cities, one of several requests as the situation continued to deteriorate.[98] Specifically, US intelligence had reported that the Soviets had dispatched dozens of experts in sabotage and street fighting from the Moscow intelligence training school to Paris and that they had since dispersed throughout France to instruct communist sympathizers.[99] Caffery subsequently reported that a source close to the communists described recent meetings between PCF and Soviet officials in Paris in which they stressed parallel preparations for illegal and underground activities in the case of emergency and continued growth of legal party groups with an eye to success in the October municipal elections.[100]

Likewise, French intelligence also noted an uptick in communist preparations. One source in contact with the PCF claimed that militants in eastern France would be armed with paradropped Italian and Yugoslav equipment and that arms depots had already been constituted in Nancy, Longwy, and Meurthe et Moselle.[101] French intelligence also "confirmed" the reconstitution of the international brigades, Soviet arms deliveries in the north of France, and immigration from the Low Countries, all with the purpose of assisting a communist seizure of power, charges that the Interior Ministry would repeat again later that autumn.[102] Perhaps most importantly, French authorities in contact with US military attachés noted American preoccupation with this activity. Rumors of the brigades, arms caches, and parachutages, one official stated, led the Americans to the conclusion that this activity was part of a grand design to organize shock troops and facilitate communist control at the opportune moment.[103] That summer and fall, even though these claims were nearly impossible to verify, French accounts like these continued to inform US intelligence reporting about communist subversive activity.[104]

As tensions mounted, the State Department on August 19 sent a request from the CIG to their representatives in France and Italy and asked for any intelligence on communist capabilities and intentions.[105] Caffery believed that the situation in France hinged on whether the government could feed and provide for the public during the next winter, which depended on US economic assistance. Should the political and economic situation in France deteriorate to the extent that armed conflict broke out or Moscow ordered a coup, he warned, the PCF could mobilize 50,000 "hardened and well-armed militants" in Paris alone. Caffery again maintained that the communists were strong enough to seize power; the question of whether they could hold Paris remained.[106]

During the lead-up to the October elections, Caffery and the CIG reported the increased possibility of de Gaulle's return, and, in a remarkable shift from years past, suggested he might indeed be best positioned to save France from communists. De Gaulle's popularity continued to rise, Caffery said, because PCF efforts to block recovery and Molotov's walk-out from the Paris ERP negotiations showed that they did not want to see an independent and prosperous Europe. There was also, in France, the growing conviction that they must have a strong government, and that de Gaulle was the only figure with enough prestige and authority to control anti-communist forces that were "a definite majority" but remained "incoherent and impotent" because of divisions within and between the parties.[107]

With communists allegedly inciting "l'événement" and de Gaulle poised to exploit it, Hillenkoetter wrote Truman about the very real possibility of a serious European crisis in which the French position was most critical. The French suffered from a balance of payments problem and would exhaust their dollar resources before Congress could implement the ERP; at the same time, a worldwide grain shortage had forced them to reduce their bread ration, prompting violent tirades against the government by PCF leaders. Any further reductions, he warned, could undermine stability and threaten the emergence of communist governments "either through peaceful or violent means." This situation, he wrote, greatly increases the possibility that France will turn to an extremist solution – the communists or de Gaulle – which could lead to civil war.[108] With these concerns in mind, embassy officials pressed for guarantees of economic assistance to France before the October elections and the cold winter set in again. Without it, an Interior Ministry source told Caffery, the Ramadier government was doomed; while it might profit de Gaulle in the short term, it would likely benefit only the PCF in the long run.[109] Subsequent CIG reporting underscored the necessity for immediate aid to Europe to forestall revolution; there were indications the Soviets had directed the PCF to prepare large-scale strikes and mass demonstrations to coincide with the current strike wave and anti-government protests in Italy.[110]

Behind the scenes, anti-communist French officials continued to advocate for American intervention. On September 8, MRP Senator Jules Boyer warned US War Department official Colonel Charles Bonesteel that "communist propaganda in France was becoming extremely successful" and American information programs were "ineffective." The situation, Boyer and a friend said, was becoming "extremely dangerous in light of the

October municipal elections," and they feared that "unless urgent and effective action was taken, the communists might win a substantial portion of these elections in rural areas." Bonesteel believed "it [was] almost pathetic that the French ... are almost openly begging for some sort of intelligent objective leadership from the outside," but in fact they had laid out a concept for a robust culture and information program that would presage American efforts in years to come.[111] Caffery reported that Socialist, MRP, and Gaullist editors of French provincial newspapers had also recommended US efforts to counteract communist propaganda.[112]

The CIA released its first "Review of the World Situation," just two weeks before the October elections in France. The estimate stressed the critical situation in France and its importance to US security interests. "The greatest danger to the security of the United States," it asserted, "is the possibility of economic collapse in Western Europe and the consequent accession to power of communist elements." The CIA did not believe that the USSR would resort to overt military aggression. Their strategy in France was thus to prevent recovery, blame the United States for distress, identify it with imperialism and reaction, and to exploit weakness and instability to bring communists to power. CIA analysts argued thus that stabilization and recovery in Western European nations should be prioritized as it would likely "curb Soviet aggressiveness" and "stabilize the international situation." Relatedly, they noted resurgent nationalism and conflict in the colonial areas of Western European powers, which also hindered recovery thus placing traditional American liberal policies in "apparent conflict with its interest in supporting friendly European governments."[113] The effect of the estimate was apparent when President Truman, Secretary Marshall, and Admiral Leahy met with members of Congress two days later. Truman and Marshall warned that France and Italy would fall to the communists if aid was not made available by the first of the year.[114]

In Paris, sources close to Ramadier reminded Caffery of their anti-communist actions to garner more aid. They underscored French alignment with the United States and their opposition to "heavy communist pressure to reenter the government" but argued that the prospect of one of the worst winters in French history without aid would cause the government to collapse, after which there would be no prospect of keeping the communists out.[115] Caffery also relayed reports of communist "probes" of government resolve. PCF militants had attempted to block a shipment of sugar to Germany, which Caffery viewed as an electoral stunt but also "evidence communists are seriously testing the authority of the state."[116] In Marseille, Cecil Gray in Marseille noted recent communist manifestations. If the PCF planned on violent action after the elections, he wrote, these events "might well be compared to patrol attacks in a military campaign seeking out soft spots for an eventual all-out offensive."[117]

THE COMINFORM

In late September, State Department officials learned that PCF leaders Jacques Duclos and Etienne Fajon had gone to Poland for high-level meetings.[118] Caffery reported that an "ex-member of Comintern" told his staff that the reestablishment of the Comintern was inevitable. He noted the participation of all Eastern European parties plus the French and Italian communist parties; the presence of Soviet Communist Party leaders Andrei Zhdanov and Georgy Malenkov further suggested this was a revived instrument of Soviet imperialism. Caffery' sources in Paris saw this as "an open declaration of ideological, social, and economic war upon all countries that haven't already succumbed ... to Soviet power."[119] Another report from Belgrade suggested that the timing of the new Cominform signaled European communism's intent to mount an "all out winter drive against France and Italy" before US aid could be effective.[120] Subsequent reports further detailed the activities of the conference, including Zhdanov's review of the international situation and declaration of two opposed camps. One dispatch from Warsaw indicated that a source of "questionable reliability" claimed that the Cominform had assigned France first priority as the object of a political attack with the aim of establishing a communist regime. Soviet policy was thus believed to be one of "aggressive warfare against the western world by every means short of military action." They now seemed willing to risk war, wagering that the US democratic system made it virtually impossible to go to war except in retaliation for clear military aggression.[121] Reports like these suggested the need for strong displays of resolve. Leahy was especially interested in them, marking each one for the president's attention.[122]

French observers carefully monitored American interpretations of the new Cominform. In Washington, DC, Bonnet reported, news of the conference had shocked public opinion even if US officials were unsurprised by the decisions made in Warsaw, which they viewed as a continuation of the USSR's more hardline policy and determination to make the Marshall Plan fail. Many journals, Bonnet wrote, believed the Soviets had left their revolutionary stage and were embarking upon a Napoleonic one. As a result, disparate factions in America and abroad had come together on the necessity of aid to prevent Western Europe from falling to the communists. As Walter Lippmann had put it, "la guerre à froid" was now a reality.[123]

There were conflicting views in France over the Cominform's significance. Charpentier in Moscow reported that the Soviets had packaged it as a defensive mechanism to resist imperialist aggression and expansion, thus reminiscent of Lenin's 1906 declaration at the Stockholm Congress, "to keep its victory, the Russian Revolution needs foreign reserves." But it remained unclear why this new coordination had been made public when maintaining secrecy would have presented the same advantages and none of the drawbacks.[124] However, Ambassador Jean Payart in Belgrade believed Stalin's objective was to isolate France from the United States and "to carry the Iron Curtain to the Atlantic and make sure that France is not the head of the American bridge, but becomes instead the advanced bastion of the Soviet world."[125] Other observers viewed the Cominform as nothing other than "the unrolling of an offensive against the United States"; the French and Italian parties had now been accepted as allies in the defense of Europe. They also believed the Soviets would lead an open fight against colonial interests and Western zones of influence.[126]

On October 10, Hillenkoetter wrote Truman about the formation of the Cominform. He reiterated that the Soviets desire to strengthen control over their satellites, improve coordination, and "serve notice" to the French and Italian parties that they were not their own masters and must adhere to the Kremlin's policies. The Soviets apparently recognized that the legal path to power for Western parties had narrowed; according to the CIA, their goals now focused on preparing a core of militants capable of direct action and subversion to undermine Western governments. In the longer term, he said, the Cominform would replace the Comintern as the Kremlin's "tool for attaining world domination."[127]

Despite a few indications that challenged the view of the Cominform as a sign of an all-out Soviet offensive against the West,[128] Paris and Washington, DC, both failed to grasp the basis for the creation of the Cominform and what had happened at the meetings in Poland. Originally conceived as a way for communist parties to exchange information and to organize a new journal, the intent behind the conference shifted after August 1947 to creating a new organization for interparty coordination. This was, as Anna di Biago argues, due only in part to the announcement of the Marshall Plan but also to the fact that the Soviets found themselves with limited access to information. A letter from Zhdanov to Maurice Thorez that June expressed unease over PCF expulsion from the government, not because of its consequences for the political situation in France but because the Soviet government had been in the dark. "Many people think," Zhdanov wrote, "that the French communists concerted their action with the CC of the VKP(B). You yourselves know that this is not true … the steps you have taken were wholly unexpected." It is also important to note that Moscow hesitated to adjust the nature of the conference for fear that it would be seen as a new Comintern; meanwhile, Soviet officials still deemed communist participation in coalition governments as positive.[129] Most importantly, the criticism levied against the PCF was not a call to revolution but an inducement to sharpen the fight for inclusion in the government, here meaning pressure on the government as a "party of opposition" through electoral successes coupled with powerful pressure by the masses in the form of strikes. "Nobody is recommending putschism," Polish leader Wladyslaw Gomulka explained. Zhdanov added "it is hardly expedient to reveal to one's enemy one's choice of tactics and proclaim one's unwillingness to choose one or another form of struggle" because "if you tell the enemy you are not armed, the enemy will say: fine, all the easier for me to deal with you." It is important to note too that Cominform delegates criticized the PCF for acting independently from Moscow, for excessive "legalism" and compromise with other parties, and for failing to recognize soon enough American imperialist designs in France,[130] accusations that certainly belied claims in US and French reporting – and in recent scholarship[131] – that the PCF had been intent on an illegal seizure of power for some years and that they were nothing more than Moscow's puppets.

One week before the municipal elections slated for October 19, PCF leader Maurice Thorez spoke at a rally in Marseille. His speech clearly outlined communist policy. He decried government incapacity and economic malaise, and he sharpened attacks on Anglo-American imperialists and the fascist "campaign of hatred and division" run by de Gaulle. The British and Americans, he said, had deprived France of German coal and reparations. Moreover, the Marshall Plan – which the PCF opposed for favoring the German aggressor over the French victim – aimed to divide Europe into two camps and undermine French sovereignty. The creation of the Cominform, he argued, was to alert the masses to these dangers and to organize the forces of "democracy and peace" against those of "reaction and imperialist war." The Soviets, he claimed, would help France without political conditions. Thorez further denounced the war in Indochina and proclaimed solidarity with the people of Viet Nam and "the martyrs of Spain and Greece."[132] Notably, Thorez did not call for insurrection and revolution; the speech was, instead, a political stump speech.

Just days before the elections, the new US military attaché in Paris Brigadier General F. J. Tate followed up on alleged parachuting of weapons to communists in eastern France reported earlier that summer. His staff had tried and failed to secure eyewitness accounts; however, his office still deemed it "probable" that the drops had occurred. While the "basic informant" was of "doubtful character," an interview with another informant who produced papers showing his work with Allied intelligence during the occupation gave them reason to believe the reports. Their claims were entirely speculative, based on hearsay. This informant had heard from other sources that they had seen container drops to waiting communists in the same region, and while their contents were unknown, they believed they were submachine guns. Interior Ministry intelligence officials had been informed, but it inexplicably took them two weeks to investigate. When they returned to the drop zones, they found only broken tree branches, trampled earth, and Russian-type cigarette butts.[133]

One week later, General Tate again reported alleged parachuting of arms to communist militants, this time in France's Ardennes region. His source was a British journalist who relayed information from an Interior Ministry official who claimed to have witnessed the delivery of unidentified items on the night of October 12. He stated that the ministry knew about the drops and where the materials were hidden but had chosen not to interrupt the activity or seize the caches in order to protect their network of informants inside communist groups. Neither the aircraft nor the contents of the packages had been identified, yet Tate accepted this version of events: "[I]t is obvious that the materials are ... either arms, ammunition, or funds to support communist party activities."[134] There was no indication of the origin of the planes, who might be flying them or what their intentions were, or any examination if it was even plausible for a Soviet-sponsored plane to fly into the Ardennes without detection. As with other similar reports, this intelligence could not be corroborated.

ELECTIONS

French municipal elections on October 19 delivered a big victory for de Gaulle and the RPF, which gained almost 40 percent of the vote, a clear defeat of the PCF and the left on the local level. The PCF earned 28.8 percent, the SFIO 19.5 percent, and Bidault's MRP 9 percent. In Washington, DC,

Bonnet reported the results had been well-received, especially the gains for the anti-communist RPF and the PCF's failure to retain its position as the largest party in France. US officials were also buoyed by overwhelming support for the ERP. At the same time, they feared further polarization of French politics that could undermine recovery efforts. The official US position, Bonnet wrote, was to avoid appearance of interference in French affairs while reaffirming their anti-communist attitude.[135]

European Division Chief John Hickerson wrote that the unification of noncommunist Frenchmen had been partially achieved not around the political center but further to the right around de Gaulle. This was, he argued, a gesture of despair by moderate voters disgusted with government incapacity and seeking a "man on horseback to save them from the greater evil of communist government." He assumed that de Gaulle would soon retake power and indicated that, as much as they might find it distasteful, it was in US interest that this noncommunist grouping succeed.[136] Soon after, the CIA reported Gaullist probing the possibility of American support. A source close to de Gaulle had told Caffery that he was in no hurry and that he might demand concessions before forming a government in the event Ramadier should fall. These conditions would likely include a constitutional revision and that he be given "full powers" for a specified period. De Gaulle would also likely request substantial financial assistance from the United States.[137]

Other French military officials took advantage of the possibility of communist action to promote their agendas. Just days after the elections, the US military attaché in Paris reported that French Chief of Staff General Georges Revers and Deputy Director of French Intelligence Colonel Fourcault had, with Ramadier's approval, approached them to request staff talks between the US joint chiefs and French military representatives to work out closely coordinated military plans. Revers claimed, somewhat unbelievably given manpower shortages, that one million Frenchmen under thirty could be raised to fill twenty to forty divisions if the United States were to furnish them equipment and that this force would be capable of "holding a Soviet advance long enough to secure French port areas and landing beaches for US troops if needed." Furthermore, "the threat of war could be almost certainly eliminated if the USSR were faced by early spring with a carefully planned and well-coordinated US–UK–French military program."[138] The following day, General Tate added that Fourcault was unable to explain his reasons for believing war inevitable in two to five years, the basis for their request for US military aid and talks. Tate noted that Revers' position as an active leader of anti-communist networks made it "highly probable that a US commitment for military aid would be at least partially diverted for use by resistance forces."[139]

As they often did, rumors of a communist coup again circulated in the immediate aftermath of the elections. On October 22, 1947, Frederick B. Lyon in the State Department wrote Hickerson that "a very good source" in Paris – one of Lyon's French friends – had telegraphed him information a few minutes before. The source reported, "due to the fear of a communist coup next week in Paris all police and certain troops are being mobilized. Real trouble is expected." Lyon could not, however, guarantee the accuracy of the report.[140] In southwest France, a hotbed of communist agitation, Cecil Gray reported the PCF had used the CGT to penetrate the local police and prefectures. "With the ostensible purpose of organizing government workers," he charged, "the CGT infiltrates the public service offices with communists, who form secret cells serving as sources of information for the communist party on matters of a secret and confidential nature."[141]

French intelligence also reported that the PCF had established a new political-military unit, led by a Soviet colonel and headquartered in Geneva; the propaganda arm was to be in Paris, the military organization in Montpellier.[142] A subsequent report indicated that far-right elements in Paris were circulating a rumor according to which the Quai had intercepted a telegram from Moscow to the PCF, which could not be translated in its entirety. They claimed that Moscow had instructed the PCF to "make an operation around 18 hours," the date undetermined. Communists were allegedly "to go by car in groups of five to the homes of certain anti-communists and kidnap them."[143]

Soon after, the French public voted once more in run-off elections. Bonnet again reported the results had given hope to Americans who feared the French government would turn toward a communist police state. This reassurance, he said, would lead to a more liberal attitude in Congress on aid to "nations who prove their desire to help themselves economically and politically." More journalists believed the elections in France demonstrated how "a simple promise of [American] aid can rally anti-communist forces." However, the Americans did not necessarily believe the PCF had lost ground, and they feared the PCF would abandon their tactics since Liberation and turn to violent action, a possibility that would imperil their hopes for European recovery.[144]

On October 29, 1947, Maurice Thorez delivered a speech before the PCF Central Committee, in which he clearly signaled a change in communist strategy and objectives. The PCF would transition from tactics of a party of government to "new sharpened methods of struggle." Caffery believed Thorez had abandoned any pretense of patriotism and saw the speech as "a declaration of loyalty toward the Soviet Union." The United States, with the help of the French Socialists, Thorez charged, was attempting to colonize France toward eventual world domination. He further engaged in self-criticism, enumerating the errors and opportunism of party militants and PCF leaders and their failure to note and confront the imperial and anti-democratic forces operating on behalf of the United States, while underestimating the power of labor and a mass movement. Caffery believed this provided "clear indication of a planned intensification of 'mass' tactics."[145] As Irwin Wall has pointed out, however, class war and revolution were absent from Thorez's speech. He had "simply clarified the terms of the PCF's demand for a government with itself in a preponderant role."[146] This was not about revolution; it was about returning to a Popular Front.

THE RIGHT OF DIVORCE

The summer after eviction from the French government, PCF leaders sought to correct unfavorable public opinion resulting from its recent colonial policy. In early July, Étienne Fajon vehemently denied his party had fomented or encouraged rebellions in Indochina and Madagascar. He claimed that foreign powers, and especially the United States, coveted the colonies as areas of investment, new markets, and strategic bases, and he accused reactionary elements in the colonies and certain government circles of encouraging foreign penetration. Notably, he observed the right of the colonized to self-determination and separation as put forward by the 1928 Soviet treatise on the colonies. However, the "right of divorce," Fajon argued, did not signify its necessity. Complete separation of these areas from France would open them up to "the expansion of international reaction," and it was better for them to achieve their aims within the French Union. To the colonized, he declared, the communists were their only true friends in France.[147]

Meanwhile, French sources and US intelligence continued to underscore the communist tendencies of liberation movements in the French empire, even as local US representatives expressed doubt about these claims. In one instructive episode, an aide to General Raoul Salan, the commander of French forces in northern Indochina, claimed that the Viet Minh was "exclusively communistic" and pointed to French intelligence reports that the Soviets had sent a team to reorganize Vietnamese military forces. Vice-Consul James O'Sullivan believed these teams were likely something more benign – White Russian musicians traveling in China – and the French consul in Kunming admitted to a US representative there that the report was likely a "fabrication of French military intelligence in Indochina."[148] O'Sullivan observed that French declarations about the Viet Minh's communism had been more frequent in the past two weeks. He believed that French insistence on this point could presage repression; colonial authorities had also emphasized Vietnamese communism in the months before the Haiphong incident of the previous year.[149] Echoing remarks by OIR the previous year, O'Sullivan further remarked that it was "curious that the French discovered no communist menace in the Ho Chi Minh government until after September 1946 when it became apparent that the Vietnam government would not bow to French wishes."[150]

US intelligence and French authorities continued to stress the danger. In contrast to the CIG Daily Summary, which largely reproduced the reporting and views of local US representatives, CIG Intelligence Reports warned that the government in Hanoi was a dictatorship under the control of the communist Viet Minh, who used the secret police to control the population and extend communist control over the whole of the nation.[151] Later, another CIG intelligence report analyzed an alleged fragment of a Viet Minh textbook used for communist indoctrination. In general, the report linked the text to Soviet theories and support for the USSR against Western imperialists.[152] It was strikingly similar to a longer report allegedly obtained by an American intelligence agent in Hanoi and passed to French police officials, which purported to provide further proof of close relations between the Comintern and Indochinese communists as well as the revolutionary objectives of the Viet Minh.[153] On September 15, the political adviser to the high commissioner in Indochina sent a report on communist activity to officials in Paris, echoing much of earlier reports, but also made an argument that would resonate with Americans: "nationalist forces against which France fights are in reality communist forces."[154]

Caffery in Paris again questioned O'Sullivan's assessments in Hanoi. He did not think it was curious at all that the French only became aware of the communist menace in Ho's government until after September 1946. In the months before, he said, the Vietnamese government had eliminated pro-Chinese nationalists and other moderate elements. Ho had reorganized the government in September 1946, and this had resulted in the increased influence of extremist, pro-communist elements in the

Viet Minh. Caffery inaccurately wrote that France itself had only realized the worldwide menace of communism after the Paris Peace Conference. Currently, he said, the eviction of the communists from the government and the growing anti-communism of other political parties has "naturally increased interest and distrust in the communist tendencies in Ho Chi Minh's government." The PCF's open support for Ho and the Viet Minh had also illuminated the issue, he claimed. "French communists," Caffery argued, "had never varied in their slogan that independence of Vietnam must be entrusted to Ho Chi Minh and to Viet Minh and no others."[155] This assessment was disingenuous at best, and it is worth noting that Cominform delegates in Poland that fall criticized Fajon's July speech and the PCF for its adherence to "independence within the framework of the French Union," even after its expulsion from the government.[156]

OIR analysts challenged Caffery's view from Paris. They argued that French negotiator Emile Bollaert did not intend to negotiate in good faith with the Vietnamese. Bollaert's speech of September 10, in which he presented France's "final" offer to Vietnam, provided only limited internal autonomy and unification of the three kys, but demanded French control of the military and foreign policy, and a governmental structure in which French officials would retain administrative control. He also suggested that the present government be replaced with a "qualified" government to which the French could devolve limited powers. OIR analysts bluntly stated that these proposals retracted promises made in the March 6 agreement and that the French government was likely certain that its offer would not be accepted. Instead, this was an appeal to overthrow Ho's government and the opening salvo in a political and military campaign against Hanoi. OIR analysts also rejected French military optimism about the outcome; after nine months of warfare, the French military had only limited territorial gains and were not in a position to dictate terms. Even though this reporting very clearly reflected State Department reports from Saigon and Hanoi, it met resistance. George Abbott, who would later replace Reed as the US consul in Saigon, wrote Wallner in the Western European Division that he had been "worried for some time by the anti-French, pro-Vietnam slant of the material on Indochina put out by OIR," the latest example of which was the September 24 report. "Certainly," he said, "*Humanité* would love to quote certain passages." "It is obvious," Abbott continued, "that we are in for a long world-wide struggle for a position with our friends in Moscow, and it would be a very serious error to permit a communist-controlled Government ... in Indochina." Abbott argued that Ho's communist allegiance was more apparent each day, and he was himself looking into intelligence that the PCF had sent Ho significant amounts of cash. Nonetheless, he complained, OIR persisted in advocating negotiations with Ho.[157]

French officials understood that the Viet Minh's ideological orientation was an essential question for US officials. On October 30, a French report on American activity in Indochina noted that "the day when French propaganda succeeds in proving one or the other, the American attitude will be less hesitant in France's regard." The same report also indicated that peace and order were required for American economic ambitions in the region. The Vietnamese had not yet demonstrated the ability to maintain peace and stability; for the time being "order is synonymous with the French presence." French analysts also noted that former Ambassador William Bullitt, then on a fact-finding trip to Vietnam in September and October, was eager to know whether the Viet Minh and Ho Chi Minh were communist. He acknowledged the US government had no document proving Ho's affiliation or his links with Moscow. "If one exists," Bullitt hinted to his French counterparts, "it was certain that its exploitation would have a good effect in American public opinion."[158] Here US officials conflated two separate issues. Few doubted that Ho was a communist, but this did not necessarily imply alignment with Moscow.

In North Africa, it was already apparent that the United States was moving away from Arab nationalists in favor of France. American officials maintained contact with nationalist leaders but were increasingly preoccupied by the degree of communist influence on the masses. In early July, Ambassador Bonnet confronted Loy Henderson about US contacts with a Moroccan nationalist. While Henderson reaffirmed American commitment to French control of North Africa, Bonnet was especially struck by his anti-communist zeal. Henderson was married to a White Russian and had served as William Bullitt's adviser in Moscow, and he seemed "consumed" with diminishing communist influence in the region. He felt the French had not done enough to suppress communism there, even as they repressed Arab nationalists, giving them no option but to accept communist support. Embassy Counselor Armand Bérard repeatedly refuted Henderson's claims and tried to show him the excessive role he attributed to communists in North Africa and the dangers of American sympathy with Arab nationalism.[159] Later, Bonnet reported that the Americans' overriding anti-communism dictated their support for French control, but they maintained contact with nationalists in case the situation blew up. For them, North Africa was the first link in a line of defense against the Soviet world, which passed through Greece, Turkey, Iran, India, and finally, Indochina.[160]

The possibility of an alliance between communists and nationalists seemed more likely given the situation in Europe and the intercession of PCF and Soviet officials. On September 11, French resident general in Tunis Jean Mons reported that the PCT had approached nationalist Destour leader Salah Ben Youssef with a document from the PCF Central Committee, according to which Soviet ambassador to the United Nations Andrei Gromyko was "prepared to support the legitimate claims of the Arab World" once he received assurance from nationalist leaders about an entente with universal communism. Destourian leaders reported that Tunisians were hostile to communist ideology, but "if Russia or the communists take up defense of North Africans, the Tunisian people would without hesitation rally to their side." The French report noted the suppleness of the nationalist position; this was due, Mons argued, to the fact that this demarche had more scale to it because "it came not only from the PCF, but from a nation like the Soviet Union, which engages on Middle Eastern issues." It was likely, he said, that the nationalists intended to use these offers to blackmail the French government. Even if the communists ultimately failed to reach an agreement with nationalists, the ensuing political confusion would only benefit the Soviets on the international level even if the same success escaped local communists.[161]

When French officials outlined proposed reforms for North Africa in October, Caffery enthusiastically endorsed them.[162] In Tunis, however, American Vice-Consul Donald Dumont warned that US acceptance of the French proposals would amount to turning their back on the principles for which they fought the last war. He acknowledged that the department had concerns beyond North Africa in consideration here; "the growing power of communism and the possibility it may sweep over France is obviously the fundamental element which must enter into any decision regarding American policy in North Africa." The French, he said, were acutely aware of American preoccupation with communism in North Africa and will not fail to point out that the most effective way of checking communism is by maintaining peace and security, which only they could do through strong control over the Arab population. Finally, Dumont warned, "despite our deep concern lest communism gain control of France ... we should not shut our eyes to the far-reaching consequences which could result from the endorsement of a French program ... that now appears so limited in scope as to be irreconcilable with the democratic principles for which we stand."[163]

TIPPING POINT

On November 1, Caffery reported that Maurice Thorez and other PCF officials were en route to Moscow to celebrate the thirtieth anniversary of the October Revolution. Notable among this contingent was Laurent Casanova who led communist shock troops during the German occupation and was now, Caffery alleged, "charged with organization of a communist military apparatus in France, which would be thrown into action at Moscow's orders."[164] Several days later, noncommunist left and trade union sources told him that the Cominform declaration – allegedly advocating a change from parliamentary maneuvers to revolutionary mass action and from extreme anti-German nationalism to extreme anti-American nationalism – and Thorez's October "mea culpa" speech had shaken the noncommunist left and given ammunition to anti-communist trade unionists. Now was the time to strike hard, these sources said; if anti-communist opposition within and outside of the CGT were adequately financed, they could defeat the communists in the labor movement within a year. Moreover, "should these Soviet patriots lose the machinery of the CGT they would be deprived of their greatest weapon."[165]

The view that communists had suffered reverses because of US aid to Western Europe and their open subservience to Moscow coexisted with the belief that these setbacks could lead the Soviets to push them into action, precipitating a civil war. Marshall told Truman on November 7 that the United States should "strengthen in every way local forces of resistance ... and persuade others to bear a greater part of the burden of opposing communism."[166] These views were reflected in the CIA's Review of the World Situation, which detailed communist losses attributable to the Truman Doctrine and Marshall Plan on one hand, and the Cominform on the other. CIA analysts concluded, "the danger of communist accession to power in France appears to have been eliminated, although the communists retain the capability to precipitate a civil war in France, particularly in opposition to accession to power by de Gaulle." But they also believed that if interim US aid alleviated suffering in France during the winter and there remained the fair prospect of an effective recovery program, then the conditions upon which a de Gaulle return depended would not exist and a center coalition around Socialist leadership could yet survive.[167]

On November 12, 1947, serious unrest broke out in Marseille, seeming to realize the French and American governments' worst fears. US Consul Cecil Gray reported that the disorders were communist-led and inspired.

Rioters had seized the Palais de Justice, broken into the city hall and ransacked offices, nightclubs, and bars. Shots had been fired, wounding thirty and killing one. American and British flags, on display for Armistice Day, had been torn down. While there was apparent calm in the streets the next morning, strikes had been called among port, metallurgy, construction, and chemical workers.[168] In Paris, French intelligence reported that communist circles claimed the PCF had reconstituted its clandestine organization under the supervision of a Russian officer, in order to be ready for any eventuality.[169] Another report indicated that the party had instructed local militants in at least one location to occupy municipal and police offices and arrest the mayor, police commissioner, inspectors, and other dangerous political adversaries in the RPF. The same report conveyed intelligence from the Rhône Department that "the purpose of the communists is to seize power following a coup, of which the success must be assured from the moment action is taken."[170] Days later, the French Interior Ministry released a statement disclosing the discovery of three arms caches in southern France. The official statement did not indicate for whom the weapons were intended,[171] but the fact that the government had released the information at a time when France was threatened by unrest seemed to confirm reports that the arms were meant for PCF revolutionaries.

On November 17, Pierre Charpentier in Moscow suggested the communist parties had decided circumstances were favorable to begin action in France and Italy "at a crucial moment in the fight between US imperialism and the USSR, while the Marshall Plan has not yet produced an effect, while the economic and financial situation is serious in Western Europe, while social conflicts are developing there, at a moment which may constitute the last chance for communist parties." It was possible, he wrote, that they had reached a turning point, and that "the risk of unleashing movements with a revolutionary character in France and Italy had been accepted by Moscow with all of its possible consequences even including war."[172] The following day, widespread strikes erupted in France. Viewed alongside rumors of arms cache discoveries, alleged weapons drops and new international brigades, the strikes seemed like a prelude to insurrection.[173]

Soon after, French ambassador to the Soviet Union Georges Catroux expounded on the views expressed by Charpentier in the November 17 telegram, which detailed Soviet actions – namely the Cominform declaration and recent attacks on the United States at the United Nations – that seemed if not a prelude to war then at least a risk that might lead to it.

In one of the most astute contemporary assessments of Soviet intentions in France, Catroux asserted that, as paradoxical as it might sound, the Soviets' aggressive attitude was one they believed might actually spare them the war they feared. They had felt threatened ever since the announcement of the Truman Doctrine in March, because the United States was on their doorstep in Greece and Turkey, and because they saw the Marshall Plan as an instrument that could unite Western Europe against them and lead to American preeminence in the West, a sure sign of capitalist encirclement. Recourse to war was not then possible, but they felt they must act to weaken their adversaries; their weapons would be propaganda calculated to unmask the dangerous designs of the United States, create a coalition of nations around the USSR, and create a bulwark against a threatened war. The first objective remained: destruction of the Marshall Plan. France and Italy were the essential pieces of the Western bloc, and they had local parties powerful enough to bring in the working class and crush the Socialists who supported US policy. It remained to be seen, Catroux wrote, if, as Charpentier concluded, this action risks the conflict they most hope to avoid.[174]

In Washington, DC, US officials observed French strikes with unease. On November 22, Admiral Leahy wrote in his diary that communist-instigated rioting directed by Moscow had spread in France and Italy. In France, it had caused the collapse of the Ramadier government, and it threatened the present government of Italy.[175] Two days later, Robert Schuman formed a government, but it left Caffery despondent. This was the climax of one of France's longest political crises, yet the government remained incapable of addressing France's grave problems: "plus ça change, plus c'est la même chose." It was difficult to see how the government would succeed; to him, it seemed like one step closer to the ultimate showdown between the PCF and de Gaulle.[176] In late November, Irving Brown, the European representative for the American Federation of Labor, told the US embassy in London that the strikes in France were a precursor to a general strike, which would be used by the PCF to seize power. However, he too sensed growing opposition to the communist domination of the CGT; if the government dealt strongly with the strikes they may collapse and the communist leadership repudiated.[177]

French intelligence also weighed the possibility of a communist coup. They argued that the PCF hoped to maintain the discontent of the working class, conserve its combative ardor and win the sympathy of lukewarm elements to oppose a Gaullist seizure of power. Communist sympathizers and militants seemed to think that the power struggle had begun. Many also thought the party would soon be dissolved and its leaders arrested; they thought it "better to fight now and take their chances."[178] Additionally, Jean de Beausse, the chargé d'affaires in Warsaw, wrote Bidault that he had learned from a good source that, "in inviting the democracies to come if need be to the aid of the insurgent French working class against an eventual dictatorship of General de Gaulle," Thorez had not spoken as carelessly as some had thought. Sources told him that this was discussed at the inaugural Cominform meeting, where its representatives had decided that should the PCF decide to resort to weapons, "the workers of Piedmont and Lombardy would rise up to open the Po Valley and the Eastern European democracies would advance to the Italo-Yugoslav frontier." Moreover, the "imminent" nature of an uprising in France had justified "the synchronization of the strikes in northern Italy and those on French territory."[179] On November 29, the Service de Documentation Extérieure et de Contre-Espionnage (SDECE – French foreign intelligence) reported that Thorez had left the impression "that civil war was imminent in France" with his Polish colleagues and that he had studied the possibility of the return to France of foreigners who played an active role in wartime communist militias.[180]

On November 29, noncommunist trade unionists told Caffery that the PCF and the Soviets would gladly call a general strike to bring about a collapse and the formation of a communist government; however, most felt that the PCF was not strong enough to force a general strike in the face of growing opposition from segments of the trade union movement. Still, the communists would likely continue to work to affect production, create disorder, and paralyze the national economy. While communist circles reported that Stalin had ordered Thorez to sabotage the Marshall Plan without resort to armed action, these anti-communist observers pointed out that Soviet intelligence agents ran the communist strike committee and were determined to create the utmost disorder short of armed rebellion.[181]

Anti-communists in Italy in contact with US intelligence likewise linked the strikes in France and Italy to a broader communist attempt to seize power. US military attaché in Rome John Willems reported that a very high Italian government source had given him a document about the Cominform, which he believed "authoritative." According to the report, the Soviet Politburo was "directing a coordinated all-out communist campaign to take over the French and Italian governments by violence rather than constitutional methods." The use of a general strike to block the implementation of the ERP was but an initial stage, and subsequent actions would not be restricted to this method. However authoritative Ambassador James Dunn and General Willems considered the document, the CIA suggested otherwise. Its analysts believed that it was one of three things: an Italian government plant to expedite interim aid by showing the urgency of anti-Soviet countermeasures, a Cominform plant to spur the PCI and PCF to action but with no real intention to take the course indicated, or an authentic indication of Soviet plans. The analysts noted their belief that neither the PCI nor the PCF had the capacity to seize power without substantial outside support, which would involve the risk of a major conflict the Soviets presently hoped to avoid,[182] suggesting, at least, that the intelligence was an Italian attempt to encourage aid.

In Washington, DC, Bonnet noted American sympathy and support for French government efforts to end social conflict. They did not want to delay interim aid or embarrass the French government. Nothing, Bonnet said, suggested that Marshall Plan aid was in peril. Even press hostile to US policy had chosen to highlight communist agitation and countermeasures taken by the French government.[183] And on December 2, Bonnet again noted US officials' "very strong desire to help us resist what they consider a communist offensive directed from Moscow" – the very view encouraged by their anti-communist sources – and their frequent inquiries about assistance. Bonnet took the opportunity to emphasize the usefulness of immediate aid and American sympathy with French government views for the settlement of the German problem.[184] The same day, Ambassador Douglas cabled US Representative John Vorys, a member on the select committee for foreign aid, to express Marshall's (then in London) grave concern over the "critical situation in France," where he believed there was a "very real struggle for power." "If we are not to run the serious risk of losing France," Marshall argued, Congress must act quickly to approve interim aid. He added, "this is not, I promise you, a cry of 'wolf, wolf' but brute reality." The situation had deteriorated, but a promise of aid would strengthen favorable forces in France and enable them to prevent "a flagrant attempt to seize power."[185]

French sources maintained a delicate balance between showing Americans that French efforts (with crucial American assistance) to thwart communism were succeeding while also reminding them that the threat was still present. In early December, ex-communists told Caffery that their former party had been driven to an impasse by Soviet policy – which they noted, was not entirely approved by the majority of PCF leadership – from which they could only extricate themselves by going underground. The Soviets were well-aware of the damage done to the political prospects of the French and Italian parties, but were more interested in preparing fifth columns for eventual war between the United States and the Soviet Union.[186] The next day, Robert Schuman told Caffery that the situation had improved and he was confident he would defeat communist efforts to throw him out of office. Anticommunist trade unionists told him too that they were optimistic about strike developments; several of the strikes had failed, they said, because "a majority of the French public now realize the anti-national character" of the PCF.[187]

Not long after, an Interior Ministry official told Caffery that they had new information that had clarified their views on Soviet and PCF intentions. As other reports had earlier surmised, the official now argued that Moscow viewed the Marshall Plan as an instrument for capitalist encirclement, and that they needed to ensure its failure by neutralizing assistance to France and Italy. Legal tactics had not worked, and they had thus adopted a program of revolutionary activity to disrupt the Marshall Plan and prepare the way for communist control. Thus, the source now claimed, "the present action ... is designed not to grab power by a coup d'état at this time but rather to cause the present democratic governments in Western Europe to collapse ... under strong communist blows" against political, social, and economic structures. They hoped that his would lead the United States to abandon Europe, leaving the door open for communist control. The Interior Ministry reiterated other reports that Thorez had forbidden the use of firearms, telling CGT militants that if they did their job, "living conditions would so deteriorate and there would be such widespread misery that a new and desirable situation would be created" to recapture the masses.[188]

Privately, French officials also noted new information that Thorez wanted a more moderate policy. "A good source" reported Thorez's comments to a communist parliamentary group, in which he lamented that some militants had let themselves be swept up in events to the point that they started believing in revolution. In fact, the objectives of communist agitation had been twofold: to bring pressure on the Foreign Ministers Conference in London (especially on the question of the German settlement and participation in the ERP) and to prevent American implementation of the Marshall Plan. However, he warned, "the tactic of sabotage they had envisioned to impress the U.S. ran the risk of civil war and world war and must be abandoned." Instead, he argued, the sabotage of the Marshall Plan should be accomplished through regular strikes that can be resumed in three months. In the meantime, they must continue to negotiate and – as Zhdanov had argued – maintain the appearance of intransigence to obtain the maximum.[189] Subsequent reports suggested that Stalin had accepted Thorez's defense of a more moderate policy during their recent meetings at Sochi,[190] and that Moscow did not wish to push plans for agitation in France and Italy to the point of civil war and had issued instructions to the PCF to stop the strike movement when the government began to mobilize.[191]

While the French government demonstrated determination and strength against the communist threat, de Gaulle's emissaries continued to engage US officials. On December 15, Wallner wrote to the embassy that he had spent the evening with Gilbert Renaud (also known by his nom de guerre Colonel Remy), whom Wallner found "inspired confidence." Renaud had served in Gaullist intelligence services during the war, was a close confidant of de Gaulle, and currently involved in the RPF. He told Wallner that the general would return to power in March, but could not explain how, except that he would only do so at the invitation of the French people in a general election, and that constitutional reform "must, of course accompany this invitation." Renaud was sure to underscore de Gaulle's anti-communist agenda: he would outlaw the PCF, imprison its leaders, and dissolve the CGT.[192] Two days later, de Gaulle's press officer explained that the general anticipated continued communist efforts to sabotage French recovery, leading to another serious economic breakdown in February or March. De Gaulle reportedly believed that the Schuman government was "ineffective and helpless" and would be unable to prevent another economic collapse, leading to his recall to power.[193]

Other French sources kept up the drumbeat. A high official in the Interior Ministry confided to Caffery that he was deeply troubled by news that communist leaders had ordered their militants to dig in and step up agitation even though they know the strike battle is lost. Prefectures all over France reported "flying squads of hardened communist shock troops . . . are being shuttled about to combat the police," and in some cases, are deliberately "provoking" the police to fire on them and demonstrating crowds. This source concluded that whatever the cost the PCF had orders to "follow a line of action which will inevitably call for governmental action against the party," and drive it underground, where it would await future use in an international conflict.[194] Schuman himself told Caffery that French police had arrested a dozen Soviet nationals in Marseille, and had definitive proof that the men were "leaders in the troubles" there and that one of them recently received "a considerable sum of money from Russia."[195]

Interior Minister Jules Moch also asked a member of the US embassy to call on him, during which he took the occasion to warn that the government victory over the PCF was not final and that he anticipated another showdown in February or March unless the government could prevent it through the procurement of critical foodstuffs like wheat, milk, and meat. He said that American interim aid was "splendid" and would help them maintain the bread ration, but he did not think they could increase it without special aid. Moch also took the occasion to show his interlocutor the latest communist instructions, which called for an all-out attack on the Socialists as slaves of American imperialism and other anti-government and anti-American propaganda designed to foster mistrust; they also allegedly assured their followers of "substantial funds from Moscow for this 'crusade' against American imperialism" and the ERP.[196]

In the aftermath of the strikes, Bonnet could happily report alignment of French and American views. The London Conference of Foreign Ministers broke up without resolution on German issues on December 15, 1947, but Bonnet reported that US officials in Washington, DC, were "nearly unanimous that the western powers could not wait for another conference to settle the status of western Germany." He further noted that the Soviet attitude, and Molotov's attacks on the Anglo-American powers and the French government underscored the similarity of Western powers' views in the face of Soviet action. Soviet attacks on the Marshall Plan had also reinforced their conviction of the necessity of rebuilding Western Europe and settling the German issue once and for all.[197]

On December 17, the US Congress approved the "Foreign Aid Act of 1947," a major boon to the French government and anti-communists. Caffery reported that many observers expected the CGT to lose two-thirds of its membership for its role in the failed strikes. The ambassador suggested that French workers were ahead of labor leaders in fomenting a split in the union, which occurred just days later. The CIA acknowledged a wave of defections from the CGT, but they pointed out that noncommunist elements were still a minority in the CGT and that Caffery's "two-thirds" estimate was too high.[198] A founder of the new "Force Ouvrière" in the Marseille region told Cecil Gray that they had set January 30, 1948, as their deadline for organizing new recruits because they had reason to believe that at the end of January or beginning of February 1948, the communists would unleash a second wave of disorder "far more violent and serious than those which the country has just passed through." Instead of the "unorganized masses" they relied upon in November, this time the PCF would use "experts in violence" like those who had sabotaged the railroads during the recent strike.[199]

Post-strike intelligence estimates noted French efforts to combat PCF designs but suggested that the communists still posed a dangerous threat. On December 17, the CIA released its third Review of the World Situation, the first since strikes broke out in France. This assessment repeated much of its previous analysis of the French situation, that the Soviets' primary objective was to defeat the ERP by bringing about economic collapse, and that they were willing to sacrifice the political futures of the French and Italian parties to larger Soviet interests. It praised the "strong and effective" efforts of the new Schuman government to defeat this major communist effort to disrupt the economy and declared that the French Army had proven capable of dealing with any potential insurrection. France, the report continued, had "successfully passed its first real test against the economic power inherent in the communist hold on labor." However, the government still faced continued hardship – work stoppages had cost two million tons of coal and decreased production by 40 percent in November – and renewed communist efforts to damage the government and recovery efforts through increased use of "violent acts of coercion and sabotage by trained and reliable, militant underground units."[200]

CIA intelligence reports detailed, with some specificity, how the PCF had been forced to adjust their operational plans considering growing anti-communism to refocus from a general uprising to a more targeted action by militants. One report, released the same day as the CIA estimate, argued that the strikes in Marseille were part of a larger communist assault on France. The original plan of attack, which had called for an assault on Paris and the use of forces in the south "deployed under the pretext of helping Spanish republicans against Franco" to proclaim a series of "Soviet governments" with a capital in Toulouse, had been adjusted in response to disaffection of the masses with the PCF and CGT, redeployment of paramilitary communist groups after the communist expulsion in May, and Ramadier's order to Revers to prepare for anti-communist action. According to the new plan, Paris was to be cut off from the border regions by paramilitary groups and chains of cells extending from Brest to the Midi, where they planned to rise up and "proclaim local Soviets." Routes to Italy were to be kept open so that Italian communists could establish contact with communist centers in the Midi in the event of a successful insurrection in Italy.[201]

Soon after, Bonnet noted the effects of this reporting on the administration. Journalists Stewart and Joseph Alsop described Truman's recent
declaration that "never in its history, even in the course of two world
wars, has the United States had its security so in danger," as an assertion
founded on the "numerous facts brought to him each day by the CIA."[202]

One December 22, the CIA reported that the French War Minister
Henri Teitgen desired military discussions with the United States. He
suggested that France would be willing to grant the United States basing
privileges on French territory. "France," he said, "has now openly
declared itself against the USSR and on the side of the western world."
He also indicated that if the United State offered guarantees to French
security, there would be "no difficulty" in working out a solution for the
control of Germany. While he was heartened by government success
against communist-directed strikes in November, he expected another
wave of disorder in late January.[203] Georges Bidault broached the issue
again several days later, reiterating the desire for military talks. "By
definitely aligning itself with the West" and "by arresting and expelling
Soviet agitators," he observed, France has "exposed itself to possible
Soviet reprisals."[204]

As the year came to a close, the CIA released ORE 64, "The Current
Situation in France," which rehashed the agency's views as enumerated in
previous summaries and World Situation briefs, with the concurrence of
the three military departments. Notable, however, was sharp dissent by
OIR. ORE had rightly emphasized the strategic importance of France,
they said, but had presented an unbalanced view confined almost exclusively to France's role in a future war, thus "slurring over the vital and
dynamic contribution which French political leadership and economic
potential are expected to make to U.S. strategic aims for peace." OIR
analysts also roundly disagreed with ORE's assessment of the consequences for communist domination of France as "overly pessimistic"
and its description of communist tactics as an "all-out effort to create
disorder" to prevent de Gaulle's return to power. This phrase, they
argued, suggested communist paramilitary forces would initiate civil
strife, which they deemed unlikely. To ORE's suggestion that de Gaulle
"might" take an authoritarian approach, OIR declared that he *would*, as
evidenced by his attitude but also by his recent speeches. They further
argued that ORE's assessment of the economic situation "overplays
the effects of the November-December strikes and work stoppages" and
"fails to mention the economic difficulty with greatest immediate
political implications, namely acute shortages of bread, meat, and fats."

OIR further noted that ORE had failed to give the French credit for the successes of the Monnet Plan. They also suggested that France's shift to a Western orientation could not be understood with only reference to its failure to act as a mediator between the two blocs but because of the domestic isolation of the PCF.[205] These disparities reflected fundamentally different views of the situation in France but also the rivalry between the two organizations over analysis of the French situation.

FROM EUROPE TO THE EAST

As that autumn's strikes had spread over France, the CIA reported that continuing conflict in Southeast Asia would affect American interests in Europe and the Far East. First, the human and material resources of the region were key for European recovery. At the same time, colonized populations viewed French efforts to reestablish control as having the support of the United States. In as much as the ERP enhanced the French position at home and in the colonies, it would increase resentment of the United States, which would be exploited by communist propaganda against US imperialism.[206] A month later, the CIA reported that the Soviets were intensifying their activities in the Far East in an attempt to divert world attention from "possible Soviet reverses in Europe" or perhaps "to induce the US to divert part of its efforts and resources from Europe to the East." This would not necessarily imply Soviet abandonment of its efforts in Europe but the recognition that unsettled conditions in Asia offered rewarding opportunities for the eventual expansion of Soviet influence.[207]

Not long after, the CIA examined the situation in French North Africa. The region was of major strategic importance as a potential base for operations in Europe or the Near East, and for its richness in minerals. In Soviet hands, however, it could neutralize US positions in the Azores and Cape Verde islands and cut important lines of communication. The present domestic turmoil in France, the report continued, plus the drain of colonial wars in Indochina and Madagascar and rising Arab nationalism, seriously threatened the status quo. While there was no immediate danger of a revolt, France's failure to implement meaningful reform could cause the situation to deteriorate. Nationalism was not new in North Africa but had gained after the war due to communist propaganda and agitation, the French loss of military power and prestige, a poor economy in France, and the return of nationalist leaders. The report noted that the nationalists were receiving some moral support from the Soviets through local communist parties, but these parties had little weight while they only demanded autonomy in the French Union. However, they claimed, if the nationalists succeeded in independence, the small, well-organized, and well-financed communists might take advantage of unsettled conditions to take control of the movement, "paving the way for communist control of the whole region." Future tactics, however, "would depend on the internal political situation in France, the position of the French Communist Party, and ultimately, upon orders from Moscow."[208]

Once again, OIR analysts dissented. They disagreed with the contention that the nationalists and the French government were hopelessly deadlocked; a peaceful solution was still possible. They also argued that the CIA had "overemphasized the possibility that communist strength and influence would increase." The opposite was also possible; that is, there would be no united front and the PCF's setbacks in the metropole would, in turn, weaken local parties. Finally, they disagreed with the claim that communists would take control if the nationalists triumphed in North Africa. Even if peace came through revolution, the nationalists would likely win because they were Arab parties while the communist parties were European.[209]

By the end of the year, despite the deepening war in Indochina and nationalist agitation in North Africa, French officials could breathe easier. As French delegate to the UN Guardianship Council Roger Garreau remarked, the danger to French colonialism, "if not warded off, is at least put off." At the same time, the boldness of the colonial powers was growing. The division of political positions between anti-communists and communists served the colonial powers, he said. American adherence to anti-communism, for example, had helped them to forget their normal concerns, and it permitted France to surmount its colonial flaw: "One gets the feeling, to hear the debates, that France is thus absolved."[210] For American officials, French colonizers may have committed the original sin of denying liberty to the colonized, but at least they were "believers." Better that than godless communists who deserved no absolution. During the war, American intelligence experts and diplomats may have intended do things differently than French colonizers, but by 1948 they had themselves become imperial agents as they shed their anti-colonial cloak in favor of France's orientalist, anti-communist one.

*****

As the Cold War deepened around the globe, American diplomats and intelligence analysts struggled to make sense of communist activity in France and her empire. It was no easy task to reconcile the vast streams of information at their disposal. Some of the uncertainty stemmed from legitimate confusion about PCF activity and rhetoric; some from ideological rigidity; some was related to poor intelligence and analytic tradecraft, including worrisome intelligence gaps, lack of corroborating evidence, and failure to account for a bevy of self-interested sources. As a result, in 1947, they offered ominous assessments that ensured that US policymakers felt compelled to assume and operate upon worst-case scenarios.

The atmosphere created by alarmist reporting and by real instances of PCF and Soviet intrigue in France convinced US policymakers to act. The Truman Doctrine indicated American aid for Greece, but at its core was an expression of determination to stem the communist tide in Western Europe. The Marshall Plan and the intermediate aid packages were also responses to fears of a French collapse that year. Both helped to shore up anti-communist forces in France, many of whom had been sources for much of the reporting on the French situation. But these same alarmist reports also deepened the pro- and anti-communist divide. By the summer, the PCF openly opposed the government; that fall, it embarked upon an ill-conceived series of strikes to paralyze the French economy and force their return to the government. Their failure to do so, and their now undeniable allegiance to Moscow, was a mortal blow from which they would never fully recover. And, as Allison Drew has pointed out, the PCF's expulsion from the government and emphasis on thwarting American imperialism in Europe left communist parties in the colonies "freer to develop [their] own positions, and [their] discourse became more militant."[211]

Conclusion

How Intelligence Becomes Policy

By the end of 1947, the Cold War had frozen the French political landscape – and Franco-American relations – into a recognizable pattern. US officials saw France as weak, wrought by political turmoil and a communist party determined to sow chaos to undermine the French government and American plans in postwar Europe, and by war with communist-inspired liberation movements overseas. French weakness and propensity toward revolution suggested the necessity for American intervention to stave off communist influence and protect France and Western Europe from Soviet aggression, and to prevent France's empire from falling into communist hands.

In subsequent years, American interference in French affairs only accelerated and intensified. Emboldened by their covert support for the noncommunist Force Ouvrière split from the communist-led Confédération Générale du Travail in late 1947, American officials turned to other clandestine means to combat communism in France, beyond their already overt support for French military and economic recovery. US ambassador to France Jefferson Caffery maintained his secretive contacts with Charles de Gaulle about his possible return to power and suggested ways he could appeal to noncommunist labor, and the US government continued covert subsidies for French trade unions. In the coming years, American officials also sought to combat a Soviet peace campaign through CIA encouragement and funding of a French countereffort and friendly political parties, intellectuals, and media. And in 1951, President Truman created the Psychological Strategy Board to combat the expansion of Soviet power. A special task force was established for France, which produced the "Psychological Operations Plan for the Reduction of Communist Power in France," a broad strategy with concrete measures for the American and French governments to combat the threat posed by the PCF and global communism. At the same time, American support for French efforts to reestablish control over France's colonies became less tepid and more active, as their opposition to the PCF and the Soviet Union foreclosed the possibility of accommodation with communist and nationalist movements.

Even as the weakness and revolution narrative prevailed well into the postwar era, however, there were growing questions about the intelligence upon which it rested. The intelligence itself reveals the persistence of dissent, fissures within and among the intelligence agencies charged with assessment of the French situation, and grave concerns about the sources of American diplomatic and intelligence analysis. These issues assumed public importance in mid-1948 when *New York Times* columnist Hanson Baldwin exposed some of the difficulties facing the nascent CIA. As an example, Baldwin reported that many intelligence reports generated by the CIA and other more established agencies including Army G-2, the State Department, and the FBI during recent riots in Bogotá[1] were "virtually unevaluated and undigested intelligence"; most read like "clippings from *The Daily Worker*[2] and were so generalized they could scarcely be interpreted as accurate forecasts of the revolt."[3] At the same time, he argued, the CIA lacked "sufficient stature to command full confidence" or to challenge the evaluations of other service estimates, which often overstated the communist threat based on their own institutional interests.[4] Baldwin's exposé suggested these problems were not confined to specific episodes but plagued American intelligence more generally.

Some CIA analysts began to doubt the most alarmist intelligence on the reformation of "international brigades," covert parachuting of weapons to communist militants, the founding of the new Cominform, and the French strikes in late 1947 – intelligence which, for the past four years, had accumulated, building the narrative of French weakness and communist intrigue, and underpinning hardening American policy. In fact, investigations into some of the most sensational claims in France failed to yield one case where the intelligence could be definitively confirmed with first-hand eyewitness accounts or other intelligence sources. In early June 1947, for example, local police and communist leaders in southern France stated that they knew "absolutely nothing of international brigade headquarters" in the region that was allegedly directing training for guerilla operations in Greece.[5] Some weeks later, a British Foreign Office spokesman revealed that Britain too was investigating Greek reports about international brigades but had been unable to "prove or disprove" them.

Further, the French Foreign Ministry denied that volunteers for such a brigade had been recruited in southern France.[6]

Reflecting upon these issues in early 1948, the CIA warned that intelligence on the international brigades was problematic, and that intelligence coverage of the issue had been a "fiasco" and should be a warning to those concerned with more recent Cominform matters. Between March and November 1947, the analysts wrote, a stream of reports had come in from across the globe describing the "recruitment, training, and movement of international brigades" to assist Greek guerillas fighting the government. In 1946, an "almost equal volume of intelligence" reported on international brigades in southern France. However, it was now accepted, they argued, "that both series of 'brigades' were notional."[7]

CIA analysts also came to question the veracity of rumors about communist parachutages over postwar France.[8] In some cases pranksters or other benign activity could explain the rumors. A pro-American French "super prefect" seemed to confirm this concern: "so far," he said in early 1948, "security agents and police [have] been unable to find a single person who had actually seen such a parachuting." In his opinion, these reports were "a complete fabrication of Communist origin."[9] Whether invented by the PCF to scare the French public into acquiescence or by other factions to encourage American financial and military assistance, the prefect's assertion raised serious questions about the efficacy and sources of US intelligence; it also undermines assertions that intelligence officers concerned with France were not relentlessly anti-communist and "performed fairly well" on the matter.[10]

Likewise, French newspaper *Le Monde* discovered that alleged "signal lights" of Soviet planes and communist weapons drops that had so intrigued the public were actually the work of hoaxers. Other activity could be attributed to a soldier on leave who enjoyed setting off fireworks. In some cases, it was proven that an incident simply never happened.[11] These rumors had circulated and, exploited by one group or another, had found credence. "As if the real perils [facing France] do not suffice," one writer lamented, "the French learn each day about the existence of conspiracies which make the secret activities under the Occupation look like child's play." These were troubled times, and they allowed this kind of information to flourish. In an age of ideological fervor, falsehoods had become an effective response to the other side: "In a suspicious world, no one lingers to unravel the threads of the fable ... from shadowy pseudo-dangers, we thus help to create authentic peril."[12]

Press reporting also suggested that the presence of arms caches were not all indicators of communist intrigue. France, occupied by the Germans and ravaged by war, was awash in weapons. Local reports gave a number of explanations: some citizens had kept the arms they had during the German occupation and failed to turn them into the police; others may have intended to sell them on the black market; some of the weapons may have been destined for Spain or Palestine; some belonged to right-wing groups. Writing in March 1948 about the seizure of five tons of arms destined for Jewish fighters in Palestine, the *New York Times* reminded readers that "the [French] police have later found it necessary to revise the figure of the amount of arms found and the statements of the purposes for which they were gathered and hidden."[13] The *Washington Post* recalled that discoveries of arms caches had "given rise to reports that both the right and left were receiving arms from abroad." Spanish fascists, Italian arms traffickers, and rightist elements in the French occupation zone of Germany were possible sources of arms for French rightists, while PCF militants could look to the Soviet zone of Germany for weapons. One official reportedly lamented, "During the war we had one Maquis – now we have two of them arming against each other."[14]

Similar problems plagued intelligence coverage of the founding of the Cominform in the autumn of 1947. CIA analysts cautioned that the "large proportion of reports received from informants (directly, or through friendly police or security services)" had been based on "opinion, guesswork, creative imagination and rumor." These reports ranged from "nonsensical generalities to highly plausible specific statements of purported fact." CIA experts further warned, "however specific they may be, if statements made are not supported by factual evidence that can be independently confirmed, they cannot be considered as possessing adequate reliability." Even though embassy analysis and CIA current intelligence had claimed for months that the new Cominform was a resurrection of the prewar Communist International and a Soviet tool for directing a communist fifth column and fomenting revolution in France, these analysts reported that "not a single confirmed report on the clandestine coordination or action aspects of the Cominform [had] been received thus far." These analysts also observed that "any international Communist or Communist-front organization is automatically charged by a wide variety of sources (from professional anti-Soviet paper mills to jittery police, security, and government officials) with highly 'secret' participation in espionage, sabotage, and revolutionary activities." At the same time, "almost virtual ignorance of the actual clandestine methods employed by the communist movement now, and for the past thirty years, combined with fear of the unknown, promotes the production of innumerable myths, scare-reports, and provocations."[15] In the absence of information, these embassy and intelligence analysts fell back on their shared mindset and their emotional communities, without stopping to consider the hidden assumptions governing their views or possible alternative explanations.

Finally, regarding Soviet or Cominform direction of the French strikes in 1947, CIA analysts observed that the PCF had decided in late September not to call a general strike unless there was a right-wing putsch; its official policy was to stand for increased production. PCF officials resisted calls for a change in policy at the inaugural meeting in Poland, but the CIA believed they had been overruled by the Soviets, who had pushed for strikes. While Thorez had delivered the "mea culpa" speech in late October and initiated strikes as ordered at the conference, they said, the PCF still refrained from calling a general strike, nor was the term used in communist propaganda. "The actual tactics employed," CIA analysts argued, "showed a degree of subtlety and caution which is remarkable in view of the fire-eating propaganda which is now the usual Communist stock in trade." Furthermore, "during the French strikes, despite their obviously vital nature, discretion was by no means thrown to the winds." The CIA had no information to prove that the Cominform directed the French strikes; it was also unlikely that the Cominform supervised the day-to-day activities of other parties.[16] Analysts had "over-interpreted" what evidence they had and failed to assess it "relative to any available evidence to the contrary."[17]

Subsequent CIA analysis further observed that chatter among French police, government, and lay circles of "directives from Moscow" reported by "highly reliable sources" had not held up under critical inspection, and they warned that "more fabrications are likely to pop up in areas where communist capabilities produce serious apprehension as to their 'illegal' intentions." Intelligence analysis of the general threat posed by communism, they said, had been confused by "countless preconceptions, uncritical generalizations, and sensational nonsense." The postwar period had produced a significant trove of "uninformed or fabricated reportage" on the subject, usually from "highly unobjective anti-Soviet sources and professional intelligence merchants."[18]

The minutes of the inaugural Cominform meeting suggest the validity of these CIA concerns; they also reveal the great fallacy of the prevailing narrative of French weakness and revolution and of reigning assessments of communist capabilities and intentions. Ill-informed and caught off guard by events in France, communist officials criticized the PCF for "excessive infatuation with parliamentary methods of struggle" since Liberation and for maintaining the possibility of a French path to Socialism,[19] which suggests that the PCF had not considered launching a "coup" or illegal methods to "seize power" between Liberation and the strikes of 1947. Nor were Cominform officials recommending they turn to putschism. Instead, their criticism was meant to force the PCF to sharpen the struggle in opposition to the government and American imperialism through advocacy of working class interests and strikes.[20] This was not to "seize power" but to show their strength with the masses and force their return to the government. Cominform delegates also criticized PCF officials for the party's colonial policy and its advocacy of independence within the French Union, belying assertions that they had been secretly fomenting rebellion against the French colonial regime.[21]

The sources of US intelligence on much of this revolutionary activity came largely from informants in the French Interior Ministry and transnational and transimperial webs of right-leaning observers and ex-communists now hostile to the PCF, whose own information was often the recycled product of rumor and anonymous sources. In some cases, US intelligence experts had no access to the source and were completely reliant on French security services who were unsurprisingly loath to share all their information. At the same time, analysts failed to recognize and account for serious gaps in intelligence collection, and they fell victim to unmitigated cognitive biases that assumed all communist activity must be toward a common, revolutionary end. Too often, they missed important factors in France that militated against worst-case scenario assumptions.[22]

As Francis Balace has documented, many of the fantastical stories that had so intoxicated allied officials and intelligence services (including the US military attaché in Brussels, Colonel Robert Solberg)[23] originated with a single Belgian source known to be viscerally anti-communist; his reports were later dismissed as *"une affaire rocambolesque,"* pure fantasy.[24] The 1946 War Department intelligence plan had acknowledged as such: "the great preponderance" of reports on communists had come from "the large number of anti-Communist groups and individuals ... ranging from ... Socialist[s] and right-wing parties, government officials, and business and clerical figures to anti-Soviet émigrés and professional informants."[25] Some of them had been plucked from French prisons, guilty of collaboration and working for German intelligence in the last

war but possessing desirable skills in a new Cold War.[26] Many hoped to
encourage American involvement in French affairs to their benefit; others
hoped to convince their counterparts of the necessity for immediate
financial and military assistance in order to stave off communism in
France and rebuild the French military as a bulwark against Soviet
expansionism in Western Europe. While there were some cases in which
US intelligence and diplomatic officials acknowledged their informants'
possible motives, serious reflection on the personal and political objectives
of these sources – and their impact on American assessments of the
situation in France and US foreign policy – was rare; as a result, their
significant influence remained hidden within the secret dossiers they
passed to US officials.

The most profound problem with the prevailing narrative, however,
lay in its inherent bias and failure to account for French and colonized
agency, its estimates based upon simple calculations of power. Privately,
OIR analysts regarded the CIA's ORE 64 "The Current Situation in
France" to be a "distressingly poor paper" and a "childish generaliza-
tion," another "a good example of ORE putting France's worst foot
forward."[27] In their formal dissent, OIR complained that the report had
"slurr[ed] over the vital and dynamic contribution which French political
leadership and economic potential are expected to make to US strategic
aims for peace" and failed to give the French credit for positive gains they
had made since Liberation.[28] Indeed, embassy and intelligence analysis
had surveyed the French situation through a lens of weakness from the
outset of the Liberation and early postwar eras. They viewed French
officials as unable to solve their nation's domestic and colonial problems
or to withstand Soviet pressure without outside help. They regarded the
PCF as a foreign party, closely directed by handlers in the Soviet Union.
And they failed to account for the agency of the colonized in the French
empire. Over time, they came to see liberation movements in the French
colonies not as indigenous responses to oppressive colonialism but as
closely connected to the interests of the PCF and the Soviet Union.
Indeed, once strident anti-colonialists, many of these American rappor-
teurs came to adopt the very same orientalist views of the colonized and
France's *mission civilisatrice* as their French contacts. Annoyed by the
"captious attitude" and tone of OIR comments, CIA officials dismissed
the criticism and claimed that OIR dissent had not taken issue with any of
their major conclusions.[29] In fact, these disagreements were larger than a
battle over specific conclusions; OIR criticism was a rejection of their very
approach to the French problem. Failure to recognize agency and

initiative meant that CIA and embassy analysis also failed to identify and understand local sources of discontent or the influence of state and private transimperial actors.

Despite serious concerns raised by mid-level CIA and OIR analysts, the prevailing narrative survived. It did so, in part, because the CIA and State Department remained internally divided on the matter. State Department (European Division, the Paris embassy, and local representatives in the colonies), OIR, and CIA analysis in many cases reflected their institutional identities and pedigree. CIA Intelligence Reports – based on contact with French intelligence and government sources with interests in securing American assistance and military commitments – continued to report the same alarmist stock about communist coups and arms drops for the remainder of the decade. CIA estimates – moderated somewhat by a more thorough analysis and a review process – were more sanguine but still viewed PCF activity as inseparable from the march of global communism. Within the State Department, the OIR and foreign service officers posted to the empire remained a marginalized bastion of optimism while analysis from the secretive EUR/X unit under Raymond Murphy and Caffery's embassy in Paris continued to paint dark images of France on the brink. According to CIA officials, this same embassy analysis made up 90 percent of the material incorporated into the CIA's Daily Summary, read each morning by Truman and his advisers.[30]

Rumors of communist conspiracies – even though largely unproven – meant that the narrative of French weakness and revolution persisted unchallenged. The heightening of international tensions, the renewal of strikes in France, and the expulsion of communist ministers from the French government created a favorable atmosphere for rumor, even if it contradicted other reports that suggested moderation on the part of the PCF and the Soviets.[31] These rumors took flight on the whispers of sources across Europe, North Africa, and Southeast Asia. This intelligence sustained a psychology of fear, which meant, for the foreseeable future, that communist activity in France could only be viewed in relation to alarmist reports of communist preparations to seize power, and communist-led national liberation movements in the empire as part of a global conspiracy. This only increased the gulf dividing French workers with legitimate grievances and a government charged with French security and order.

Across the Atlantic, intelligence bolstered hardening American policy. Intelligence expert Paul Pillar has rightly noted that it is unlikely that specific pieces of intelligence or individual reports drive policy.[32]

However, this study of intelligence on revolutionary activity in France demonstrates that streams of intelligence can have a cumulative effect, and that it is, in fact, a major source of the images that over time drive American decision-makers in their consideration of US policy options. While there were certainly other important aspects of Franco-American relations in these critical post-Liberation years, the communist threat preoccupied US officials in ways that other issues did not, and it made intelligence on this perceived threat more significant. Rather than moderating the views of American officials on the ground or keeping policy arguments in Washington, DC, honest, alarmist reports were meant to shock; they heightened fear and encouraged action. Moreover, the sheer volume of these reports over time normalized an extreme view of the situation in France. Most of the intelligence that underpinned the prevailing narrative was, at best, oversimplified and devoid of context and nuance, and it led to policy that similarly lacked sophistication. This view persisted despite the discredit of these sources, and the United States continued to intervene in French affairs for decades to come. Intelligence directly influenced American decisions (and their timing) to offer France vital loans, to engage in anti-communist propaganda and cultural programs in France, to consider adjustments in military posture, to contest the communist hold over labor. And when French officials laid down the imperial mantle, American anti-communists picked it up again in Vietnam.

French officials themselves privately noted that rumors of communist conspiracies deformed American images of France, fostering the belief that there existed in France a state of open warfare between communist and anti-communist forces, and relatedly, that France could not be counted as a trusted ally.[33] They also understood that reports of revolutionary activity contributed to the American belief that the PCF and Soviets had determined that the time had come to begin action in France.[34] The prevailing narrative of French weakness and revolution thus also encouraged decisive action by the French government to demonstrate its legitimacy and outmaneuver political rivals in order to convince American officials that they could manage the communist threat, with some assistance. Secretly, they carefully managed American perceptions through their exchanges with US intelligence experts and diplomats. Publicly, this took the form of anti-communist rhetoric and measures by French authorities, including most famously, the expulsion of the PCF from the ruling coalition in 1947. This basic formula also continued to provide a convenient way for French factions to delegitimize their rivals. Charles de Gaulle, accused in 1944 of harboring communist sympathies only to reemerge at the head of an anti-communist movement in 1947, found himself again the target of political rivals in 1948 and 1949 who claimed he would be soft on communism if he returned to power. This narrative was also one factor in the French determination to demonstrate strength in the colonies through brutal repression of national liberation movements. Ultimately, it also fed the paranoia of PCF leaders and their revolutionary turn. On February 25, 1949, just three months after communist officials had again supported another wave of strikes in France, Maurice Thorez famously affirmed that the French people would never wage war against the Soviet Union, even if the Soviets invaded French soil.[35] In the years to come, the PCF – no longer a party of the government – became a party of obstruction, suspicion, and bitterness.

US analysis on France reveals the complex relationship between intelligence and the formulation of American foreign policy in the early Cold War. In 1944 and 1945, OSS, military, and embassy analysts together provided comprehensive coverage of developments in France and contrasting narratives about the French situation. There was no formalized use of red-teaming or competitive analysis at this time; however, contrary views espoused by the OSS on one hand, and military and embassy analysts on the other, at least offered US officials alternative viewpoints from which to consider policy options. By the end of 1945, however, the disbandment of the OSS and the marginalization of its successor organizations in the State Department meant that the reified view of French weakness and revolution prevailed without any real challenge to the flawed assumptions upon which it was based. As CIA expert and OSS R&A veteran Sherman Kent noted a few years later, the Nazis had called this *Kampfende Wissenschaft*, or knowledge to further the aims of state policy.[36]

While some of these difficulties could have been assuaged with better tradecraft – most notably competitive analysis, better coordination, and a more scientific approach to intelligence assessments – methods more widely practiced by intelligence officers in years to come – responsibility cannot rest solely with the early Cold War intelligence community. President Truman preferred current intelligence to in-depth studies of a particular situation. Thus, he relied heavily upon the CIG/CIA Daily Summary instead of more comprehensive analyses, which would have provided a more profound and complex understanding of the French situation. At the same time, Truman did not want independent judgments on the intelligence provided to him. As late as 1950, Director of Central

Intelligence Roscoe Hillenkoetter remarked that his job as he understood it was "to collect and disseminate, not evaluate."[37] Furthermore, Truman's closest adviser on military and intelligence matters, Admiral William Leahy, asked OIR to stop sending him its reports, most likely because he had what he needed to make his case from other intelligence agencies, and he was not interested in other theories. Truman, not one for nuance, was pleased with this situation, as were anti-communists in State Department and military circles. The administration's preferences effectively bounded CIA analysis, hindering full examination of critically important issues.

This book's focus is necessarily confined to the role of US intelligence in the formulation of American policy for France in the early Cold War, but it demonstrates, through careful examination of intelligence alongside the diplomatic record, and by privileging American *and* French views, methods that scholars of US intelligence and foreign relations can apply to other historical episodes and important relationships, and to more broad analyses of the nexus between intelligence and policy. American leaders rely on intelligence to assist them in making important policy decisions, and it must be taken into account to understand American relationships with the world. Whether intelligence drives policy (or the reverse) is a point worth arguing, but singular focus on this question runs the risk of obscuring the full spectrum of intelligence available to policymakers. It is equally, if not more, important to identify and understand specific ways intelligence impacts the policy-making environment through systematic examination of the intelligence–policy nexus across time. The intelligence bureaucracy has evolved since its formative postwar years with important advances in analytic tradecraft and awareness of the dangers of politicization, but subsequent episodes demonstrate that the dynamics that govern those essential human interactions at the intelligence profession's core persist, as does a "chronic lack of long-term perspective" that would allow intelligence officials today to appreciate the insights that these formative episodes have for current policy.[38]

The French episode demonstrates that intelligence that bolsters administration policy is no less important than the rare occasion when intelligence drives policy in another direction. It is also important to consider those instances when intelligence contradicted the president's policy preferences, even if decision-makers ultimately dismissed it. This case also underscores a perennial intelligence challenge, that is, determining the intentions of people and movements, especially those tied to figures who might not behave rationally according to norms. At the same time, as this account shows, scholars and practitioners must also consider the role of state and private, transnational and transimperial sources, and more informal methods of pressure and influence rather than remaining confined to traditional, official exchanges between governments; otherwise, they risk missing key aspects of important relationships.

Much of the current body of literature on intelligence analysis focuses on strategic surprise. There have been numerous accounts of intelligence failures to predict signal events – the Tet Offensive in Vietnam, the Yom Kippur War, the collapse of the Soviet Union, 9/11. But there has been too little emphasis on those cases in which analysis pointed to something that failed to happen because – like the crisis in France – they are difficult to untangle. But one of the key legacies of American intelligence on France in those years, beyond the myriad persistent implications for Franco-American relations, was that US officials did not see the episode clearly at the time and they drew erroneous conclusions about the efficacy of the intelligence and its impact on US policy. In the French case, US officials ultimately viewed the lack of a communist coup as proof that their programs and intervention had worked; except for a few CIA and OIR analysts, no one suggested that the intelligence had been overblown or wrong, that perhaps there was no coup because French communists never intended to launch one.

In the immediate aftermath of the French crisis of 1947, US officials drew lessons from their experiences in France and Italy, namely, the means they had developed to intervene in the internal affairs of other regimes through aid to impoverished populations, military assistance and targeted funding for friendly factions, and campaigns to influence the voting public against a communist choice. The very next year, in 1948, even as some CIA analysts privately began to question much of the intelligence on the communist threat in Europe, the CIA launched its first covert operation to influence Italian elections. The Christian Democrats – America's choice – prevailed. Yet, as Kaeten Mistry has shown, US officials in Italy, as in France, failed to appreciate the role of local actors in shaping American involvement, and ultimately, the efficacy of the intervention. In the coming decades, the belief in a worldwide communist conspiracy and US engagement with webs of anti-communist sources contributed to continued American interventions in European affairs and across the Global South.

The Cold War is over, but the French case continues to provide key insights into the intelligence crises of the twenty-first century. In 1940s France, there had been little proof of much of the clandestine revolutionary activity attributed to French communists, much less evidence of a communist coup, but there was convincing intelligence on Soviet intrigue in Europe, which led US officials to exaggerate the evidence on PCF machinations. There was also very little intelligence on Saddam Hussein's weapons of mass destruction (WMD) program in Iraq in 2002 and 2003, but there was plenty of evidence on the nuclear programs of other rogue actors, which suggested that Saddam likely possessed a similar program.[39] In both cases, US officials pointed to their sources and alleged eyewitness accounts to bolster the narrative; and in both cases, much of intelligence those sources provided either could not be confirmed or were eventually proven to be outright fabrications. Would the United States still have endeavored to prop-up anti-communist regimes in France without alarmist intelligence? Probably, but perhaps not to the extent or degree, or with the rapidity, that it did. Likewise, the United States may have intervened in Iraq without the evidence provided by CURVEBALL and self-interested political exiles, but it would have been much more difficult to make the case for intervention to the American people and to US allies. In both cases, ignorance over the role a web of transnational sources played in shaping US responses to the crises obscured an important influence upon US policy.

The Iraq case underscores continued challenges for intelligence analysis that were evident in France and its empire. US analysts understood much about Saddam Hussein's capabilities but little about his intentions due to the opacity of the regime but also due to amnesia regarding the broader historical and geopolitical dynamics that might explain his behavior. Critics of the analysis on Iraq point to the problem of "groupthink" in leading intelligence analysts "to interpret ambiguous evidence as conclusively indicative of a WMD program and to ignore or minimize evidence" to the contrary.[40] Similar dynamics shaped American analysis of the French situation after the disbandment of the OSS six decades before. As *Contesting France* demonstrates, OSS analysts did not suffer from historical amnesia and better understood the broader contours of French politics and society than their counterparts in the State Department and military. Their marginalization meant that there was no challenge to entrenched views that seeded groupthink. Likewise, as the WMD Commission pointed out, US officials in 2003 failed to use caution when seeking "agent intelligence" on WMD,[41] much like some of their predecessors in the State Department, Paris embassy, and military intelligence in the early Cold War, then in contact with sources across France and its empire. The details and lessons of the French case are worth revisiting, in part, because they remain relevant today.

Notes

Acknowledgments

1 A reference to Dean Acheson's biography, *Present at the Creation: My Years in the State Department* (New York: W. W. Norton, 1969).

Introduction

1 Harold Callender, "The Great Challenge That Confronts France: Can This Divided Country Unite Its Resources to Resist a Foreign Tyranny That Threatens It?" December 7, 1947. *New York Times (hereafter NYT)*, p. 47. The reference to "two Western countries" is to France and Italy, which were also experiencing strikes.

2 Announced in June 1947, the Marshall Plan would not go into effect until the following spring.

3 "Douglas to Secretary of State," December 2, 1947. *Foreign Relations of the United States (hereafter FRUS) 1947 Volume III* (Washington, DC: GPO, 1972), 807–808.

4 Joseph and Stewart Alsop, "If Russia Grabs Europe," *Saturday Evening Post* 220, no. 25 (December 20, 1947), 15.

5 Ibid., 15.

6 Ibid., 15.

7 Mary Nolan, *The Transatlantic Century: Europe and the United States, 1890–2010* (Cambridge: Cambridge University Press, 2012), 166–167, 170.

8 Tony Judt, *Postwar: A History of Europe since 1945* (New York: Penguin Books, 2006), 35.

9 Ibid., 35.

10 Ibid., 35–40, 79, 86.

11 Barbara Rosenwein, "'AHR' Conversation," 1494.

12 See Richard Immerman, "Intelligence and Strategy: Historicizing Psychology, Policy, and Politics," *Diplomatic History* 32, no. 1 (2008): 5. www.jstor.org .proxyau.wrlc.org/stable/24916053.

13 Veronika Heyde's study of reciprocal influence between noncommunist resistance elements in Europe and American groups, including the OSS, on the idea of European unification demonstrates one effective way to examine interaction between various factions on a specific issue. *De l'Esprit de la Résistance Jusqu'à l'Idée de l'Europe* (P.I.E. Peter Lang, 2010).

14 Charles Luguet, "Notes établies au poste de Washington & au passage à Londres par le général Luguet," January 10, 1944. Dossier 1, Politiques Internationales, Archives du Général de Gaulle (hereafter ADG), Archives Nationales (Pierrefitte-France) (hereafter AN).

15 IRIS (1945) was subsequently renamed the Office of Research and Intelligence (1946), the Office of Intelligence Coordination and Liaison (1946–1947), and the Office of Intelligence Research (OIR) (1947–1957). Presently, State Department Intelligence falls under the Bureau of Intelligence and Research (INR).

16 Here used to mean "nationalists."

17 Luguet, "Notes établies..."

18 See Irwin Wall, *The United States and the Making of Postwar France, 1945–1954* (Cambridge: Cambridge University Press, 1991), 5; Martin Zahniser, *Uncertain Friendship: American-French Diplomatic Relations Through the Cold War* (New York: John Wiley & Sons, 1975), 241–242 and 264; John Young, *France, the Cold War, and the Western Alliance, 1944–1949: French Foreign Policy and Postwar Europe* (New York: St. Martin's Press, 1990), 224–228; Frank Costigliola, *France and the United States: The Cold Alliance since World War II* (New York: Twayne Publishers, 1992), 50–51, 58 and 78. For contrasting views, which underscored American dominance and, consequently, French weakness and dependence, and viewed France as an American "colony," see Alfred Grosser, *La IVe République et sa politique extérieure* (Paris: Librairie Armand Colin, 1972), 221 and 399–405. See also Annie Lacroix-Riz, *La Choix de Marianne: les relations franco-américaines de la libération aux débuts du Plan Marshall, 1944–1948* (Paris: Messidor, 1986), 11, 122, 214–216.

19 A reference to Geir Lundestad, "Empire by Invitation? The United States and Western Europe, 1945–1952," *Journal of Peace Research* 23, no. 3 (1986): 263. See also Lundestad, *The United States and Western Europe since 1945* (Oxford: Oxford University Press, 2003), 1–18.

20 William Hitchcock, *France Restored: Cold War Diplomacy and the Quest for Leadership in Europe, 1944–1954* (Chapel Hill: The University of North Carolina Press, 1998), 9. See also Michael Creswell, *A Question of Balance: How France and the United States Created Cold War Europe* (Cambridge, MA: Harvard University Press, 2006).

21 Alessandro Brogi, *A Question of Self-Esteem: The United States and the Cold War Choices in France and Italy 1944–1958* (Westport, CT: Greenwood Press, 2001). Brogi argues that, in their foreign relations, French officials pursued prestige as a matter of both appearance and substance. If France appeared to be (and was treated as) a world power, then it could use this

prestige to produce actual power in the future. Brogi argues that recent accounts that stress European initiative and their ability to "instruct the Americans and contest their leadership" have gone too far. While he recognizes French influence over Western affairs, he also points to its limits and the "profound constraints in which they conducted their diplomatic actions" (pp. 2 and 9). Ultimately, prestige politics failed to produce as much power as French officials had hoped and did not significantly alter the postwar "power hierarchy" of the West (pp. 262 and 265).

22 For an examination of the everyday diplomacy of intelligence liaison, see Jason Dittmer, "Everyday Diplomacy: UKUSA Intelligence Cooperation and Geopolitical Assemblages," *Annals of the Association of American Geographers* 105, no. 3 (2015): 604–619. https://doi.org/10.1080/00045608 .2015.1015098.

23 Jeffrey James Byrne, *Mecca of Revolution: Algeria, Decolonization, and the Third World Order* (Oxford: Oxford University Press, 2016), 8.

24 Philippe Buton, *Les lendemains qui déchantent: le Parti Communiste Français à la libération* (Paris: Presses de la Fondation Nationale des Sciences Politiques, 1993), 11–12. See also Stéphane Courtois and Marc Lazar, *Histoire du Parti Communiste Français* (Paris: Presses Universitaires de France, 2000).

25 Costigliola, *France and the United States*, 4–5.

26 See, for example, Kaeten Mistry, *The United States, Italy, and the Origins of the Cold War: Waging Political Warfare, 1945–1950* (Cambridge: Cambridge University Press, 2014).

27 Michael Werner and Benedicte Zimmerman, "Beyond Comparison: Histoire Croisée and the Challenge of Reflexivity," *History and Theory* 45, no. 1 (February 2006): 43, 49.

28 See Frank Costigliola, "Reading for Emotion," in *Explaining the History of American Foreign Relations* (Cambridge: Cambridge University Press, 2016), 363; Julie Livingston, "'AHR' Conversation: The Historical Study of Emotions," *The American Historical Review* 117, no. 5 (December 2012): 1490.

29 See Peter Stearns, "Emotions History in the United States: Goals, Methods, and Promise," in *Emotions in American History*, ed. Jessica Gienow-Hecht (Brooklyn: Berghan Books, 2010), 25; Costigliola, "After Roosevelt's Death: Dangerous Emotions, Divisive Discourses, and the Abandoned Alliance," *Diplomatic History* 34, no. 1 (January 2010): 7; Costigliola, "Unceasing Pressure for Penetration: Gender, Pathology, and Emotion in George Kennan's Formation of the Cold War," *Journal of American History* 83, no. 4 (March 1997): 1337.

30 Costigliola, "Reading for Emotion," 359. Ilaria Scaglia, in her study of emotions in interwar internationalism, points out that "many individuals and institutions used [emotions] strategically to attain particular goals and shaped their behavior accordingly." Scaglia, *The Emotions of Internationalism, Feeling International Cooperation in the Alps in the Interwar Period* (Oxford: Oxford University Press, 2020), 11.

31 A reference to Odd Arne Westad's pivotal study *The Global Cold War*, in which he urged scholars to view the Cold War not as a European but a global phenomenon in which similar processes played out across the developed and developing worlds (Cambridge: Cambridge University Press, 2007), 3.

32 Kristin Hoganson and Jay Sexton, "Introduction," in *Crossing Empires: Taking U.S. History into Transimperial Terrain*, eds. Kristin Hoganson and Jay Sexton (Durham: Duke University Press, 2020), 1–5.

33 Christoph Kamissek and Jonas Kreienbaum, "An Imperial Cloud? Conceptualising Interimperial Connections and Transimperial Knowledge," *Journal of Modern European History* 14, no. 2 (2016): 165–166.; Mark Atwood Lawrence, *Assuming the Burden: Europe and the American Commitment to War in Vietnam* (Berkeley: University of California Press, 2007), 6–7, 13. See also Kathryn Statler's pathbreaking work, *Replacing France: The Origins of American Intervention in Vietnam* (Lexington: the University Press of Kentucky, 2007), 278.

Chapter 1

1 Charles Glass, *Americans in Paris: Life and Death under Nazi Occupation* (New York: Penguin, 2010), 353.

2 As quoted in ibid., 351, and in "Paris Ghost City, Repatriate Says," *NYT*, March 17, 1944, 4.

3 Glass, 387.

4 François Darlan, commander of Vichy's armed forces, had hinted his willingness to cooperate with the United States in North Africa in the event of a landing. The invasion underway, Darlan ordered resisting Vichy forces to cease fire, after which he was recognized as the local civilian authority in North Africa. He was assassinated the next month, in December 1942.

5 William Koren, "Franco-American Relations in Paris," October 30, 1944. Box 1162, Intelligence Reports 1941–1945, RG 226, National Archives and Records Administration II (hereafter NARA).

6 Ibid.

7 Ibid.

8 Jay Allen, as quoted in Martin Weil, *A Pretty Good Club: The Founding Fathers of the U.S. Foreign Service* (New York: W. W. Norton, 1978), 121.

9 Barry M. Katz, *Foreign Intelligence: Research and Analysis in the Office of Strategic Services, 1942–1945* (Cambridge, MA: Harvard University Press, 1989), 2.

10 Weil, 47.

11 Mowrer, as quoted in ibid., 127.

12 ibid., 119.

13 Annie Lacroix-Riz, *De Munich à Vichy: L'assassinat de la Troisième République 1938–1940* (Paris: Armand Colin, 2008). De Gorostarzu may have also been the father of another de Gorostarzu implicated in the right-wing Organisation Armée Secrète (OAS) putsch in 1961.

14 "Lisbon Telegram," January 6, 1944. Box 5141, 851.00, RG 59, NARA.

15 "Reasons Underlying This Government's Lack of Confidence in General de Gaulle," January 20, 1944. Box 5141, 851.00, RG 59, NARA. H. Freeman Matthews, "Note," February 29, 1944. Box 17, Chairman's File – Leahy, RG 218, NARA. Matthews, "Memo of Conversation," March 6, 1944. Box 5151, 851.01, RG 59, NARA.

16 "Reasons Underlying This Government's Lack of Confidence in General de Gaulle," January 20, 1944. Box 5141, 851.00, RG 59, NARA.

17 Jean Lacouture, *De Gaulle: The Rebel 1890–1944*, trans. Patrick O'Brien (New York: W. W. Norton, 1990), 346.

18 "Glassford to Secretary of State," February 4, 1944. Folder 3, Box 5150, 851.01, RG 59, NARA.

19 Ibid.

20 Stephen Ambrose, *Ike's Spies: Eisenhower and the Espionage Establishment* (New York: Random House, 1981), 20.

21 Richard Harris Smith, *OSS: The Secret History of America's First Central Intelligence Agency* (Guilford, CT: Lyons Press, 2005), 37 and Lacouture, 418.

22 "Matthews to Leahy," February 29, 1944. Prime-President 1943, Box 17, Chairman's File – Leahy, RG 218, NARA.

23 "W. Walton Butterworth to W. Perry George," August 26, 1944. Box 5153, 851.01, RG 59, NARA.

24 "Matthews Memo of Conversation with Laurent," March 6, 1944. Folder 1, Box 5151, 851.01, RG 59, NARA.

25 "Diary," spring/summer 1945. Chapter XIII, Box 25, Charles Bohlen Papers, LOC.

26 "Dossier Mornay," January 25, 1944. Box 166, February 1943–April 1945, Naval Aide's Files A-16 France and Free French, Map Room Papers, Franklin D. Roosevelt Presidential Library (hereafter FDRL).

27 Weil, 123.

28 "Dossier Mornay," January 25, 1944 and Robertson, 112.

29 Keith Jeffrey, *The Secret History of MI-6, 1909–1949* (New York: Penguin, 2010), 398.

30 Wilhelm F. Flicke, *War Secrets in the Ether: Part III*, trans. Ray W. Pettengill (Washington, DC: NSA, 1953), www.nsa.gov/public_info/_files/friedmanDocuments/Publications/FOLDER_265/41760949080010.pdf, 247–248.

31 "France" and "The Growth of Revolutionary Feelings in France," forwarded January 27, 1944. Folder 3, Box 5150, 851.01, RG 59, NARA. See also "The Internal Situation in France," forwarded February 3, 1944. Folder 4, Box 5141, 851.00, RG 59, NARA.

32 Coversheet, "The Internal Situation in France," February 3, 1944.

33 "Underground, Communists, and Invasion Aid," March 13, 1944. Box 772, Intelligence Reports, RG 226, NARA.

34 Jean-Pierre Laurent, "Paul Vignaux, inspirateur de la 'Deuxième gauche': récits d'un exil français aux États-Unis pendant la Seconde guerre mondiale," *Matériaux pour l'histoire de notre temps: Les États-Unis et les refugies politiques européens: des années 1930 aux années 1950*, no. 60 (2000): 48–56.

35 Valentine Weiss and Thierry Guilpin, "Fonds Geneviève Tabouis 17 AR 1-269, Répertoire numérique détaillé" (Paris: Archives Nationales, 2010), 4 and 10. Also, Robert Murphy, *Diplomat among Warriors* (New York: Doubleday, 1964), 26.

36 "De Gaulle's Politics and the French Underground," May 23, 1944. Box 900, Intelligence Reports, RG 226, NARA.

37 "Internal Conditions in France," April 14, 1944. Box 875, Intelligence Reports, RG 226, NARA.

38 "Marshall Memo to the President," April 15, 1944. Box 20, JCS Chairman's File – Leahy, RG 218, NARA.

39 "Mott Report," April 11, 1944. Box 20, JCS Chairman's File – Leahy, RG 218, NARA.

40 Ibid.

41 "Marshall Memo for the President," April 18, 1944. Box 166, February 1943– April 1945, France and Free French, Naval Aide's Files, Map Room Files, FDRL.

42 Ibid.

43 Harris Smith, 37–38 and 44–45.

44 "Current Political Situation in France," April 20, 1944. Box 837, Intelligence Reports, RG 226, NARA.

45 "Secretary of State to the Ambassador in the Soviet Union," April 8, 1944. *Foreign Relations of the United States: 1944, Volume 3* (Washington, DC: GPO, 1965), 675–677.

46 Wall, 30.

47 "Memorandum," September 1944. Folder 6, Box 5141, 851.00, RG 59, NARA.

48 "France: Political Groups and Revolutionary Movements," September 21, 1944. Box 1110, Intelligence Reports, RG 226, NARA.

49 "Hoppenot à MAE," October 16, 1944. Dossier 119, P4712, Politique Extérieure, Amérique, Centre des Archives diplomatiques du ministère des Affaires étrangères (La Courneuve – France) (hereafter MAE).

50 Ibid.

51 "Caffery to Secretary of State," October 20, 1944. *FRUS: 1944, Volume 3* (Washington, DC: GPO, 1965), 742–743.

52 "Communist-Sponsored Manifestation in Honor of French Martyrs," October 12, 1944. Box 5142, 851.00, RG 59, NARA.

53 Wall, 96 and Ted Morgan, *Reds: McCarthyism in Twentieth Century America* (New York: Random House, 2003), 378.

54 "Murphy to Bonbright," November 11, 1944. Folder 3, Box 5142, 851.00, RG 59, NARA.

55 Ibid.

56 For a discussion of politicized analysis see Robert Kennedy, *Of Knowledge and Power: The Complexities of National Intelligence* (Westport, CT: Praeger Security International, 2008), 105–107.

57 Walter Lippmann, "Today and Tomorrow: Report from France," *The Washington Post (hereafter WP)*, December 2, 1944.

58 Ibid.

59 Katz, 13.

60 Ibid.

61 Ibid., 14.

62 Ibid.

63 Hughes, as quoted in Ibid., 182.

64 Ibid.

65 Ibid.

66 "Morale," January 11, 1944. Box 640, Intelligence Reports, RG 226, NARA.

67 Ibid.
68 "Political Resume," February 5, 1944. Box 685, Intelligence Reports, RG 226, NARA.
69 Ibid.
70 "The Current Line of the Communist Party in Algiers," February 24, 1944. Box 731, Intelligence Reports, RG 226, NARA.
71 Ibid.
72 "Summary of Views on Communists in Resistance Movement," March 3, 1944. Box 735, Intelligence Reports, RG 226, NARA.
73 Ibid.
74 "Comments made early in December by a French Officer who has just returned from France regarding the Resistance movements there," sent by Chapin to Secretary of State, March 8, 1944. Folder 2, Box 5151, 851.01, RG 59, NARA.
75 Ibid.
76 "Report from Argus to Regis on Conversations with French Resistance Leader," forwarded to Roosevelt on April 3, 1944. Roll 23, M1642, Records of OSS Washington Director's Office, RG 226, NARA.
77 Ibid.
78 "Unification of the Resistance," April 7, 1944. OSS Weekly Airgram No. 22. Box 801, Intelligence Reports, RG 226, NARA.
79 Ibid.
80 Ibid.
81 "France: Increased Persecution of the Maquis," May 1, 1944. Roll 31, M1642, Records of OSS Washington Director's Office, RG 226, NARA.
82 "Current Franco-American Tension," June 1, 1944. Box 896, Intelligence Reports, RG 226, NARA.
83 Lt Col Roger Griswold, "Violence to be Expected in France by Certain Circles," n.d. Roll 38, A3556, Donovan Select Files, RG 226, NARA.
84 Ibid.
85 Ibid.
86 Ibid.
87 Ibid.
88 "The Communists and the Invasion," June 29, 1944. Box 941, Intelligence Reports, RG 226, NARA.
89 Ibid.
90 "Ramon Guthrie, Poet, Dies at 77." *NYT*, November 23, 1973: 38. *ProQuest Historical Newspapers*. www.proquest.com/.
91 "Report on Impressions of the French Situation," June 29, 1944. Roll 50, M1642, OSS Director's Files, RG 226, NARA.
92 Ibid.
93 Although the Bourbon flag was white, Guthrie here is likely using black and red as a general reference to reaction and revolution, respectively.
94 Ibid.
95 Ibid.
96 Ibid.
97 Ibid.
98 Koren, "Franco-American Relations in Paris."

99 Ibid.

100 Ibid.

101 "Official Dispatch, Bern to Director OSS," October 23, 1944. Folder 1, Box 5142, 851.00, RG 59, NARA.

102 Ibid.

103 "Comment on Memorandum of Colonel Fabry," forwarded to Roosevelt on October 31, 1944. Roll 30, A3556, Donovan Select Files, RG 226, NARA.

104 Ibid.

105 Ibid.

106 Ibid.

107 Ibid.

108 For a discussion of "cognitive bias," see Kennedy, 88–90.

109 For discussion of policy-neutral analysis, see James B. Bruce and Roger Z. George, "Introduction: Intelligence Analysis – The Emergence of a Discipline," in *Analyzing Intelligence: Origins, Obstacles, and Innovations*, eds. Roger Z. George and James B. Bruce (Washington, DC: Georgetown University Press, 2008), 8–9. Bruce and George argue that Donovan conceived of the OSS as a war-fighting organization, and thus never thought of his research and analysis branch as being "policy neutral" (p. 21).

110 "Le Communisme en France," January 1944. 3AG1/275, PCF, France Libérée, ADG, AN.

111 P. Collomb, "Lettre à Monsieur le Marchal, Secrétaire Général du Protectorat," April 3, 1944. Dossier 1 Maroc, Questions Coloniales 3AG1/284, ADG, AN.

112 Gabriel Puaux, "Action Communiste en milieu Musulman," May 2, 1944. Dossier 1 Maroc, Questions Coloniales 3AG1/284, ADG, AN.

113 Ibid.

114 Léon Muscatelli, "Le Préfet d'Alger à Monsieur le Gouverneur General de l'Algérie," January 26, 1944. Dossier 3 PCA, Algérie, Questions Coloniales, ADG, AN.

115 Ibid.

116 "Similitude entre le programme Neo-Destour et celui du Parti Communiste de Tunisie," February 5, 1944. Dossier 2 Tunisie, Questions Coloniales AG/3(1)/284, ADG, AN.

117 "Action et propagande communiste en milieux indigènes," April 6, 1944. Dossier 1, Questions Coloniales, 3AG1/284, ADG, AN.

118 "Communisme," May 20, 1944. Dossier 1, Questions Coloniales, 3AG1/284, ADG, AN.

119 "Parti communiste tunisien," July 24, 1944. Dossier 2, Questions Coloniales 3AG1/284, ADG, AN.

120 "Attitude du Parti Communiste," November 13, 1944. P4027, Tunisie, Direction Afrique-Levant, MAE.

121 "Situation politique générale en Algérie," November 23, 1944. Dossier 2, Algérie, 3AG4/18, Gouvernement Provisoire de la République Française (hereafter GPRF), AN.

122 "Groupements révolutionnaires Annamites," July 24, 1944. Dossier 1 Indochine, Questions Coloniales 3AG1/281, ADG, AN.

123 Ibid.

124 Ibid.
125 "Message intercepté des communistes français d'Indochine au parti communiste français," December 6, 1944. Dossier 5 Indochine, Colonies, GPRF, AN.
126 "Monsieur Doucet, représentant du PCF auprès du CNR à Monsieur Rabaud, délégué du CFLN," February 22, 1944. PCF, France Libérée 3AG1/275, ADG, AN.
127 "La Délégation du Comité Central du PCF en Afrique du Nord à Monsieur le General de Gaulle," February 26, 1944. PCF, France Libérée 3AG1/258, ADG, AN.
128 "Le Comité Central du PCF à Messieurs les membres du CFLN," March 1944. PCF, France Libérée, 3AG1/275, ADG, AN.
129 "La Délégation du Comité Central du PCF," February 26, 1944.
130 Ibid.
131 One only has to read Jean Laloy's account of de Gaulle's meetings with Stalin in 1944 to get a sense of the tension that divided the two leaders. Laloy compared Stalin and de Gaulle's handshake goodbye to two boxers at the end of a match. Dossier 1, URSS 3AG4/16, GPRF, AN.
132 "Note," February 15, 1944. Dossier 1, 3AG1/262 Politique Internationale, ADG, AN.
133 "Massigli to MAE," October 6, 1944. Dossier 51, P16879, Europe/URSS, MAE. "Activité russes en France," November 27, 1944. Dossier 73, Europe/URSS, MAE.
134 "Note," February 15, 1944.
135 Ibid. For more on de Gaulle's conception of Franco-Soviet policy in this period, see Georges-Henri Soutou, "General de Gaulle and the Soviet Union," in *The Soviet Union and Europe in the Cold War, 1943–1953*, eds. Francesca Gori and Silvio Pons (London: Macmillan Press, 1996). Soutou argues that de Gaulle was more aware of a Soviet threat than has been claimed. Even while de Gaulle sought a pact to control Germany, he also sought to balance Soviet power with a Western bloc. He was also well aware of the ideological dimensions of a global conflict and the problem of the PCF in Franco-Soviet relations.
136 Jean Laloy, "Compte Rendu," December 2–10, 1944. Dossier 1, URSS, GPRF, AN.
137 "Note pour M. le Commandant Pelabon," July 11, 1944. PCF, France Libérée 3AG1/275, ADG, AN.
138 Luguet, "Notes."
139 Ibid.
140 Hoover, "French Committee of National Liberation," August 31, 1944. Box 5153, 851.01, RG 59, NARA.
141 As Brogi argues in *A Question of Self Esteem.*
142 "M. Hoppenot à M. Bidault," December 20, 1944. *Documents Diplomatiques Français 1944*, No. 243 (Paris: Imprimerie Nationale, 1996), 468.
143 Ibid.
144 Koren, "Franco-American Relations in Paris."
145 Ambrose, 106–107.
146 Ibid.

Chapter 2

1 Russell W. Davenport, "France: Beachhead of Liberty," *Fortune*, October 1945, 204. Noted in French files on October 19, 1945. P4696, Presse, Direction d'Amérique, MAE.

2 Robert J. Donovan, *Conflict and Crisis: The Presidency of Harry S. Truman 1945–1948* (Columbia: University of Missouri Press, 1977), ix–xiv.

3 "Diary Entry," April 12, 1945. Diary 1945, Boxes 6–8, *Leahy Papers*, Library of Congress (hereafter LOC).

4 David McCullough, *Truman* (New York: Simon & Schuster, 1992), 486. Arnold Offner argued that Truman's distrust of the Soviets ran deep but acknowledged that, in 1945, Truman felt like he could "deal" with Stalin and initially sought accommodation with the Soviets, or at least to avoid antagonizing them. However, Truman's view of the Soviets began to harden in late 1945 and early 1946. Offner, *Another Such Victory: President Truman and the Cold War, 1945–1953* (Stanford: Stanford University Press, 2002), 24, 30, 48–49, and 54. Similarly, Melvyn Leffler argues that US officials in 1945 hoped to perpetuate wartime cooperation with the Soviets but felt that they had to closely monitor Soviet behavior. Truman did subscribe to the belief among administration hard-liners that the United States should display toughness, but he also sought to avoid a rift immediately after the war in Europe ended and to cultivate "a cooperative relationship based on Soviet restraint and consistent with U.S. interests." Leffler, *A Preponderance of Power: National Security, the Truman Administration, and the Cold War* (Stanford: Stanford University Press, 1992), 32–24.

5 Weil, 210–217.

6 Ibid., 220.

7 Ibid.

8 Ibid., 254. See also, Henry H. Adams, *Witness to Power: The Life of Fleet Admiral William D. Leahy* (Annapolis: Naval Institute Press, 1985). According to George Elsey, the assistant naval aide, "Truman came to office with zero background in these matters and zero information. And hence anyone who was able to provide him some solid information on what had been going on was obviously going to be very, very influential." Adams further noted that Leahy's interaction with Truman was constant and regular; he met with Truman at 9:45 each morning and often accompanied him to the Map Room (p. 283). Leahy also wrote in his memoirs that he personally selected important military and diplomatic dispatches for Truman to read each morning. William D. Leahy, *I Was There: The Personal Story of the Chief of Staff to Presidents Roosevelt and Truman Based on His Notes and Diary at the Time* (New York: McGraw-Hill, 1950), 2, 348. French officials, also noted Leahy's influence with the President. State Department records further document Leahy's participation in diplomatic meetings with French representatives, while intelligence files at the Truman Library show how Leahy marked dispatches for discussion with the president.

9 Childs, as quoted in Weil, 255.

10 "Diary," spring/summer 1945. Chapter XIII, Box 25, *Charles Bohlen Papers*, LOC.

11 See Alessandro Brogi, *Confronting America: The Cold War between the United States and the Communists in France and Italy* (Chapel Hill: UNC Press, 2011), 64.

12 Folder 1, Box 70, Collection 45, "Biographical Material," *Caffery Papers*, University of Louisiana-Lafayette (hereafter ULL).

13 *Newsweek*, "Envoy to Paris," October 2, 1944. Folder 1, Box 52, Collection 45, Paris 1944–1949, *Jefferson Caffery Papers*, ULL.

14 Jefferson Caffery to the Secretary of State, January 3, 1945. Folder 1, Box 3318, 711.00, RG 59, NARA.

15 Christopher Andrew, *For the President's Eyes Only: Secret Intelligence and the American Presidency from Washington to Bush* (New York: Harper, 1995), 145.

16 "Admiral Leahy to the Honorable Clarence Cannon," May 27, 1945. CIA Records Search Tool (hereafter CREST), NARA.

17 "OSS Paris to OSS Washington," August 23, 1945. Roll 3, M1642, OSS Washington Director's Office Admin Files, RG 226, NARA.

18 "Personnel," n.d. Folder 6, Box 7, MSS 90, Series 10 Books, *James Byrnes Papers*, Clemson University (hereafter CU).

19 "Municipal Elections in France," May 19, 1945. File 129963, Box 1497, E16, Intelligence Reports, RG 226, NARA.

20 David le Bailly, *Le Captive de Mitterrand* (Paris: Stock, 2014), Section 5.

21 "Political Observations Concerning France," June 20, 1945. File 135341, Box 1561, E16, Intelligence Reports, RG 226, NARA.

22 Faure was expelled from the SFIO in 1944 for supporting the Vichy government, and went on to form the Parti Socialiste Démocratique (PSD). Despite its origins in the Socialist Party, its policies were those of "conventional conservative groups." De Monzie was a member of the Parti Républicain Socialiste, an obscure grouping under the post-Liberation Rassemblement des Gauches Républicains (RGR), which despite being ostensibly left wing, attracted supporters of Pétain. Lamoureux was a member of the Radical Party, also grouped under the RGR. Barety was a member of the Alliance des républicains de gauche et des radicaux indépendants (ARGRI), a group of the Alliance Démocratique ranging from center left to center right. Richard Vinen, *Bourgeois Politics in France, 1945–1951* (Cambridge: Cambridge University Press, 1995), 122–123, 178–179 and L'Assemblée Nationale: Base de données des députés français depuis 1789: www.assemblee-nationale.fr/sycomore/fiche.asp?num_dept=409. All served in Third Republic governments, and all had rallied to Vichy after 1940. Two, Lamoureux and Barety, served on Vichy's National Council. At least three of the men – Faure, Lamoureux, and Barety, were declared ineligible for public office after Liberation. Oliver Wieviorka, *Orphans of the Republic: The Nation's Legislators in Vichy* (Cambridge, MA: Harvard University Press, 2009), 359–360.

23 "Memorandum of Conversation with Certain Former French Parliamentarians," July 21, 1945. Box 6229, 851.00, RG 59, NARA.

24 "Telegram #2836," May 21, 1945. Box 6229, 851.00, RG 59, NARA.

25 While de Gaulle certainly recognized the necessity for major changes in the French system to avoid a return to the prewar status quo, his conception of "reform" was rooted in constitutional changes strengthening the presidency and rebuilding the French military; in other words, ensuring the collapse in 1940 never happened again. He was not as interested in economic reforms, rebuffing Finance Minister Pierre Mendes-France's plans for price controls and monetary reforms because he thought the nation could not risk "dangerous convulsions" and upset economic activity. Jonathan Fenby, *The General: Charles de Gaulle and the France He Saved* (London: Simon & Schuster, 2011), 271–272.

26 "Caffery to Secretary of State Telegram #3330," June 6, 1945. Folder 1, Box 6235, 851.00B, RG 59, NARA.

27 Ibid.

28 "Leahy Diary," June 8, 1945. Leahy Diaries 1945, Boxes 6–8, *Leahy Papers*, LOC.

29 "Caffery to Secretary of State Telegram #6154," October 20, 1945. Box 6230, 851.00, RG 59, NARA.

30 "Caffery to Secretary of State Telegram #6182," October 23, 1945. Box 6230, 851.00, RG 59, NARA.

31 "French General Elections of October 21, 1945," November 8, 1945. Box 6230, 851.00, RG 59, NARA.

32 "Political Sentiment in France," April 23, 1945. File 127566, Box 1460, E16, Intelligence Reports, RG 226, NARA.

33 "Political Observations Concerning France," June 20, 1945.

34 Raymond Murphy, "Memorandum," May 21, 1945. Box 6229, 851.00, RG 59, NARA.

35 Ibid.

36 Ibid.

37 Usually "close" meant informants who had become disaffected with and left the communist party or anti-communist sources claiming to have inside information. There is no evidence that the embassy had any "moles" inside the PCF.

38 "Caffery to Secretary of State Telegram #2893," May 23, 1945. Box 6229, 851.00, RG 59, NARA.

39 "Caffery to Secretary of State, Telegram #4216," July 13, 1945. Box 6229, 851.00, RG 59, NARA.

40 Ibid.

41 Interview with Fanny Chipman, July 22, 1987, The Association for Diplomatic Studies and Training, 67. https://adst.org/wp-content/uploads/2013/12/Chipman-Fanny-S.pdf

42 Ibid.

43 "Observations on the Nature and Status of the PCF," July 30, 1945. Folder 1, Box 6235, 851.00B, RG 59, NARA.

44 "Communist Cache of Arms found in Nimes, France," October 11, 1945. Box 6230, 851.00, RG 59, NARA.

45 "Caffery to Secretary of State, Telegram #6259," October 27, 1945. Box 6230, 851.00, RG 59, NARA.

46 "Caffery to Secretary of State, Telegram #6580," November 13, 1945. Box 6230, 851.00, RG 59, NARA.
47 "Caffery to Secretary of State, Telegram #7265," December 19, 1945. Box 6230, 851.00, RG 59, NARA.
48 "FRANCAM Company, a Communist Propaganda Instrument," December 29, 1945. Folder 36, Box 9, Grombach Subject/Country Files 1920–1963, CIA, RG 263, NARA.
49 "Plan for Political Attack on the Communist Party," December 29, 1945. Folder 36, Box 9, Grombach Subject/Country Files 1920–1963, CIA, RG 263, NARA.
50 "Interview with Albert Bayet, Vallois, Altman, and Benedite," April 16, 1945. File 125853, Box 1442, Intelligence Reports, RG 226, NARA.
51 Eric Pace, "General Ralph C. Smith, Honored for War Bravery, Dies at 104," *NYT*, January 26, 1998; also, Sharon Tosi Lacy, "Smith vs. Smith," *HistoryNet* March 30, 2011. www.historynet.com/smith-vs-smith.htm.
52 "French Constitutional Problems," July 11, 1945. File 138804, Box 1607, Intelligence Reports, RG 226, NARA.
53 "The Political Ideas of General de Gaulle," October 5, 1945. Report #2508, M1221, INR Reports, RG 59, NARA.
54 Craig R. Witney, "Andre de Wavrin, 'Col Passy' of Resistance Fame, Dies," *NYT*, December 22, 1998. www.proquest.com. See also Douglas Porch, *The French Secret Services: A History of French Intelligence from the Dreyfus Affair to the Gulf War* (New York: Macmillan, 2003), 176–179.
55 "Transmitting Memorandum of a Conversation between a Member of My Staff and Colonel DeWavrin," November 30, 1945. Folder 2, Box 3318, 711.00, RG 59, NARA.
56 "Interview with Albert Bayet, Vallois, Altman and Benedite," April 16, 1945.
57 "Discontent among Working Classes in France," May 11, 1945. File 127629, Box 1462, Intelligence Reports, RG 226, NARA.
58 "OSS Paris Outgoing," May 18, 1945. Paris R&A, Washington/Field Station Files May-June 1945, RG 226, NARA.
59 "OSS Paris Outgoing," May 25, 1945. Paris R&A, Washington/Field Station Files May-June 1945, RG 226, NARA.
60 "OSS Paris Outgoing," June 28, 1945. Paris R&A, Washington/Field Station Files May-June 1945, RG 226, NARA.
61 "Possible Successor in Case of de Gaulle's Death," May 16, 1945. File 128110, Box 1467, Intelligence Reports, RG 226, NARA.
62 "French Constitutional Problems," July 11, 1945. File 138804, Box 1607, Intelligence Reports, RG 226, NARA.
63 The call for a sovereign, unicameral assembly to which the government would be responsible represented not only PCF views but also a political consensus among all parties against the powerful presidential regime that de Gaulle advocated. Irwin Wall, *French Communism in the Era of Stalin: The Quest for Unity and Integration, 1945-1962* (Westport, CT: Greenwood Press, 1983), 36.
64 "The Tenth French Communist Party Congress," July 12, 1945. File 138620, Box 1605, Intelligence Reports, RG 226, NARA.
65 Ibid.

66 "Brief Resume of French Postwar Problems," May 12, 1945. File 131125, Box 1512, Intelligence Reports, RG 226, NARA; "OSS Paris Outgoing," May 18, 1945.
67 "Re: Your 10521," June 15, 1945. Paris R&A Outgoing Cables, OSS Washington/Field Station Files May–June 1945, RG 226, NARA.
68 "Notes sur les États-Unis," n.d. Dossier 9, Canada/EU, GPRF, AN.
69 "Note," July 13, 1945. Dossier 9, Canada/EU, GPRF, 3AG4/19, AN.
70 "Conversation à Washington et à New York sur certains problèmes européens," August 31, 1945, No. 150, *Documents Diplomatiques Français* (hereafter *DDF*) *1945 Tome II* (Paris: Imprimerie Nationale, 2000), 385.
71 "L'opinion publique aux États-Unis," December 3, 1945. Dossier 123, P4713, Politique Extérieur, Direction d'Amérique, MAE.
72 "Télégramme reçu à la DGER le 24 novembre 1945," Volume 119, P4712, Politique Extérieur, Direction d'Amérique, MAE.
73 "Note," June 5, 1945. Dossier 2 PCF, Intérieur, GPRF, AN.
74 "Labor and Political Developments in France," June 21, 1945. Box 6229, 851.00, RG 59, NARA.
75 "Note," July 12, 1945. Dossier 2 PCF, Intérieur, GPRF, AN.
76 "Note (2)," July 12, 1945. Dossier 2 PCF, Intérieur, GPRF, AN.
77 "Inquiétudes de certains leaders du Parti Communiste sur la politique étrangère défendue par le Parti," October 2, 1945. Dossier 2 PCF, Intérieur, GPRF, AN.
78 "Attitude politique actuelle du parti communiste," October 30, 1945. Dossier 2 PCF, Intérieur, GPRF, AN.
79 "Caffery to Secretary of State, Telegram #6218," October 25, 1945. Box 6230, 851.00, RG 59, NARA.
80 "Caffery to Secretary of State, Telegram #6189," October 23, 1945. Box 6230, 851.00, RG 59, NARA.
81 "Maurice Thorez à Président Charles de Gaulle," November 15, 1945. Dossier 2 PCF, Intérieur, GPRF, AN. The 75,000 number is contested. Most historians place the number of communists killed by the Germans closer to 15,000–16,000. Whatever the figure, the PCF drew postwar credibility from the blood price its members had paid, which it exploited to the maximum for political gain.
82 "Caffery to Secretary of State, Telegram #1983," April 20, 1945. Box 3989, 751.00, RG 59, NARA.
83 "Caffery to Secretary of State, Telegram #2363," May 4, 1945. Box 3989, 751.00, RG 59, NARA.
84 Ibid.
85 "Caffery to Secretary of State, Telegram #2380," May 5, 1945. 156-1, Foreign Affairs – France, President's Secretary Files (hereafter PSF), Harry S. Truman Presidential Library (hereafter HSTL).
86 "Caffery to Secretary of State, Telegram #2381," May 5, 1945. Box 3989, 751.00, RG 59, NARA.
87 Ibid.
88 Ibid.

89 "Caffery to Secretary of State, Telegram #2412," May 6, 1945. Box 3989, 751.00, RG 59, NARA.

90 "Donovan to Truman," June 3, 1945. Roll 150, M1642, OSS Director Files, RG 226, NARA.

91 "Comments on the Coal Situation in France," May 17, 1945. File 135535, Box 1564, Intelligence Reports, RG 226, NARA.

92 "The Ambassador in France (Caffery) to the Secretary of State, Telegram #4875," August 11, 1945. *FRUS 1945 Volume IV* (Washington, DC: GPO, 1968), 703.

93 "Caffery to Secretary of State, Telegram #4895," August 13, 1945. Folder 6, Box 6235, 851.00B, RG 59, NARA.

94 "Memorandum of Conversation with de Gaulle," August 22, 1945. Subject Files France, PSF, HSTL.

95 "Conversation entre M. Bidault et M. Byrnes," August 23, 1945. No. 128, *DDF 1945 Tome II* (Paris: Imprimerie Nationale, 2000), 331–332.

96 "Brief Resume of French Post-War Problems," May 12, 1945. File 131125, Box 1512, Intelligence Reports, RG 226, NARA.

97 "Memorandum for the Secretary," May 12, 1945. Box 3989, 751.00, RG 59, NARA.

98 "Caffery to Secretary of State, Telegram # 2586," May 12, 1945. Box 6229, 851.00, RG 59, NARA.

99 "Cover Letter to MA Report," November 30, 1945. Folder 2, Box 3318, 711.00, RG 59, NARA.

100 "Report by Colonel Hammond to General Smith," November 16, 1945. Folder 2, Box 3318, 711.00, RG 59, NARA.

101 Ibid.

102 "Sawyer to Langer," May 11, 1945. Paris R&A, Washington/Field Station Files May–June 1945, RG 226, NARA.

103 "Notes for Conference with the President," July 3, 1945. Memoranda for the President 1945–1946, Foreign Affairs, PSF, HSTL.

104 Ibid.

105 Ibid.

106 Weil, 223.

107 "European Questions No. 22 Briefing Book: France," June 23, 1945. *FRUS 1945 Volume I* (Washington, DC: GPO, 1960), 252–253.

108 "Evidence of Liaison of the French Communist Party with Moscow," October 8, 1945. Folder 36, Box 9, Grombach Subject/Country Files, RG 263, NARA.

109 "Caffery Airgram to Secretary of State," December 7, 1945. Box 6230, 851.00, RG 59, NARA.

110 Ibid.

111 Ibid.

112 "MAE à Ambassade de l'Union des Républiques Socialistes Soviétiques," August 9, 1945. Dossier 73, Politique Extérieur, URSS, Europe, MAE.

113 Adrien Tixier, "Activité des ressortissants soviétiques en France," August 23, 1945. Dossier 1, URSS, 3AG4/16, GPRF, AN.

114 "M. Charpentier à M. Bidault," September 21, 1945. No. 201. *DDF 1945 Tome II*, 513–515.

115 "Entretien de M. Bogomolov avec le Général Catroux," October 15, 1945. Dossier 62, P16879, Politique Extérieure, URSS, Europe, MAE.

116 "Note pour le Ministre," October 28, 1945. No. 272, *DDF 1945 Tome II*, 663–667.

117 "Moscou et la Crise Politique Française," November 17, 1945. Dossier 1, URSS, 3AG4/16, GPRF, AN.

118 "General Catroux à M. Bidault," December 19, 1945, No. 390. *DDF 1945 Tome II*, 935–937.

119 Ibid., 936–937.

120 "Note de M. Burin des Roziers pour le Général," June 5, 1945. No. 406, *DDF 1945 Tome I*, 740.

121 "L'Amérique et les problèmes internationaux," July 5, 1945. P4696, Presse, Direction d'Amérique, MAE.

122 Ibid.

123 "Bérard à Chauvel," July 23, 1945. No. 59, *DDF 1945 Tome II*, 145.

124 Ibid., 146.

125 Ibid.

126 "Les États-Unis, l'URSS, et le problème européen," December 4, 1945. Dossier 162, P4724, Politique Extérieur, Direction d'Amérique, MAE.

127 Ibid.

Chapter 3

1 "Caffery to the Secretary of State," March 13, 1945. US Department of State, *FRUS, 1945 Volume VI China* (Washington, DC: GPO, 1962), 300.

2 Stein Tønnesson, *The Vietnamese Revolution of 1945: Roosevelt, Ho Chi Minh and de Gaulle in a World at War* (London: Sage, 1991), 310. David Marr, *Vietnam: State, War and Revolution, 1945–1946* (Berkeley: University of California Press, 2013), 118, 286–287. See also Dixie R. Bartholomew-Feis, *The OSS and Ho Chi Minh: Unexpected Allies in the War against Japan* (Lawrence: University of Kansas Press, 2006).

3 Ministère de la Guerre/La Gendarmerie en AFN, "Synthèse Mensuelle – Décembre 1944," no. 10/2, January 2, 1945. Dossier 2, Afrique du Nord, GPRF, AN.

4 General Mast, "A.s. de la propagande communiste et communisante dans la Régence," January 8, 1945. Dossier 47, P4027, Tunisie, Direction d'Afrique-Levant, MAE.

5 General Mast, "A.s. de la propagande communiste," March 14, 1945. Dossier 47, P4027, Tunisie, Direction d'Afrique-Levant, MAE.

6 "Présence d'Ali Djerad à Paris," January 27, 1945. Dossier 47, P4027, Tunisie, Direction d'Afrique-Levant, MAE.

7 "Renseignements," January 28, 1945. Dossier 47, P4027, Tunisie, Direction Afrique-Levant, MAE.

8 "A/s de la propagande communiste en Tunisie," February 24, 1945. Dossier 47, P4027, Tunisie, Direction d'Afrique-Levant, MAE.

9 La Gendarmerie, "Rapport de synthèse mensuelle du mois de Janvier 1945," February 6, 1945. Dossier 2, Afrique du Nord, GPRF, AN.

10 "Télégramme," No. 190 (Rabat), February 24, 1945. Dossier 124, P4713, Politique Extérieure, Direction d'Amérique, MAE.

11 "A/s de la situation politique des partis musulmans à la date du 11 Mars," March 13, 1945. Dossier 2, Algérie, GPRF, AN.

12 "Note sur la situation politique en milieu Musulman au Maroc Français," May 1945. Dossier 1, Maroc, GPRF, AN.

13 Ibid.

14 "Note pour M. Palewski, La situation en Algérie," June 21, 1945. Dossier 2 Algérie, GPRF, AN.

15 "Note sur la situation politique en milieu Musulman au Maroc Français," May 1945. Dossier 1, Maroc, GPRF, AN. The same intelligence report, while decrying the role of French communists in stirring up colonized populations, admitted that a grave situation existed with rising food prices and shortages, and recommended that an energetic effort be undertaken to resupply the region to avoid the troubles, which most saw coming.

16 "Notes sur les troubles de l'Algérie," May 10, 1945. Dossier 2, Algérie, GPRF, AN.

17 The PPA had been banned at the outbreak of the Second World War, in September 1939.

18 "Note à l'attention de M. le Général de Gaulle, la situation en Algérie," June 2, 1945. Dossier 2, Algérie, GPRF, AN.

19 Ibid.

20 According to Ernest Gellner, "The Sociology of Robert Montagne, 1893–1954," *Daedelus* 105, no. 1 (Winter 1976): 138–140.

21 Ibid.

22 "Attitude du parti communiste depuis les récents incidents du département de Constantine," May 28, 1945. Dossier 2, Algérie, GPRF, AN.

23 "Note à l'attention de M. le General de Gaulle – La situation en Algérie," June 11, 1945. Dossier 2, GPRF, AN.

24 "La situation en Algérie," June 2, 1945. Dossier 2, Algérie, GPRF, AN.

25 "La situation en Algérie," June 11, 1945. Dossier 2, Algérie, GPRF, AN; "Synthèse Mensuelle Mois d'Octobre 1945," November 1, 1945. Dossier 2, Afrique du Nord, GPRF 3AG4/17, AN; "A.S. Collusion du Parti Communiste Tunisien et du Neo-Destour," December 19, 1945. Dossier 47, P4027, Tunisie, Direction d'Afrique-Levant, MAE.

26 "A/s: Meeting communiste à l'occasion du passage de M. Llante," October 23, 1945. Dossier 47, P4027, Tunisie, Direction d'Afrique-Levant, MAE.

27 "A/s: attitude de l'URSS et des communistes," February 9, 1945. Dossier 296, Syrie-Liban, Direction d'Afrique-Levant, MAE.

28 "Des partis communistes syrien et libanais," April 21, 1945. Dossier 296, Syrie-Liban, Direction Afrique-Levant, MAE.

29 "Le voyage de Mr. Solod, dans le Nord Syrien," December 6, 1945. Dossier 2, Levant, 3AG4/12, GPRF, AN.

30 "Les États-Unis, la Crise de Syrie et le Proche Orient," August 7, 1945. Dossier 161, P4723, Direction d'Amérique, MAE.

31 "A/S de la diffusion d'un tract," July 3, 1945. Dossier 2, Questions Politiques, Algérie, Direction d'Afrique-Levant, MAE.

32 Ibid.

33 Matthew Connolly, *A Diplomatic Revolution: Algeria's Fight for Independence and the Origins of the Post-Cold War Era* (Oxford: Oxford University Press, 2002), 48.

34 "Élections à l'Assemblée Constituante – Parti Communiste," December 10, 1945. Dossier 2, Algérie, GPRF, 3AG4/18, AN.

35 "Collusion du PCA et du PPA," December 11, 1945. Dossier 2, Algérie, GPRF, 3AG4/18, AN.

36 "A/S de l'évolution de la politique communiste en Algérie," December 27, 1945. Dossier 2, Algérie, GPRF, 3AG4/18, AN.

37 "Élections à l'Assemblée Constituante – Parti Communiste," December 10, 1945.

38 "Collusion du PCA et du PPA," December 11, 1945. Dossier 2, Algérie, GPRF, 3AG4/18, AN.

39 Adrien Tixier, "Activité panarabe en Algérie," December 17, 1945, and "Activité nationaliste et panarabe en Algérie," December 13, 1945. Dossier 2, Algérie, GPRF, 3AG4/18, AN.

40 "Collusion entre les nationalistes et le PCA," December 19, 1945. Dossier 2, Algérie, GPRF, 3AG4/18, AN. See also "Note au sujet de l'activité du parti communiste algérien," December 26, 1945. Dossier 2, Algérie, GPRF, 3AG4/18, AN.

41 Ibid.

42 "A/s Collusion du Parti Communiste Tunisien et du Neo-Destour," December 19, 1945. Dossier 47, P4027 Tunisie, Direction d'Afrique-Levant, MAE.

43 "A/s de l'évolution de la politique communiste en Algérie," December 27, 1945. Dossier 2, Algérie, GPRF, 3AG4/18, AN.

44 Ibid.

45 "J. Royère, Consul de France à Kunming à son excellence le General Pechkoff, Ambassadeur de France en Chine a Tchongking," February 23, 1945. Dossier 168, Politique Intérieur Indochine, Direction d'Asie-Océanie, MAE.

46 "Le Viet Minh," June 13, 1945. Dossier 168, Politique Intérieur, Indochine, Direction d'Asie-Océanie, MAE.

47 "Attitude des principales puissances dans la question de l'Indochine," August 1945. *DDF* 1945 Tome II, 188–189. In reality, Roosevelt had pressured both Britain and France to move their colonial possessions toward independence, moves that both nations resisted. Roosevelt's intransigence on Indochina and perceived flexibility on India was less the result of different goals than the fact that he envisioned Great Britain as one of the four great powers after the war and wished to maintain Allied unity. Of note, British Prime Minister Winston Churchill also told Roosevelt that he would resign if he continued to press the matter. By contrast, Roosevelt held French leaders and France's *mission civilisatrice* in contempt; French weakness further convinced him to insist on trusteeship for Indochina. For FDR's views on the French and British colonies, see Srinath Raghavan, *India's War: World War II and the Making of Modern South Asia* (New York: Basic Books, 2016), 37; Fredrik Logevall, *Embers of War: The Fall of an Empire and the Making of America's Vietnam* (New York: Random House, 2012), 44–60.

48 "L'Amérique et les problèmes internationaux," P4696/Presse, Direction d'Amérique, MAE.

49 "Attitude des principales Puissances dans la question de l'Indochine," No. 72, August 1945. *DDF 1945 Tome II*, 188–191.

50 Logevall, 94.

51 "Note à l'attention de M. le Directeur General de la DGER," September 1, 1945. Dossier 161, Politique Intérieur, Indochine, Direction d'Asie-Océanie, MAE.

52 "Note à l'attention de M. le Directeur General de la DGER," September 17, 1945. Dossier 161, Politique Intérieur, Indochine, Direction d'Asie-Océanie, MAE.

53 "Projet de Télégramme à Washington," September 21, 1945. Dossier 5 Indochine, Colonies, GPRF, AN.

54 "Télégramme, No. 5472-5473," October 31, 1945. Dossier 128, P4714, Politique Extérieure, Direction d'Amérique, MAE.

55 Philippe Devillers, *Histoire du Viet-Nam de 1940 à 1952* (Paris: Éditions du Seuil, 1952), 170.

56 "A. Torel à General Catroux," September 30, 1945. Dossier 161, Politique Intérieur, Indochine, Direction d'Asie-Océanie, MAE.

57 Ibid.

58 Charles de Gaulle, "Note pour Monsieur Bidault," December 7, 1945. Dossier 1 URSS, 3AG4/16, GPRF, AN.

59 "Général Leclerc au Général de Gaulle," October 13, 1945, No. 247, *DDF 1945 Tome II*, 612.

60 Ibid.

61 "Nguyen Van Thao à Florimond Bonté," n.d. Dossier 5 Indochine, Colonies, GPRF, 3AG4/23, AN.

62 Ibid.

63 Strategic Services Unit (History Project), *War Report: OSS Volume II – Operations in the Field* (Washington, DC: US GPO, 1949), 441.

64 Ronald Specter, "Allied Intelligence and China, 1943–1945," *Pacific Historical Review* 51, no. 1 (1982): 24–26.

65 SSU History Project, *War Report: OSS Volume 2*, 438.

66 Specter, 27.

67 SSU History Project, *War Report: OSS Volume 2*, 440.

68 "General Pechkoff, Ambassadeur de France à Tchoung-King à M. Bidault, MAE," No. 37, January 21, 1945. *DDF – 1945 Tome I (1er Janvier–30 Juin)*, 69–72.

69 DGER, "Activité Révolutionnaire Annamite," February 21, 1945. Dossier 168, Politique Intérieure, Indochine, Direction d'Asie-Océanie, MAE.

70 "Activité de Major Patti," October 17, 1945. Dossier 128, P4714, Direction d'Amérique, MAE.

71 General Tai Li was the Chinese government's chief of secret police.

72 Paul Helliwell, as quoted in Specter, 37–38.

73 Melvin Gross, as quoted in Specter, 39.

74 SSU History Project, *War Report: OSS Volume 2*, 440.

75 "Helliwell to Davis and Coughlin," August 16, 1945. Container 199, A1-154 Field Station Files – Indochina, RG 226, NARA.

76 "Interview with Archimedes L. A. Patti, 1981," 04/01/1981, WGBH Media Library & Archives, accessed March 8, 2016, http://openvault.wgbh.org/catalog/vietnam-bf3262-interview-with-archimedes-l-a-patti-1981.

77 Archimedes Patti, *Why Vietnam? Prelude to America's Albatross* (Berkeley: University of California Press, 1982), 67 and 81.

78 Logevall, 101–102.

79 Ray Galecki, as quoted in Bartholomew-Feis, 315.

80 Vu Dinh Huynh, as quoted in, Bartholomew-Feis, 315.

81 SWNCC, "Policy with Regard to Indochina," 35/11, May 25, 1945 and "Suggested Reexamination of American Policy with Respect to Indo-China," 35/10, May 1, 1945. Roll 5, LM 54, SWNCC Case Files, CREST, NARA.

82 "'Magic' – Diplomatic Summary," March 27, 1945. Box 15, A1 9006, RG 457, NARA.

83 "Attitude of French in French Indo-China towards Americans," March 28, 1945. File 126754, Box 1453, Intelligence Reports, RG 226, NARA.

84 "Charles de Gaulle to Harry Truman," May 15, 1945. 156-1, Foreign Affairs – France, PSF, HSTL.

85 SWNCC, "Suggested Reexamination of American Policy with Respect to Indo-China," 35/10, May 1, 1945. Roll 5, LM 54, SWNCC Case Files, 43.

86 Tønnesson, 16.

87 Logevall, 88–89.

88 H. Freeman Matthews, "Memorandum for the Secretary," May 12, 1945. Box 3989, 751.00, RG 59, NARA.

89 Marr, *Vietnam*, 307.

90 Patti, 125.

91 Richard J. Aldrich, *Intelligence and the War against Japan: Britain, America and the Politics of Secret Service* (Cambridge: Cambridge University Press, 2000), 306.

92 Ibid., 311.

93 The "Deer Team" was special operations team of OSS agents parachuted into Indochina with the mission to establish contact with the Viet Minh in order to equip and train the Vietnamese for operations against the Japanese. David G. Marr, *Vietnam 1945: The Quest for Power* (Berkeley: University of California Press, 1997), 286–287.

94 SSU History Project, *War Report: OSS Volume II*, 453.

95 McArthur was then the Supreme Commander of Allied Forces for the Southwest Pacific Area. Army and Navy commanders alike had excluded the OSS from their sectors in the Pacific, which forced OSS Chief William Donovan "to fight the Japanese in the only region left open to him, the distant China-Burma-India Theater." CIA, "The OSS in Asia," www.cia.gov/library/publications/intelligence-history/oss/art09.htm.

96 William L. Langer, *In and Out of the Ivory Tower* (New York: Neale Watson Academic Publications, 1977), 197.

97 Cora Du Bois, as quoted in Susan C. Seymour, *Cora du Bois: Anthropologist, Diplomat, Agent* (Lincoln: University of Nebraska Press, 2015).

98 Aldrich, 342–343.

99 Tønnesson, 350.

100 Patti, 330.
101 Harris Smith, 301.
102 Harris Smith, 302 and 323.
103 "The League of Independence of Indo-China," n.d., and "Franco-Jap Squabble in Indo-China," n.d. File 124840, Box 1429, Intelligence Reports, RG 226, NARA. Tønnesson maintains that the writer was Ho Chi Minh. Tønnesson, 310.
104 "French Colonial and Guerilla Forces," July 6, 1945. File 136350, Box 1575, Intelligence Reports, RG 226, NARA.
105 Cora du Bois, *Social Forces in Southeast Asia* (Minneapolis: University of Minnesota Press, 1949), 71.
106 Ibid.
107 OSS R&A, "Indochina's War-Time Government and Main Aspects of French Rule," July 10, 1945. Box 21, R&A 1715, RG 226, NARA.
108 Harold C. Deutsch and Lt. (JG) John K. Sawyer, "Your Request for Information re Weekly French Intelligence Report," January 1, 1945. Roll 86, A3556, Donovan Select Files, RG 226, NARA.
109 Early on, French officials identified Cline as a member of the Counter Intelligence Corps. Ministère de la Guerre/La Gendarmerie en AFN, "Synthèse Mensuelle – Décembre 1944," no. 10/2, January 2, 1945, Dossier 2, Algérie, GPRF, AN. However, by February of 1945, they had correctly identified him as an OSS officer. "Activité américaine au Maroc," February 14, 1945. Dossier 124, P4713, Direction d'Amérique, MAE.
110 "French Navy – Personnel – Communist Penetration," February 9, 1945. File 117040, Box 1334, Intelligence Reports, RG 226, NARA.
111 "Communism in Algiers," April 24, 1945. File 128162, Box 1467, Intelligence Reports, RG 226, NARA.
112 "La situation en Algérie," June 2, 1945. Dossier 2, Algérie, GPRF, AN; "General Political Impression – Northern French Africa," June 19, 1945. File 136506, Box 1577, Intelligence Reports, RG 226, NARA.
113 Ibid.
114 "General Political Impression – Northern French Africa," June 19, 1945. File 136506, Box 1577, Intelligence Reports, RG 226, NARA.
115 "Communist Meeting in Oran," January 2, 1945. File 108170, Box 1217, Intelligence Reports, RG 226, NARA; also "L'Action Algérienne – Clandestine Arab Newspaper," March 16, 1945. File 118701, Box 1354, Intelligence Reports, RG 226, NARA.
116 "Anti-French Sentiment/Political Opinions," January 6, 1975. File 108954, Box 1227, Intelligence Reports, RG 226, NARA.
117 "Activities of Nationalists," April 2, 1945. File 121396, Box 1383, Intelligence Reports, RG 226, NARA.
118 "Cancellation of Voyage of Resistance Council Investigating Committee to North Africa," February 9, 1945. File 113620, Box 1288, Intelligence Reports, RG 226, NARA.
119 "Police Action Against Native Political Groups," March 30, 1945. File 121036, Box 1379, Intelligence Reports, RG 226, NARA.

120 "French Sensitivity over American Influence on Algerian Nationalism," April 17, 1945. File 127058, Box 1456, Intelligence Reports, RG 226, NARA.
121 "Disorders in Algeria," May 17, 1945. File 130515, Box 1506, Intelligence Reports, RG 226, NARA.
122 "Estimate of the Situation," May 24, 1945. File 131523, Box 1515, Intelligence Reports, RG 226, NARA.
123 "Effect of French North African Situation in France," May 11, 1945. File 127640, Box 1462, Intelligence Reports, RG 226, NARA.
124 "Riots – Setif and Guelma Areas, 8–12 May," May 24, 1945. File 131525, Box 1515, Intelligence Reports, RG 226, NARA.
125 "OSS Paris Outgoing," May 18, 1945. Paris R&A, Washington/Field Station Files May–June 1945, RG 226, NARA.
126 "Memorandum for the President: Current Foreign Developments," June 1, 1945. Folder 2, Box 154, PSF Subject File – Foreign Affairs, HSTL.
127 "OSS Paris Outgoing," June 8, 1945. Paris R&A, Washington/Field Station Files May-June 1945, RG 226, NARA.
128 "OSS Paris Outgoing," June 1, 1945. Paris R&A, Washington/Field Station Files May-June 1945, RG 226, NARA.
129 "Telegram 3269," June 3, 1945. Telegrams/France, PSF – Foreign Affairs, HSTL.
130 "Telegram NIACT 3296," June 4, 1945. Telegrams/France, PSF – Foreign Affairs, HSTL.
131 "Memorandum for the President," June 4, 1945. Folder 2, Box 154, Current Foreign Developments, PSF – Foreign Affairs, HSTL.
132 "Approach to the United States by the League of Arab States Regarding the Uprising in Algeria," June 21, 1945 to October 5, 1945. *FRUS 1945 Volume VIII* (Washington, DC: GPO, 1969), 30–32.
133 "Memorandum by Under Secretary of State (Acheson) to the Secretary of State," October 9, 1945. *FRUS 1945 Volume VIII*, 43–48.
134 "Conference with the Chiefs of Mission in the Near East with President Truman on November 10, 1945." *FRUS 1945 Volume VIII*, 11.
135 Ibid., 13–14.
136 Tønnesson argued that the French had already lost in Indochina before war ever broke out in 1946. Tønnesson, 1.

Chapter 4

1 Jules Moch, quoted in Jean Lacouture, *De Gaulle: The Ruler 1945–1970*, trans. Alan Sheridan (New York: W. W. Norton, 1991), 119.
2 Louis Joxe, quoted in Lacouture, 120.
3 Maurice Thorez, quoted in Lacouture, 121.
4 "Caffery to the Secretary of State, Telegram no. 316," January 21, 1946. *FRUS 1946 Volume V* (Washington, DC: GPO, 1969), 402–403.
5 Lacouture, 123.
6 Bidault, as quoted in Lacouture, 122.

7 Gregory F. Treverton describes this function of intelligence as it related to the Iraq War in "Intelligence Analysis: Between 'Politicization' and Irrelevance," in *Analyzing Intelligence: Origins, Obstacles, and Innovations* eds. Roger Z. George and James B. Bruce (Washington, DC: Georgetown University Press, 2008), 100.

8 Weil, 246.

9 Ibid.

10 Katz, 188; Weil, 243, 246–247.

11 "Notes," January 5, 1946. Longhand Notes, PSF, HSTL; see also Arnold Offner, *Another Such Victory: President Truman and the Cold War 1945–1953* (Stanford: Stanford University Press, 2002), 117–124.

12 "Souers Interview," December 15, 1954. Folder 5, Student Research File/CIA, HSTL; "NIA Directive No. 1," February 8, 1946. Michael Warner, ed., *The CIA under Harry Truman* (Honolulu: University Press of the Pacific, 2005), 35.

13 "War Department Intelligence Review (hereafter WDIR)," No. 1, February 14, 1946. WDIR File – February 1946, Naval Aide to the President Files, HSTL; "CIA Chronology," Student Research File/CIA, HSTL.

14 Melvyn Leffler, *A Preponderance of Power: National Security, the Truman Administration, and the Cold War* (Stanford: Stanford University Press, 1992), 100, 137.

15 Ibid., 102.

16 "MAE à AMBAFRANCE et LEGAFRANCE…," January 28, 1946. Dossier 119, P4712, Politique Extérieure, Amérique, MAE.

17 "Bonnet à MAE," January 28, 1946 and "La crise politique française vue par la presse américaine," January 31, 1946. Dossier 119, P4712, Politique Extérieure, Amérique, MAE.

18 "Télégramme reçu à la DGER," February 2, 1946. Dossier 119, P4712, Politique Extérieure, Amérique, MAE.

19 "Caffery to the Secretary of State, Telegram No. 647," February 9, 1946. *FRUS 1946 Volume V*, 412–413.

20 "Bonnet à Bidault," March 13, 1946. No. 190, *DDF 1946 Tome I*, 419; Leffler, 103.

21 Kennan argued that there were no legitimate Soviet interests and that it was impossible to placate Soviet leaders determined to preserve their rule at home. They would seek global expansion and to exploit any vulnerability in the West. While it was impossible to appeal to reason in negotiations with Soviet officials, Kennan maintained that the USSR's basic weakness meant that its leaders would respond to American "manifestations of force." See Leffler, 108.

22 "Bonnet à Bidault," March 13, 1946.

23 In February, War Department intelligence developed a set of Essential Elements of Information (EEIs), requesting coverage of worldwide communist activity and Soviet leadership of the communist movement. "War Department Intelligence Plan," February 18, 1946. CREST, NARA.

24 Arthur Krock, "In the Nation: The President's Secret Daily Newspaper," *NYT*, July 15, 1946. www.proquest.com.

25 On the evolution of ex-Communists' views, see Richard Crossman, ed., *The God That Failed* (London: Hamilton, 1950). See also John V. Fleming, *The Anti-Communist Manifestos: Four Books That Shaped the Cold War* (New York: W. W. Norton, 2009). Isaac Deutscher, a defender of the Soviet experiment but critic of Stalinist tyranny, famously called a converted anti-communist an "inverted Stalinist" who "brings to the job lack of scruple, the narrow-mindedness, the disregard for truth, and the intense hatred with which Stalinism has imbued him." Quoted in David Caute, *Isaac and Isaiah: The Covert Punishment of a Cold War Heretic* (New Haven: Yale University Press, 2013), 171.

26 "H. Freeman Matthews to the Secretary of State," February 29, 1946. Folder 1, Box 6235, 851.00B, RG 59, NARA.

27 "The Communists Seek Heavy Arms," March 5, 1946. Folder 1, Box 6235, 851.00B, RG 59, NARA.

28 Durbrow was Chipman's counterpart in Rome, and later an official in the State Department's European Division.

29 Durbrow, as quoted in Ted Morgan, *A Covert Life: Jay Lovestone: Communist, Anti-Communist, and Spymaster* (New York: Random House, 2011), 149–150.

30 "New Anti-Communist Political Group in Formation," February 12, 1946. Box 6231, 851.00, RG 59, NARA.

31 "De Gaulle's View of the International Situation," March 4, 1946. Roll 1, M1656, SSU Reports 1945–1946, NARA.

32 "Development of the Anti-Communist Political Grouping," March 8, 1946. Roll 1, M1656, SSU Reports 1945–1946, NARA.

33 "CIG Daily Summary," March 13, 1945. CREST, NARA.

34 "Summary of Daily Bulletins of an Official French Agency," March 14, 1946. Box 1, Records of Office of Western European Affairs French Desk 1941–1954, RG 59, NARA.

35 There was truth to this claim. *La Tribune des Nations* was founded in 1946 with the help of Soviet subsidies. Its founder was a secret PCF member and worked for Polish intelligence. Andrew and Mitrokhin, *The Sword and the Shield*, 462–463.

36 "Communist Influence in the French Press," March 19, 1946. Roll 1, M1656, SSU Reports, NARA.

37 "Communists and Non-Communists in French Trade Union," March 27, 1946. Roll 1, M1656, SSU Reports, NARA; "CIG Daily Summary," April 17, 1946. CREST, NARA.

38 "WDIR," March 28, 1946. WDIR File – March 1946, Naval Aide File, HSTL.

39 "WDIR," April 25, 1946. WDIR File – April 1946, Naval Aide Files, HSTL.

40 Mark Elliott, "The Soviet Repatriation Campaign," in *The Refugee Experience: Ukrainian Displaced Persons after World War II*, eds. Wsevold W. Isajiw, Yury Boshyk, and Roman Senkus (Edmonton: Canadian Institute of Ukrainian Studies Press, 1992), 349. Former Soviet Air Force Colonel Vasili Kotov levied similar charges in "Stalin Thinks I'm Dead," *Saturday Evening Post* 220, no. 31, January 31, 1948.

41 "Soviet Measures to Enforce Repatriation," March 22, 1946. Roll 1, M1656, SSU Reports, NARA.

42 "Department of State to Amembassy Paris," March 22, 1946. Box 3989, 751.00, RG 59, NARA.

43 "Caffery to the Secretary of State," Telegram #1407 and #1418. March 23, 1946. Box 3989, 751.00, RG 59, NARA.

44 Ibid.

45 "Comments and Recommendations of Counselor of Embassy George F. Kennan, at Moscow Concerning Policy and Information Statement of March 1, 1946," April 1, 1946. Folder 2, Box 3318, 711.00, RG 59, NARA. Kennan's biographers note that he too believed that the Soviets aimed for a communist seizure of power in France, primarily through political rather than military means, and that this posed a serious threat for US national security. Wilson Miscamble, *George Kennan and the Making of American Foreign Policy 1947–1950* (Princeton: Princeton University Press, 1992), 74. John Lewis Gaddis, *George F. Kennan: An American Life* (New York: Penguin, 2011), 286. Irwin Wall points out that Kennan failed to understand the sources of the PCF's popularity, attributing it the French public's failure to understand communist objectives. Wall, *The United States and the Making of Postwar France*, 59.

46 "Communist Party of France," April 3, 1946. Box 3, French Desk, Subject Files, RG 59, NARA.

47 Ibid.

48 "Caffery to the Secretary of State," Telegram #1580, April 4, 1946. Box 3989, 751.00, RG 59, NARA.

49 "Caffery to the Secretary of State," Telegram #1595. April 4, 1946. *FRUS 1946 Volume V*, 421–422.

50 "Wallner to Bonbright," January 30, 1946. Box 3991, 751.00, RG 59, NARA; "Memorandum of Conversation," January 30, 1946. *FRUS 1946 Volume VIII* (Washington: GPO, 1971), 19.

51 "Bidault à tous les postes diplomatiques," March 7, 1946. No. 160, *DDF 1946 Tome 1*, 367.

52 "WDIR," March 21 and 28, 1946. WDIR File – March 1946, Naval Aide File, HSTL.

53 "Political Information-A66642," March 28, 1946. Roll 1, M1656, SSU Intelligence Reports, NARA.

54 Lawrence, 21.

55 "Political Information-A66643," March 29, 1946. Roll 1, M1656, SSU Intelligence Reports, NARA.

56 "Note pour M. Palewski," January 12, 1946 and "Note à l'attention de M. Palewski au sujet du rapprochement du Parti Communiste avec le PPA," January 18, 1946. Dossier 2, Algérie, GPRF, AN.

57 "Note pour le Résident Général de France à Rabat," January 26, 1946. No. 69, *DDF 1946 Tome 1*, 148.

58 "L'offensive de la politique soviétique," March 1, 1946. No. 148, *DDF 1946 Tome 1*, 312–316.

59 "Beynet à Bidault," March 4, 1946. No. 154, *DDF 1946 Tome I*, 355–357.

60 "Attitude de la Légation soviétique," March 4, 1946. Dossier 296, Syrie-Liban, Afrique-Levant, MAE.

61 "Mast à MAE," March 13, 1946. Dossier 47, P4027, Tunisie, Direction d'Afrique-Levant, MAE.

62 "Relations franco-américaines en Tunisie," March 27, 1946. Dossier 124, P4713, Politique Extérieure, Direction d'Amérique MAE.

63 "Rapport de la Légation d'Égypte à Damas sur le mouvement Communiste," April 29, 1946. Dossier 296, Syrie-Liban, Direction d'Afrique-Levant, MAE.

64 "Communist Propaganda in Algeria," March 18, 1946. Roll 1, M1656, SSU Reports, RG 226, NARA.

65 Drafted by the leftist majority in the French assembly and favored by the PCF, the constitutional referendum called for a unicameral legislature and a weak presidency.

66 "Memorandum of Conversation," May 1, 1946. Folder 7, Box 90, MSS 90, Series 5: State Department, *James Byrnes Papers*, CU.

67 "Chipman to Matthews," May 1, 1946. Box 3990, 751.00, RG 59, NARA.

68 "Caffery to the Secretary of State," May 2, 1946. *FRUS 1946 Volume V*, 434–435; "Daily Summary," May 4, 1946, CREST, NARA.

69 "CIG Daily Summary," May 3, 1946. CREST, NARA.

70 "Memorandum by Deputy Director of Office of European Affairs," May 6, 1946. *FRUS 1946 Volume V*, 436–438.

71 "Diary," May 3, 1946. Leahy Diary 1946, Boxes 6–8, *Leahy Papers*, LOC.

72 "Caffery to the Secretary of State," May 6, 1946. *FRUS 1946 Volume V*, 438–440. (The date is likely a typographical error; the State Department received the message on May 6, but the message was sent on May 4.)

73 "Caffery to the Secretary of State," May 7, 1946. *FRUS 1946 Volume V*, 447–449. Also, "Caffery to Secretary of State, Telegram #2212," May 7, 1946. Box 6231, 851.00, RG 59, NARA.

74 "Recent Interview with General de Gaulle," May 6, 1946. Roll 2, M1656, SSU Reports, RG 226, NARA.

75 "CIG Daily Summary," May 6, 1946. CREST, NARA.

76 "CIG Daily Summary," May 8, 1946. CREST, NARA.

77 "Diary," May 8, 1946. Leahy Diary 1946, Boxes 6–8, *Leahy Papers*, LOC.

78 "Communist Aspirations and Plans," May 8, 1946. Roll 2, M1656, SSU Reports, RG 226, NARA.

79 "Soviet Penetration – Western Europe," May 10, 1946. Roll 2, M1656, SSU Reports, RG 226, NARA; "Chairman, Reporting Board to Bonbright," May 10, 1946. Folder 1, Box 6235, 851.00B, RG 59, NARA.

80 "CIG Daily Summary," May 11, 1946. CREST, NARA.

81 "The High Strategy of the French Communist Party," May 10, 1946. Box 6235, 851.00B, RG 59, NARA.

82 Ibid.

83 Ibid.

84 "Bonnet à Bidault," May 21, 1946. No. 349, *DDF 1946 Tome I*, 795–796.

85 "Massigli à Chauvel," May 28, 1946. No. 369, *DDF 1946 Tome I*, 832.

86 "CIG Daily Summary," June 4, 1946. CREST, NARA.

87 "Caffery to the Secretary of State," June 22, 1946. *FRUS 1946 Volume V*, 465.
88 "WDIR," June 6, 1946. WDIR File – June 1946, Naval Aide File, HSTL.
89 "Bonnet à MAE," June 3, 1946 and June 5, 1946. P4696, Presse, Amérique, MAE.
90 "WDIR," June 13, 1946. WDIR File – June 1946, Naval Aide File, HSTL.
91 "Herriot Refuses to Join Ministry," *NYT*, June 21, 1946. ProQuest Historical Newspapers, p. 8.
92 "WDIR," June 27, 1946. WDIR File – June 1946, Naval Aide File, HSTL.
93 "CIG Daily Summary," June 21, 1946. CREST, NARA.
94 "Interview with de Gaulle," June 24, 1946. Roll 2, M1656, SSU Intelligence Reports, RG 226, NARA.
95 "Reflections on Present Communist Policy in France," June 28, 1946. Folder 1, Box 6235, 851.00B, RG 59, NARA.
96 "Les découvertes de dépôts d'armes," *Le Monde*, June 19, 1946. www.lemonde.fr/recherche/.
97 "Arms Depots in SW France," August 7, 1946. Roll 3, M1656, RG 226, NARA.
98 "Comment furent découvertes près de Villeneuve-sur-Lot 600 caisses d'armes et de munitions," *Le Monde*, June 17, 1946. www.lemonde.fr/recherche/; "Terrorists Blast Haifa Railway Shops," *WP*, June 18, 1946, 1. ProQuest Historical Newspapers (151886758); see also Maud Mandel, *Muslims and Jews in France: A History of Conflict* (Princeton: Princeton University Press, 2014), 15–16, 30
99 "Communist Militants Enter France via Italy," June 10, 1946. Roll 2, M1656, SSU Reports, RG 226, NARA.
100 "Clandestine Soviet Transmitters and Arms Smuggling from Switzerland to France," June 10, 1946. Roll 2, M1656, SSU Reports, RG 226, NARA.
101 "Communist Militants Training in Southern France," June 18, 1946. Roll 2, M1656, SSU Reports, RG 226, NARA.
102 "Pro-Soviet Activities in Grenoble Region," July 2, 1946. Roll 3, M1656, SSU Reports, RG 226, NARA.
103 "Alleged Communist Activities in the South of France," July 23, 1946. Box 6231, 851.00, RG 59, NARA.
104 "Spanish Communist Activities in France," July 31, 1946. Box 6231, 851.00, RG 59, NARA.
105 "Russian Strategic Objectives," August 7, 1946. Roll 3, M1656, SSU Reports, RG 226, NARA.
106 "Russia Is Reorganizing Civil War Cadres throughout Europe," October 25, 1946. Box 9, Grombach Subject/Country Files 1920–1963, RG 263, NARA; "Communist Paramilitary Activity in Southwest France," October 8, 1946. Roll 5, M1656, SSU Reports, RG 226, NARA. "Russia Is Reorganizing Civil War Cadres throughout Europe," October 25, 1946. Box 9, Grombach Subject/Country Files 1920–1963, RG 263, NARA. Some of these reports originated with the Pond, a shadowy intelligence unit then operating under the War Department, led by French-born US Army officer John Grombach.

As Mark Stout has pointed out, "Grombach was constantly on the lookout for communist subversion" (p. 72). Stout, "The Pond: Running Agents for State, War and the CIA," 69–82.

107 "ORE 1: Soviet Foreign and Military Policy," July 23, 1946. CREST, NARA.

108 "Daily Summary," July 18, 1946 and July 29, 1946. CREST, NARA.

109 "Caffery to Secretary of State," July 29, 1946. Box 6231, 851.00, RG 59, NARA.

110 "Wallner to Hickerson," August 2, 1946. Box 6231, 851.00, RG 59, NARA.

111 "Entretiens Catroux-Molotov," August 12, 1946. No. 93, *DDF 1946 Tome II*, 232–234.

112 "Bidault à tous les postes diplomatiques," August 13, 1946. No. 94, *DDF 1946 Tome II*, 234–235.

113 "Daily Summary," August 26, 1946. CREST, NARA.

114 "French Communist Party Policy and the Forthcoming Elections," September 18, 1946. Roll 4, M1656, SSU Reports, NARA.

115 "Policy and Information Statement on France," September 15, 1946. Folder 2, Box 3318, 711.00, RG 59, NARA.

116 Ibid.

117 Georges Bidault, for example, told Byrnes that if France received no satisfactions on Germany then it would exist in a state of insecurity that would be seized upon by "diverse elements" for their own electoral ends. Measures must be taken, he said, before the elections in November. "Conversations entre M. Bidault et M. Byrnes," September 23, 1946. No. 166, *DDF 1946 Tome II*, 423–426.

118 "Policy and Information Statement on France," September 15, 1946. Folder 2, Box 3318, 711.00, RG 59, NARA.

119 CIG, "Special Study No. 4: Soviet Military Intentions," September 18, 1946. CREST, NARA.

120 "Opinion: General de Gaulle's Political Position," October 15, 1946. Roll 5, M1656, SSU Reports, RG 226, NARA.

121 "WDIR," October 17 and 24, 1946. WDIR Files – October 1946, Naval Aide Files, HSTL.

122 "Penetration of Communist Parties: Preliminary Brief," October 14, 1946. CREST, NARA.

123 "Caffery to the Secretary of State, no. 4254," October 29, 1946. *FRUS 1946 Volume V*, 468–470.

124 "WDIR," October 31, 1946. WDIR Files – October 1946, Naval Aide Files, HSTL.

125 "Smith to the Secretary of State, Telegram #1428," May 4, 1946. Box 3990, 751.00, RG 59, NARA.

126 "CIG Daily Summary," June 17, 1946. CREST, NARA.

127 "Memo of Conversation," May 1, 1946. Folder 7, MSS 90 Box 12, Series 5: State Department, *James Byrnes Papers*, CU.

128 "CIG Daily Summary," May 10, 1946. CREST, NARA.

129 "The High Strategy of the French Communist Party," May 10, 1946.

130 "Article du *New York Times* sur la Tunisie," May 20, 1946. Dossier 124, P4713, Politique Extérieure, Direction d'Amérique, MAE.

131 "French Overseas Possessions Policy and Information Statement," May 15, 1946. Box 3319, 711.00, RG 59, NARA.

132 "Voyage à Moscou de MM. Nicolas Chaoui et Mustapha el Ariss," June 11, 1946. Dossier 296, Syrie-Liban, Direction d'Afrique-Levant, MAE.

133 "Union des Patriotes Soviétiques Foreign Infiltration," May 21, 1946. Box 6231, 851.00, RG 59, NARA.

134 After the French conquest of Vietnam in the late nineteenth century, colonial officials divided the country into three administrative sections (or "kys") of Tonkin, Annam, and Cochinchina.

135 "Caffery to the Secretary of State, no. 3323," July 7, 1946. *FRUS 1946 Volume VIII*, 48–49.

136 "Ho Chi Minh's Position," July 23, 1946. Roll 3, M1656, SSU Reports, RG 226, NARA.

137 "Ho Chi Minh's Position," July 23, 1946; "French Communist Party Support of Ho Chi Minh," August 30, 1946. Roll 4, M1656, SSU Reports, RG 226, NARA.

138 Logevall, 137.

139 Ibid., 142–144.

140 "Note du Département – Relations du Viet Nam avec les représentants américains au Tonkin," September 2, 1946. No. 129, *DDF 1946 Tome II*, 312–319.

141 "Acting Secretary of State to the Consul at Saigon (Reed)," September 9, 1946. *FRUS 1946 Volume VIII*, 57.

142 "Caffery to the Secretary of State," September 11, 1946. *FRUS 1946 Volume VIII*, 58.

143 "The Consul at Saigon (Reed) to Secretary of State," September 17, 1946. *FRUS 1946 Volume VIII*, 59.

144 "The Vice-Consul at Hanoi (O'Sullivan) to Secretary of State," November 1, 1946. *FRUS 1946 Volume VIII*, 62–63.

145 "Les Communistes chinois au Tonkin," November 7, 1946. Dossier 174, Politique Intérieur, Indochine, Direction d'Asie-Océanie, MAE.

146 "VA-257," July 31, 1946. Folder 4, Box 3319, 711.00, RG 59, NARA.

147 "Anti-American Sentiment in Algiers," June 13, 1946. Folder 4, Box 3319, 711.00, RG 59, NARA.

148 "VA-257," July 31, 1946.

149 "WDIR," August 22, 1946. WDIR Files – August 1946, Naval Aide Files, HSTL.

150 "Labonne à Bidault," August 9, 1946. Dossier 65, Maroc 1944–1955, Direction Afrique-Levant, MAE.

151 "Mouvement nationaliste et propagande Communiste au Maroc," August 10, 1946. Dossier 65, Maroc 1944–1955, Direction Afrique-Levant, MAE.

152 "Mast à MAE," August 16, 1946. Dossier 47, P4027, Tunisie, Direction d'Afrique-Levant, MAE.

153 "Parti Communiste," August 19, 1946. Dossier 47, P4027, Tunisie, Direction d'Afrique-Levant, MAE.

154 "Barbe à M. Ali Mohamed," September 9, 1946. Dossier 258, Tunisie, Direction d'Afrique-Levant, MAE.

155 "Daily Summary," August 13, 1946. CREST, NARA.
156 "Daily Summary," August 19, 1946. CREST, NARA.
157 "Daily Summary," August 24, 1946. CREST, NARA.
158 "Inquiétudes Américaines sur le Mouvement Communiste en Tunisie," August 27, 1946. Dossier 47, P4027, Tunisie, Direction d'Afrique-Levant, MAE.
159 "WDIR," September 12, 1946. WDIR File – September 1946, Naval Aide Files, HSTL.
160 "Daily Summary," July 20, 1946. CREST, NARA.
161 "Daily Summary," September 13, 1946. CREST, NARA.
162 "Daily Summary," September 16, 1946. CREST, NARA.
163 "Policy and Information Statement, France," September 15, 1946.
164 "Policy toward North Africa," October 2, 1946. Folder 4, Box 3319, 711.5, RG 59, NARA.
165 "Habib Bourguiba, Leader of the Neo-Destour Party," October 4, 1946. Box 3, Records of the French Desk, Subject Files, RG 59, NARA.
166 "Policy toward North Africa," October 2, 1946.
167 Ibid., 1946.
168 "Preliminary Estimate of the Results of the French Parliamentary Elections," November 10, 1946. Box 1, Records of the French Desk, Subject Files, RG 59, NARA.
169 "WDIR," November 14, 1946. WDIR – November 1946, Naval Aide Files, HSTL.
170 "WDIR," November 21, 1946. WDIR – November 1946, Naval Aide Files, HSTL.
171 "Daily Summary," November 21, 1946. CREST, NARA.
172 Ridgway was then the US military representative at the United Nations.
173 "Memo of Conference with Lt Gen Billotte," November 18, 1946. Box 1, Records of the French Desk, Subject Files, RG 59, NARA.
174 "Memorandum for the President," November 26, 1946. Box 20, JCS Chairman's File – Leahy, RG 218, NARA.
175 "Bonnet à MAE," December 17, 1946. Dossier 119, P4712, Politique Extérieure, Direction d'Amérique, MAE.
176 "Caffery to the Secretary of State," December 18, 1946. *FRUS 1946 Volume V*, 477–478.
177 "Daily Summary," December 19, 1946. CREST, NARA.
178 "Memo of Conversation: Indochina," November 12, 1946. Box 2, Records of the French Desk, Subject Files, RG 59, NARA.
179 See, for example: "L'Activité extérieure du gouvernement de Hanoi dans certaines pays du Sud Est Asiatique," November 13, 1946. Dossier 161, Politique Intérieure, Indochine, Direction d'Asie-Océanie, MAE.
180 "Activités Soviétiques en Indochine," November 14, 1946; "Renseignement," November 22, 1946; "Le propagande Communiste en Extrême-Orient," November 27, 1946. Dossier 174, Politique Intérieure, Indochine, Direction d'Asie-Océanie, MAE.
181 "Caffery to Secretary of State, No. 5857," November 29, 1946. *FRUS 1946 Volume VIII*, 63.

182 Pierre Brocheux, in *Ho Chi Minh: A Biography*, trans. Claire Duiker (Cambridge: Cambridge University Press, 2007) notes that Ho was out of step with party emphasis on "class struggle" early on, preferring emphasis on nationalism and class collaboration (p. 64). This deviation, and Ho's relative autonomy in Vietnam, remained a source of tension with Soviet officials. William Duiker, in *Ho Chi Minh* (New York: Hyperion, 2000) points out "Stalin had only fitful interest in Asia and could not be counted on to throw the weight of the Soviet Union on the side of revolutionary forces there" (p. 343). He also notes "links between the Indochinese Communist Party and Moscow had been virtually non-existent since World War II" (p. 391). Most importantly, Duiker argues that Stalin doubted Ho's ideological orthodoxy; his suspicion was further aroused when Ho approached the United States in late 1945. Stalin refused to recognize the DRV in 1947 when he recognized Sukarno's Indonesia. Nikita Khrushchev describes Stalin's antipathy for Ho still on display during the latter's visit to Moscow in 1950; Stalin's behavior, Khrushchev said, was "offensive, infuriating" (p. 421).
183 "D'Argenlieu à Bidault," November 30, 1946. No. 270, *DDF 1946 Tome II*, 655.
184 "O'Sullivan to Secretary of State," December 3, 1946. *FRUS 1946 Volume VIII*, 64–65.
185 "Caffery to Secretary of State," December 3, 1946. *FRUS 1946 Volume VIII*, 65–66.
186 "Caffery to Secretary of State," December 4, 1946. *FRUS 1946 Volume VIII*, 66.
187 "Acting Secretary of State to Consul at Saigon," December 5, 1946. *FRUS 1946 Volume VIII*, 67–69.
188 "Caffery to Secretary of State," December 7, 1946. *FRUS 1946 Volume VIII*, 70.
189 "The Secretary of State to Certain Missions Abroad," December 17, 1946. *FRUS 1946 Volume VIII*, 72–73.
190 "Recent Developments in French–Vietnam Relations," December 18, 1946. Box 3, Records of the French Desk, Subject Files, RG 59, NARA.
191 Ibid.
192 "Bulletin de renseignements 19 Décembre," December 20, 1946. Dossier 180, Politique Intérieure, Indochine, Direction d'Asie-Océanie, MAE.
193 "Appel à la résistance fait par Ho Chi Minh au people," December 19, 1946. Dossier 168, Politique Intérieure, Indochine, Direction d'Asie-Océanie, MAE.
194 "Secretary of State to Certain Diplomatic and Consular Officers," December 20, 1946. *FRUS 1946 Volume VIII*, 74–75.
195 "Memorandum by the Director of the Office of Far Eastern Affairs (Vincent) to the Under Secretary of State (Acheson)," December 23, 1946. *FRUS 1946 Volume VIII*, 75–77.
196 "Memorandum of Conversation by Mr. Charlton Ogburn Jr of the Division of Southeast Asian Affairs," December 31, 1946. *FRUS 1946 Volume VIII*, 83–84.
197 "Conflict in Indochina," December 27, 1946. Box 2, Records of the French Desk, Subject Files, RG 59, NARA.

198 Mark Atwood Lawrence, *Assuming the Burden: Europe and American Commitment to the War in Vietnam* (Berkeley: University of California Press, 2005), 6–7, 13.
199 "Note pour le Président du Gouvernement: Actions russe et anglo-saxonne en Afrique du Nord," December 2, 1946. No. 276, *DDF 1946 Tome II*, 670.
200 Ibid.
201 "Activité communiste," December 21, 1946. Dossier 47, P4027, Tunisie, Direction d'Afrique-Levant, MAE.
202 "Note pour le Président du Gouvernement: Actions russe et anglo-saxonne en Afrique du Nord," December 2, 1946. No. 276, *DDF 1946 Tome II*, 670.
203 Leffler, 133.
204 Ibid.

Chapter 5

1 Ludwell Montague to the Assistant Director, R & E, "Production of a 'World Situation Estimate,'" November 12, 1947. CREST, NARA.
2 "Testimony on Authorizing Certain Military Missions," June 3, 1947. *Volume 6*, 142–143, George C. Marshall Papers (hereafter GCMP), George Marshall Foundation, Lexington, Virginia.
3 Dorothy Ringquist, Secretary to Fleet Admiral Leahy to Allan Evans, Director OIR, March 6, 1947. Box 19, Chairman's File Admiral Leahy, RG 218, NARA.
4 "Entretiens de M. Jefferson Caffery," July 8, 1947. Dossier États-Unis, Notes d'information 4AG/105, Archives du président de la république (Auriol) (hereafter Auriol), AN.
5 "A.S. de l'utilisation de certains membres du S.R.A. par les services spéciaux américains," September 22, 1947. Dossier États-Unis, Notes d'information 4AG/105, Auriol, AN.
6 CIG, "Daily Summary," January 6, 1947. CREST, NARA.
7 CIG, "ORE 1/1 Revised Soviet Tactics in International Affairs," January 6, 1947, in *The CIA under Harry Truman*, ed. Michael Warner (Honolulu: University Press of the Pacific, 2005), 99–104.
8 "Les préoccupations actuelles des chefs communistes," February 27, 1947.
9 CIG, "Daily Summary," January 29, 1947. CREST, NARA.
10 "A.S. du Parti Communiste," March 8, 1947. Responsables, 4AG/85, Auriol, AN.
11 CIG, "Communism as Related to the Spanish Problem," January 23, 1947. CREST, NARA; On May 15, for example, the State Department wrote its missions in Madrid, Paris, and Bucharest, asking for their comments on "fairly reliable" intelligence about Rumanian communists allegedly planning to join the international brigades in southern France with the objective of crossing into Spain to prepare for civil war. "A-111," May 15, 1947. Box 6235, 851.00B–851.001, RG 59, NARA.
12 "Les préoccupations actuelles des chefs communistes," February 27, 1947. Presse, 4AG/86, Auriol, AN.

13 Vincent Auriol, "Maquis Communistes," March 7, 1947, in *Journal du Septennat* (Paris: Armand Colin, 1970), 132; "Cache of Communist Arms Reported in France," March 18, 1947. Box 6232, 851.00, RG 59, NARA.

14 Harold Callender, "De Gaullists Hide Guns, Reds Charge," *NYT*, March 11, 1947, 8. ProQuest Historical Newspapers (107789541).

15 Auriol, "Complot des généraux?," March 18, 1947, 151.

16 "Paris to Secretary of State #714," February 19, 1947. Box 6235, 851.00B, RG 59, NARA.

17 "Wallner to MacArthur," January 27, 1947. Box 1, Records of the French Desk, Subject Files, RG 59, NARA.

18 "MacArthur to Wallner," February 6, 1947. Box 6235, 851.00B–851.001, RG 59, NARA. See also "Commentary on Department's Secret Instruction No. 2688," March 4, 1947. Box 3990, 751.00, RG 59, NARA.

19 CIG, "Daily Summary," February 24, 1947. CREST, NARA.

20 Intelligence Division WGDS, "Intelligence Review," February 27, 1947. Box 29, WDIR File, Naval Aide Files, HSTL.

21 Ibid.

22 Callender, "French See Perils in New U.S. Policy," *NYT*, March 14, 1947, 4. ProQuest Historical Newspapers (107702154).

23 Callender, "French Map War on Arms Caches," *NYT*, March 18, 1947, 13. ProQuest Historical Newspapers (107988428); "France Aims to Seize Hidden Arms Stocks," *WP*, March 19, 1947, 9. ProQuest Historical Newspapers (151923284).

24 "Chauvel à Massigli," March 20, 1947. *DDF 1947 Tome I* (Paris: P.I.E. Peter Lang, 2007), 541–542.

25 Intelligence Division WDGS, "Intelligence Review," March 27, 1947. Box 20, WDIR File, Naval Aide, HSTL.

26 "Caffery to the Secretary of State," March 31, 1947. *FRUS 1947 Volume III* (Washington, DC: GPO, 1972), 695–696.

27 OIR, "France's Diplomatic Position at Moscow," April 9, 1947. Intelligence Reports, M1221, RG 59, NARA.

28 "Declarations de M. William Bullitt," March 25, 1947. Dossier 95, P4704, Direction d'Amérique, MAE.

29 "Article de M. William Bullitt dans 'Life,'" May 30, 1947. P4696, Direction d'Amérique, MAE.

30 Despite his reputation as a hardliner, Byrnes in 1945 vacillated between containing and reassuring the Soviets. However, as Melvyn Leffler has pointed out, his "willingness to accommodate Soviet strategic interests was still conditioned on the Kremlin's acceptance of liberal economic and political principles." Byrnes was further criticized for making "concessions" (an unfounded charge) to the Soviets at the Moscow Conference in December 1945. Leahy was contemptuous of these efforts and tried to provide a corrective by pushing Truman toward a more hardline approach. Leffler, *A Preponderance of Power: National Security, the Truman Administration, and the Cold War* (Stanford: Stanford University Press, 1992), 40, 45–48.

31 "L'Amiral Leahy et la politique extérieure américaine," March 31, 1947. Dossier 103, P4876, Direction d'Amérique, MAE.

32 "Du nouveau Directeur d'Europe occidentale au Département d'État," April 9, 1947. Dossier 101, P4876, Direction d'Amérique, MAE.

33 "La presse américaine et le Général de Gaulle," April 18, 1947. P4696, Direction d'Amérique, MAE.

34 FBI, "French Activities," May 17, 1947. Box 6232, 851.00, RG 59, NARA.

35 "Summary of Telegrams," May 2, 1947. Box 22, State Department Briefs File, Naval Aide, HSTL.

36 French historian Annie Lacroix-Riz, in *Le Choix de Marianne*, suggests that the United States played a major role in the eviction of the PCF from the government in May 1947. She points to comments made by the US ambassador to Colombia to his French counterpart suggesting that the French should wait for disruptions that would allow them to clarify the confused situation. Furthermore, Truman and Caffery, she argues, told the French "il faut choisir," a reference, she believes, to either American aid or the PCF remaining in government (Paris: Messidor, 1985), 120–122. Irwin Wall refutes this notion. According to Wall, Ambassador Jefferson Caffery was "merely a spectator" rather than an instigator of the expulsion. *The United States and the Making of Postwar France*, 67–71.

37 Intelligence Division WDGS, "Intelligence Review," May 8, 1947. Box 20, WDIR File, Naval Aide, HSTL.

38 "Caffery to Secretary of State #1927," May 12, 1947. *FRUS 1947 Volume III*, 709–713.

39 Intelligence Division WDGS, "Intelligence Review," January 23, 1947. Box 19, WDIR File, Naval Aide Files, HSTL.

40 Intelligence Division WDGS, "Intelligence Review," May 15, 1947. Box 20, WDIR File, Naval Aide, HSTL.

41 Wall argues that PCF officials were surprised by their expulsion; they thought that the government would have to resign unless Ramadier retreated from his position on the wage issue. *French Communism in the Era of Stalin*, 56. Buton maintains that the PCF had decided to break with the Ramadier government but not with the idea of governmental participation. They hoped to precipitate a crisis, and to demand that Ramadier's successor give them one of the key ministerial posts, which had been refused them. *Les Lendemains*, 302.

42 "L'Activité du Parti Communiste," May 23, 1947. Partis Politiques – PCF, 4AG/85 Auriol, AN.

43 "Les Soviets désapprouve la maladresse dont firent preuve les communistes," June 3, 1947. Casanova, Partis Politiques – PCF 4AG/85, Auriol, AN.

44 "Marshall to AMREP Bucharest," May 15, 1947. Box 6235, 851.00B, RG 59, NARA.

45 Roscoe Hillenkoetter, "Memorandum for the President," June 6, 1947. CREST, NARA.

46 M. W. Fodor, "Uprising by Reds in Athens Likely from the Evidence," *WP*, June 14, 1947, 4. ProQuest Historical Newspapers (151935747).

47 "Caffery to Secretary of State," June 29, 1947. Box 6235, 851.00B–851.001, RG 59, NARA.

48 Joseph and Stewart Alsop, "Matter of Fact: The Politburo's Choice," *WP*, July 7, 1947, 9. ProQuest Historical Newspapers (151907645).

49 George Barrett, "U.N. Team Finds Little Evidence of 'International Brigade' in Greece," July 19, 1947, 1; "Britain Sifting Reports of 'International Brigades,'" July 16, 1947, 2; "Denials Made in France," *NYT*, June 3, 1947, 5. www.proquest.com

50 "Constitution de nouvelles brigades internationales," July 21, 1947. 4AG/85, Auriol, AN.

51 "French Minimize Greek Recruiting," *NYT*, July 22, 1947, 10. ProQuest Historical Newspapers (107872738).

52 "Récents articles sur la France et modification de l'attitude de la presse soviétique à notre égard," June 5, 1947. Dossier 52, P16879, URSS, Direction d'Europe, MAE.

53 Wall, 67–68.

54 Truman himself later said that the Truman Doctrine and the Marshall Plan were "two halves of the same walnut." Arnold Offner, *Another Such Victory: President Truman and the Cold War, 1945–1953* (Stanford: Stanford University Press, 2002), 185.

55 "Caffery to Secretary of State #2505," June 24, 1947. Box 6232, 851.00, RG 59, NARA.

56 "Memorandum for the President," June 6, 1947. DDRS. http://gdc.galegroup.com.proxyau.wrlc.org/gdc/artemis/?p=USDD&u=wash11212.

57 "Réactions des milieux diplomatiques américains sur les conflits sociaux en France," June 14, 1947. Dossier 120, P4712, Direction d'Amérique, MAE.

58 "Ramadier's Government Begins to Crack," June 25, 1947. Box 6232, 851.00. RG 59, NARA.

59 "Possible Eventualities of a Government Crisis in France," June 27, 1947. Box 1, Subject Files, Office of Western European Affairs/French Desk, RG 59, NARA.

60 "Possible Developments of Prospective French Political Crisis and Its Effect on U.S. Foreign Policy," June 28, 1947. Box 6232, 851.00, RG 59, NARA.

61 Wall, 81 and 103–105.

62 Lawrence, 158.

63 "Diplomatic Agent at Tangier to Secretary of State #488," January 13, 1947. *FRUS 1947 Volume V* (Washington: GPO, 1971), 669–671.

64 "The Diplomatic Agent at Tangier to Secretary of State," January 30, 1947. *FRUS 1947 Volume V*, 673–674.

65 "Consul at Saigon to Secretary of State," *FRUS 1948 Volume VI*, 75–76.

66 CIG, "Indo-Chinese Attempting to Come to the US," January 10, 1947. Circulated April 2, 1947. CREST, NARA.

67 "A.S. des activités du Parti Communiste Chinois en Indochine du Sud," January 21, 1947. Dossier 174, Indochine, Direction d'Asie-Océanie, MAE; "Note pour le Ministre des Affaires Étrangères," April 22, 1947. Dossier 168, Indochine, Direction d'Asie-Océanie, MAE.

68 "A.S. Habib Bourguiba," January 29, 1947. Dossier 124, P4713, Direction d'Amérique, MAE.

69 "Extraits d'un rapport de l'année 1947," n.d. Dossier 6, Algérie, Direction d'Afrique-Levant, MAE.

70 "Note sur les activités américaines en Indochine," February 18, 1947. Dossier 255, P10396, Indochine, Direction d'Asie-Océanie, MAE.

71 "Caffery to Secretary of State #1719," April 25, 1947. Box 6235, 851.00B–851.001, RG 59, NARA.
72 "Secretary of State to Embassy in France," May 13, 1947. *FRUS 1947 Volume VI*, 95–97.
73 "Secretary of State to Embassy in France," June 10, 1947. *FRUS 1947 Volume V*, 686–689.
74 Frederic L. Propas, "Creating a Hard Line toward Russia: The Training of State Department Soviet Experts 1927–1937," *Diplomatic History* 8, no. 3 (Summer 1984): 222–226.
75 "Colonial Policy of the French Communist Party," May 16, 1947. Box 6235, 851.00B–851.001, RG 59, NARA.
76 CIG, "Annamite–Russian Relations," April 17, 1947. Box 6648, 861.20, RG 59, NARA.
77 "Marshall to Paris," May 27, 1947. Box 6648, 861.20, RG 59, NARA.
78 "The Consul at Saigon to Secretary of State #260," June 24, 1947. *FRUS 1947 Volume VI*, 106–107.
79 CIG, "Daily Summary," July 2, 1947. CREST, NARA.
80 "French Report Revolution Plot Thwarted," *WP*, July 1, 1947, 1. ProQuest Historical Newspapers (151908709).
81 "Caffery to Secretary of State #2730," July 9, 1947. Box 6232, 851.00, RG 59, NARA.
82 "French Report Revolution Plot Thwarted," *WP*, July 1, 1947, 1. ProQuest Historical Newspapers (151908709). For more about Plan Bleu, see Girard, "Le Plan Bleu," in *Complots et conspirations. En France du XVIIIe au XXe siècle*, ed. Fréderic Monier (Valenciennes: Presses Universitaires de Valenciennes, 2003), 119–138; Elie Tenenbaum, "Une odyssée subversive" (PhD diss., Sciences Po, 2015).
83 Loustaunau-Lacau defended himself against these charges in his memoirs, *Mémoires d'un Français Rebelle* (Paris: R. Laffont, 1948), 344. He had "no idea if ... de Vulpian had taken part in pernicious activity or if he had recruited men or stocked arms," but claimed to have been a victim "of arbitrary measures for which the communist party and certain members of the socialist party bear responsibility."
84 "Swift Move in France Ends Plot by Right," *Argus*, July 1, 1947, 1.
85 Auriol, "Complots," July 2, 1947.
86 Girard, "Le Plan Bleu," 123–124, 131, 137.
87 Marie-Catherine Villatoux, "Les militaires français et la menace de subversion," in *Subversion, anti-subversion, contre-subversion*, eds. François Cochet and Oliver Dard (Paris: Riveneuve éditions, 2009), 67–68.
88 Girard, "Le Plan Bleu," 123–124, 131, 137.
89 It is possible that Fajon was referring to a widely believed myth circulating in French rightist circles (and within US intelligence organizations) about the postwar existence of the "Red Orchestra," an anti-Nazi espionage network that operated in Germany and occupied Europe during the Second World War. Former Nazi officials recruited into the postwar Gehlen Organization for their anti-Soviet expertise claimed that a Red Orchestra network still operated in France after the war. Richard Breitman et al., *U.S. Intelligence and the*

Nazis (Cambridge: Cambridge University Press, 2005), 306–307. It is also possible however, that Fajon's reference here to "a secret orchestra" was a more general allusion to pervasive beliefs about revolutionary networks and communist plots to seize power in France.

90 "La situation et l'activité du parti communiste," July 7, 1947. Partis Politiques PCF 4AG/85, Auriol, AN.

91 "Une émission tendancieuse de la radio soviétique," July 7, 1947. Dossier 52, P16879, Direction d'Europe, MAE.

92 "Memorandum by the Director of the Office of European Affairs to the Under Secretary of State," July 11, 1947. *FRUS 1947 Volume III*, 717–722. "Second Secretary of Embassy of France to Associate Chief of Division of Western European Affairs," October 10, 1947. *FRUS 1947 Volume III*, 766–772.

93 CIG, "Daily Summary," July 14, 1947. CREST, NARA.

94 CIG, "Daily Summary," July 18, 1947. CREST, NARA.

95 CIG, "Daily Summary," August 1, 1947. CREST, NARA.

96 CIG, "Daily Summary," August 2, 1947. CREST, NARA.

97 CIG, "Daily Summary," August 7 and 9, 1947. CREST, NARA.

98 See, for example, "Secretary of State to Officer in Charge American Mission Paris," September 24, 1947. Box 6648, 861.00, RG 59, NARA.

99 "Secretary of State to Officer in Charge of American Mission, Paris," August 6, 1947. Box 6648, 861.20, RG 59, NARA.

100 "Caffery to Secretary of State #3155," August 7, 1947. Box 6235, 851.00B, RG 59, NARA.

101 "Le Parti Communiste transforme-t-il actuellement ses groupements de base en 'troupes de choc?'," September 3, 1947. Partis Politiques PCF 4AG/86, Auriol, AN.

102 Auriol, "Les brigades internationales," October 22, 1947, and "Nouvelles Brigades internationales et stratégie soviétique," November 6, 1947.

103 Ibid.

104 Little is known about Soviet espionage and covert action in France during this period. The Mitrokhin Archive includes some revelations, including Soviet penetration of some French intelligence agencies and recruitment of friendly cipher clerks in the Foreign Office after the war, but agent recruitment slowed after the expulsion of the PCF in 1947. The KGB's Paris Residency also promoted active measures to influence western opinion, including disseminating fake memoirs and propaganda, and controlling certain newspapers. The archive also suggests that communist arms caches did exist in most countries of Western Europe but gives no specific date ranges, countries, or anticipated use, other than for "illegals." Christopher Andrew and Vasili Mitrokhin, *The Mitrokhin Archive: The KGB in Europe and the West* (London: Penguin, 1999), 360, 459, 482–484, 621.

105 "Lovett to Amembassy Paris," August 19, 1947. Box 6235, 851.00B, RG 59, NARA.

106 "Caffery to Secretary of State," August 26, 1947. Box 6235, 851.00B, RG 59, NARA.

107 "Caffery to Secretary of State," August 30, 1947. *FRUS 1947 Volume III*, 730–732. CIG, "Daily Summary," September 8, 1947. CREST, NARA.

108 "Memorandum for the President," September 3, 1947. Box 21, Chairman's File – Leahy, RG 218, NARA.

109 "Caffery to Secretary of State," September 13, 1947. *FRUS 1947 Volume III*, 749–750.

110 CIG, "Daily Summary," September 20 and 23, 1947. CREST, NARA.

111 "Improvement of US Counter-Communist Activities in France," September 8, 1947. Box 6235, 851.00B, RG 59, NARA.

112 "Caffery to Secretary of State," September 25, 1947. *FRUS 1947 Volume III*, 759–761.

113 CIA, "Review of the World Situation as It Relates to the Security of the United States CIA 1," September 26, 1947. CREST, NARA.

114 "September 29, 1947," Box 6–8 1947, Leahy Dairy, LOC.

115 "Caffery to Secretary of State," September 30, 1947. *FRUS 1947 Volume III*, 761–762.

116 "Caffery to the Secretary of State #4246," October 1, 1947. Box 6235, 851.00B, RG 59, NARA.

117 "Additional Information Regarding Communists in Marseille," October 1, 1947. Box 6235, 851.00B, RG 59, NARA.

118 "Caffery to Secretary of State #4085," September 20, 1947. Box 6235, 851.00B, RG 59, NARA.

119 "Caffery to Secretary of State #4313," October 5, 1947. Box 19, Chairman's File – Leahy, RG 218, NARA.

120 "Cannon to Secretary of State #2057," October 6, 1947. Box 19, Chairman's File – Leahy, RG 218, NARA.

121 "Griffis to Secretary of State #1618/1619," October 6 and 7, 1947. Box 19, Chairman's File – Leahy, RG 218, NARA.

122 "Caffery to Secretary of State #4323," October 7, 1947. Box 18, Chairman's File – Leahy, RG 218, NARA.

123 "Bonnet à Bidault," October 6, 1947. *DDF 1947 Tome II* (Bruxelles: P.I.E. Peter Lang, 2009), 497–499.

124 "Charpentier à Bidault," October 7, 1947. *DDF 1947 Tome II*, 505–507.

125 "Payart à Bidault," October 9, 1947. *DDF 1947 Tome II*, 517–519.

126 "Conséquences internationales de la déclaration des 9," October 13, 1947. Notes d'information 4AG/104, Auriol, AN.

127 "Memorandum for the President," October 10, 1947. Box 19, Chairman's File – Leahy, RG 218, NARA.

128 CIG, "Daily Summary," October 18, 1947. CREST, NARA.

129 Anna di Biago, "The Establishment of the Cominform," in *The Cominform: Minutes of the Three Conferences 1947/1948/1949*, ed. Giuliano Procacci (Milano: Fondazione Giangiacomo Feltrinelli, 1994), 16–22.

130 "Minutes of the First Conference," in *The Cominform*, 335–351.

131 See, for example, Buton, and Lazar and Courtois.

132 "Speech of Maurice Thorez to French Communist Party in Marseille," October 13, 1947. Box 6235, 851.00B, RG 59, NARA.

133 "Alleged Parachuting of Arms in NANCY Region," October 14, 1947. #407220, Army Intelligence Document File (hereafter AIDF), RG 319, NARA.

134 "Reported Eye-Witnessing of Parachuting into FRANCE for Communists," October 20, 1947. #407522, AIDF, RG 319, NARA.

135 "Bonnet à MAE," October 22, 1947. P4696, Direction d'Amérique, MAE.

136 "General de Gaulle and Your Press Conference," October 22, 1947. Box 2, Records of the French Desk, Subject Files, RG 59, NARA.

137 CIG, "Daily Summary," October 25, 1947. CREST, NARA.

138 CIG, "Daily Summary," October 22, 1947. CREST, NARA.

139 CIG, "Daily Summary," October 23, 1947. CREST, NARA. Here "resistance" implies opposition to a Soviet offensive in France and any potential communist occupation regime.

140 "Lyon to Hickerson," October 22, 1947. Box 6235, 851.00B, RG 59, NARA.

141 "Communist use of CGT to Penetrate Prefects and Police Force in Departments of Southwestern France," October 29, 1947. Box 6235, 851.00B, RG 59, NARA.

142 "Activité clandestine du Parti Communiste," October 24, 1947. Partis Politiques PCF 4AG/85, Auriol, AN.

143 "A.S. du Parti Communiste," October 27, 1947. Partis Politiques PCF 4AG/86, Auriol, AN.

144 "Réactions américaines aux élections municipales en France," October 27, 1947. P4712, Direction d'Amérique, MAE.

145 "Caffery to Secretary of State," October 30, 1947. *FRUS 1947 Volume III*, 795–797.

146 Wall, *French Communism in the Era of Stalin*, 63–64.

147 "Caffery to Secretary of State #A1135," July 1, 1947. Box 6238, 851.00, RG 59, NARA.

148 "Haussaire Saigon à Cominindo Paris," July 9, 1947. Dossier 255, P10396, Indochine, Direction d'Asie-Océanie, MAE.

149 "The Vice Consul in Hanoi to Secretary of State," July 3, 1947. *FRUS 1947 Volume VI*, 108–109.

150 "The Vice Consul in Hanoi to Secretary of State," July 19, 1947. *FRUS 1947 Volume VI*, 120–121.

151 "Political Information: The Viet Nam Government," July 29, 1947. CREST, NARA.

152 "Fragment of Textbook Used in Viet Mint Secret Communist School," September 3, 1947. CREST, NARA.

153 "Traduction de photocopies de documents saisis par un agent de l'Intelligence Service des USA, au siège du Comité Exécutif d'une cellule spéciale du V.M. à Hanoi," August 4, 1947. Dossier 161, Indochine, Direction d'Asie-Océanie, MAE.

154 "Rôle des communistes dans la lutte actuelle en Indochine," September 2, 1947. Dossier 174, Indochine, Direction d'Asie-Océanie, MAE.

155 "Caffery to Secretary of State," July 31, 1947. *FRUS 1947 Volume VI*, 127–128.

156 "Minutes of the First Conference," 261.

157 "Indochina: New French Offer to Vietnam," September 24, 1947; "Abbott to Wallner," October 9, 1947. Box 2, Records of the French Desk, Subject Files, RG 59, NARA.

158 "Étude sur les activités américaines en Indochine," October 30, 1947. Dossier 128, P4714, Direction d'Amérique, MAE.

159 "Bonnet à Bidault," July 5, 1947. *DDF 1947 Tome II*, 76–78.

160 "État de l'opinion américaine à l'égard de l'Union Française," July 7, 1947. Dossier 106, P4708, Direction d'Amérique, MAE. Bonnet here was referring to the American belief that in Soviet hands, North Africa could be the most important base for operations against Europe.

161 "Relations destouro-communistes," September 11, 1947. Dosser 47, P4027, Tunisie, Direction d'Afrique-Levant, MAE.

162 "Hickerson to Henderson" and Henderson cover note, October 7, 1947. Box 3989, 751.00, RG 59, NARA.

163 "Dumont to Secretary of State," October 15, 1947. *FRUS 1947 Volume VI*, 720–726.

164 "Caffery to Secretary of State #4689," November 1, 1947. Box 3990, 751.00, RG 59, NARA.

165 "Caffery to Secretary of State," November 3, 1947. *FRUS 1947 Volume III*, 797–798; "Caffery to Secretary of State #4800," November 8, 1947. Box 6235, 851.00B, RG 59, NARA.

166 "Resume of the World Situation," November 7, 1947. *Volume 6*, 238–244, GCMP.

167 CIA, "Review of the World Situation," November 14, 1947. CREST, NARA.

168 "Communist Inspired Riots and Disorders in Marseille," November 13, 1947. Box 6232, 851.00, RG 59, NARA.

169 "Activité clandestine du P.C.," November 12, 1947. Partis Politiques 4AG/86, Auriol, AN.

170 "Consignes données par le parti communiste et à appliquer sur le plan local en cas de troubles," November 13, 1947. Partis Politiques 4AG/86, Auriol, AN.

171 "Big Arms Cache Found in the South of France," *NYT*, November 22, 1947, 6. ProQuest Historical Newspapers (108030772); "Trois dépôts d'armes découvertes en quinze jours," *Le Monde*, November 24, 1947. www .lemonde.fr/recherche/.

172 "L'U.R.S.S. et les perspectives de guerre," November 17, 1947. Dossier 24, URSS, Direction d'Europe, MAE.

173 French Interior Minister Jules Moch later wrote that the strikes of 1947 (unlike 1948) were a response to real concerns about worker salaries, not an attempt to seize power. *Une si longue vie*, 340.

174 "L'URSS et la guerre," November 19, 1947. Dosser 34, URSS, Direction d'Europe, MAE.

175 Leahy, "Diary," November 22, 1947. Boxes 6–8, Leahy Papers, LOC.

176 "Evolution of Recent Government Crisis," November 25, 1947. Box 6232, 851.00, RG 59, NARA.

177 "Summary of Telegrams," November 28, 1947. Box 22, State Department Briefs File, Naval Aide File, HSTL.
178 "Les milieu communistes et l'éventualité d'un coup de force," November 28, 1947. Agitation Sociale, Partis Politiques PCF 4AG/86, Auriol, AN.
179 "M. de Beausse à M. Bidault," November 27, 1947. *DDF 1947 Tome II*, 773.
180 "Note 3," November 27, 1947. *DDF 1947 Tome II*, 773.
181 "Caffery to Secretary of State #5125," November 29, 1947. France Subject File, Naval Aide File, HSTL.
182 CIA, "Daily Summary," December 1, 1947. CREST, NARA.
183 "Bonnet à MAE," Dossier 120, P4712, Direction d'Amérique, MAE.
184 Ibid.
185 "Douglas to Secretary of State," December 2, 1947. *FRUS 1947 Volume III*, 807–808.
186 "Caffery to Secretary of State #5164," December 2, 1947. Box 6235, 851.00B, RG 59, NARA.
187 CIA, "Daily Summary," December 3, 1947. CREST, NARA.
188 "Caffery to Secretary of State," December 5, 1947. *FRUS 1947 Volume III*, 813–814.
189 "Réunion du groupe parlementaire communiste le 5 décembre," December 6, 1947. Thorez, Partis Politiques PCF 4AG/85, Auriol, AN.
190 "M. Maurice Thorez est-il allé à Sotchi?" December 7, 1947. Thorez, Partis Politiques PCF 4AG/85, Auriol, AN.
191 "Politique soviétique en Europe occidentale," December 16, 1947. Dossier 34, URSS, Direction d'Europe, MAE.
192 "Wallner to Knight," December 15, 1947. Box 1, Records of the French Desk, Subject Files, RG 59, NARA.
193 CIA, "Daily Summary," December 17, 1497. CREST, NARA.
194 "Caffery to Secretary of State," December 3, 1947. *FRUS 1947 Volume III*, 810–811.
195 "Caffery to Secretary of State # 5374," December 13, 1947. Box 3990, 751.00, RG 59, NARA.
196 "Comments of Mr. Jules Moch, Minister of the Interior, on the French food situation and information volunteered by him on activities of the Communist Party," December 17, 1947. Box 6232, 851.00, RG 59, NARA.
197 "Bonnet à Bidault," December 16, 1947. *DDF 1947 Tome II*, 911.
198 Ibid.
199 "Report Concerning Renewed Wave of Communist Violence," December 17, 1947. Box 6235, 851.00B, RG 59, NARA.
200 CIA, "Review of the World Situation," December 17, 1947. CREST, NARA.
201 "Communist Plans for the Attack on France," December 17, 1947. CREST, NARA.
202 "Si l'URSS s'emparait de l'Europe," December 19, 1947. Dossier 32, États-Unis, Cabinet du Bidault, MAE.
203 CIA, "Daily Summary," December 22, 1947. CREST, NARA.
204 CIA, "Daily Summary," December 27, 1947. CREST, NARA.
205 CIA, "ORE 64: The Current Situation in France," December 31, 1947. DDRS.

206 CIA, "CIA 2: Review of the World Situation," November 14, 1947. CREST, NARA.
207 CIA, "CIA 3: Review of the World Situation," December 17, 1947. CREST, NARA.
208 CIA, "ORE 63: The Current Situation in French North Africa," December 18, 1947. Intelligence File, PSF, HSTL.
209 Ibid.
210 "M. Garreau à Bidault," November 18, 1947. *DDF 1947 Tome II*, 732–738.
211 Allison Drew, *We Are No Longer in France: Communists in Colonial Algeria* (Manchester: Manchester University Press, 2014), 163.

Conclusion

1 Bogotá was the site of a Pan-American Conference, attended by Secretary of State George Marshall. Riots broke out after the murder of Colombian Liberal politician Jorge Eliecer Gaitán, plunging Colombia into a period of civil war known as La Violencia.
2 A newspaper of the American Communist Party.
3 Hanson Baldwin, "Intelligence – II: Older Agencies Resent a Successor and Try to Restrict Scope of Action," July 22, 1948. *NYT*, found in CIA files. CREST, NARA.
4 Hanson Baldwin, "Intelligence – III: Errors in Collecting Data Held Exceeded by Evaluation Weakness," July 23, 1948. *NYT*, found in CIA files. CREST, NARA.
5 "Denials Made in France," *NYT*, June 3, 1947, 5. ProQuest Historical Newspapers (107939499).
6 "Britain Sifting Reports of 'International Brigade,'" *NYT*, July 16, 1947, 2. ProQuest Historical Newspapers (107745917).
7 "The Cominform: September 1947–April 1948," n.d. CREST, NARA.
8 CIA, "Daily Summary," March 13, 1948. CREST, NARA.
9 "Resume of Private Conversation with the Prefect of the Rhone Regarding Communism in France," April 20, 1948. Box 6235, 851.00B, RG 59, NARA.
10 Alvarez and Mark, 64 and 274.
11 "L'intervention des gendarmes aurait fait échouer une tentative de parachutage," *Le Monde*, January 17, 1948. www.lemonde.fr/recherche/.
12 "Fausses rumeurs et vrais périls," *Le Monde*, January 20, 1948. www.lemonde.fr/recherche/.
13 "Arms for Zionists Captured in Paris," *NYT*, March 7, 1948, 2. ProQuest Historical Newspapers (108321780).
14 "French Police Raid Believed to Have Blocked Illegal Arms," *WP*, January 17, 1948, 3. ProQuest Historical Newspapers (152024037).
15 "The Cominform," n.d.
16 Ibid.
17 James Bruce, "Making Analysis More Reliable: Why Epistemology Matters in Intelligence," in George and Bruce, eds. *Analyzing Intelligence*, 182. Here

Bruce refers to intelligence in the case for Iraqi Weapons of Mass Destruction (WMD) in 2002–2003. However, his point about assessing all information, either as supportive of or undermining a particular hypothesis, applies to the French case as well.

18 CIA, "Coordination and Control of the International Communist Movement," November 1948. CREST, NARA.

19 di Biago, "The Establishment of the Cominform," 16–24.

20 "Minutes of the First Conference," 335.

21 Ibid., 261.

22 For an excellent examination of intelligence analysis and tradecraft, see Roger Z. George and James B. Bruce, eds. *Analyzing Intelligence: Origins, Obstacles, and Innovations* (Washington, DC: Georgetown University Press, 2008).

23 These contacts also reportedly included Roger Wybot of the French DST and French military intelligence. Balace, "Le 'réseau Dr. Martin' en Belgique 1945–1948 de la contre-subversion à l'intoxication," in *Subversion, anti-subversion, contre-subversion*, eds. François Cochet and Olivier Dard (Paris: Riveneuve éditions, 2009), 185.

24 Balace, 178–179.

25 "Penetration of Communist Parties: Preliminary Brief," October 14, 1946. CREST.

26 "A.S. de l'utilisation de certains membres du S.R.A. par les services spéciaux américains," September 22, 1947. E.U. Notes d'information, 4AG/105, Auriol, AN.

27 CIA, "Problems in Inter-Agency Coordination of Reports and Estimates to 1949," n.d. CREST, NARA.

28 CIA, "ORE 64: The Current Situation in France," December 31, 1947. Found in Intelligence Files, PSF, HSTL.

29 CIA, "Problems in Inter-Agency Coordination."

30 CIA, "ORE Monthly Report," March 1948. CREST, NARA.

31 See Robert Mencherini, *Guerre froid, guerre rouge. Pari communiste, Stalinisme, et luttes sociales en France, les grèves 'insurrectionnelles' de 1947–1948* (Paris: Editions Syllepse, 1998), 101–102. Some French intelligence reports suggested that PCF leaders hoped for a quick return to the government and continued to indicate to supporters that they would remain a party of government. "Activité du parti communiste," May 23, 1947. Partis Politiques – PCF 4AG/85, Auriol, AN. Subsequent reports suggested the Soviets encouraged PCF leaders to ensure their return to the government. "Par la voix de M. Molotov, les Soviets désapprouvent la maladresse dont firent preuve les communistes à l'occasion du dernier remaniement ministériel," June 3, 1947. Parti Politiques PCF 4AG/85, Auriol, AN.

32 Pillar, *Intelligence and U.S. Foreign Policy*, 5–6, 96.

33 "Article de M. William Bullitt dans *Life*," May 30, 1947. P4696, Presse, Direction d'Amérique, MAE; "Attitude des États-Unis à l'égard de la France," August 7, 1946. Dossier 119, P4712, Politique Extérieure, Direction d'Amérique, MAE.

34 "L'URSS et les perspectives de guerre," November 17, 1947. Dossier 34, Politique Extérieure URSS, Direction d'Europe, MAE.

35 Maxwell Aderath, *The French Communist Party: A Critical History (1920–1984) – From Comintern to the Colours of France* (Manchester: Manchester University Press, 1984), 152.
36 Sherman Kent, *The Intelligence Process* (Princeton: Princeton University Press, 1949), 23–24. Found in CREST, NARA.
37 Ibid.
38 Christopher Andrew, *The Secret World: A History of Intelligence* (New Haven: Yale University Press, 2018), 737–738.
39 Ibid., 736.
40 Senate Select Committee on Intelligence (SSCI), Iraq Report (2004), 18, as quoted in ibid., 740.
41 As quoted in ibid., 741.

Bibliography

Archives

United States

Clemson University
    Walter J. Brown Papers
    James F. Byrnes Papers
Franklin Delano Roosevelt Presidential Library
    Naval Aide's Files
Harry S. Truman Presidential Library
    Clark Clifford Papers
    Files Names for Offices
    President's Secretary Files
    White House Central Files
Library of Congress
    Admiral William D. Leahy Papers
    Averell Harriman Papers
    Charles E. Bohlen Papers
    Clark M. Clifford Papers
National Archives and Records Administration (NARA)
    CIA Records Search Tool (CREST)
    RG 59 State Department Central Files
    RG 84 State Department Foreign Service Posts
    RG 218 U.S. Joint Chiefs of Staff
    RG 226 Office of Strategic Services
    RG 263 Central Intelligence Agency
    RG 319 Army Staff
    RG 457 National Security Agency
University of Louisiana at Lafayette
    Jefferson Caffery Papers
Virginia Military Institute
    George C. Marshall Papers

France

Archives Nationales (Pierrefitte)
  Archives de la Présidence de la République (Auriol)
    Notes d'Information Europe
    Notes d'Information Indochine et EU
    Partis Politiques PCF
  Archives du General de Gaulle
    France Libérée
    Grand Bretagne
    Politique Internationale
    Questions Coloniales
    URSS
  Archives du Gouvernement Provisoire de République Française (1944–1946)
    Affaires Étrangères
    Afrique du Nord
    Algérie
    Canada/EU
    Colonies
    Éthiopie-Italie
    Intérieur
    Levant
    Maroc et Tunisie
    URSS
  Papiers René Pleven

Archives Diplomatique (La Courneuve)
  Cabinet du Ministre (Georges Bidault 1944–1948)
    Dossiers par pays
      Algérie, Maroc, Tunisie
      États-Unis
      France-Algérie
      Indochine/Siam
      URSS
  Cabinet du Robert Schuman (1948–1953)
    Dossiers par pays
      Afrique-Levant
      France
      Indochine
      URSS
  Direction d'Amérique
    Défense Nationale
    Politique Extérieure
    Politique Intérieure
    Presse
  Direction d'Afrique-Levant
    Algérie, 1944–1959

Maroc, 1944–1955
Syrie-Liban, 1944–1952
Tunisie, 1944–1959
Direction d'Asie-Océanie
    Indochine
        Politique Extérieure
        Politique Intérieure
Direction d'Europe
    URSS, 1944–1959
        Politique Extérieure

Published Documents

Foreign Relations of the United States 1944 Volume III. Washington, DC: U.S. General Printing Office, 1965.

Foreign Relations of the United States 1945 Volume I. Washington, DC: U.S. General Printing Office, 1967.

Foreign Relations of the United States 1945 Volume IV. Washington, DC: U.S. General Printing Office, 1968.

Foreign Relations of the United States 1945 Volume VI. Washington, DC: U.S. General Printing Office, 1969.

Foreign Relations of the United States 1945 Volume VIII. Washington, DC: U.S. General Printing Office, 1969.

Foreign Relations of the United States 1946 Volume V. Washington, DC: U.S. General Printing Office, 1969.

Foreign Relations of the United States 1946 Volume VIII. Washington, DC: U.S. General Printing Office, 1971.

Foreign Relations of the United States 1947 Volume III. Washington, DC: U.S. General Printing Office, 1972.

Foreign Relations of the United States 1947 Volume V. Washington, DC: U.S. General Printing Office, 1971.

Foreign Relations of the United States 1947 Volume VI. Washington, DC: U.S. General Printing Office, 1972.

Foreign Relations of the United States 1948 Volume VI. Washington, DC: U.S. General Printing Office, 1975.

Documents diplomatiques français 1945 Tome I. Bruxelles: P.I.E Peter Lang, 2003.

Documents diplomatiques français 1945 Tome II. Bruxelles: P.I.E Peter Lang, 2003.

Documents diplomatiques français 1946 Tome I. Bruxelles: P.I.E Peter Lang, 2003.

Documents diplomatiques français 1946 Tome II. Bruxelles: P.I.E Peter Lang, 2004.

Documents diplomatiques français 1947 Tome I. Bruxelles: P.I.E. Peter Lang, 2007.

Documents diplomatiques français 1947 Tome II. Bruxelles: P.I.E. Peter Lang, 2009.

The Cominform: Minutes of the Three Conferences of 1947/1948/1949, edited by Giuliano Procacci Milano. Fondazione Giangiacomo Feltrinelli, 1994.

Warner, Michael, ed. *The CIA under Harry Truman*. Honolulu: University Press of the Pacific, 2005.

Newspapers and Magazines (various dates)

Argus
Chicago Tribune
Fortune
L'Humanité
Le Monde
Le Monde diplomatique
Life
Look
Newsweek
The New York Times
The Saturday Evening Post
The Times of London
The Washington Post

Articles and Book Chapters

Aldrich, Richard. "British Intelligence and the Anglo-American 'Special Relationship' during the Cold War." *Review of International Studies* 24, no. 3 (July 1998): 331–351.

Barnes, Trevor. "The Secret Cold War: The CIA and American Foreign Policy in Europe, 1946–1956. Part 1." *The Historical Journal* 24, no. 2 (June 1981): 399–415.

"The Secret Cold War: The CIA and American Foreign Policy in Europe, 1946–1956. Part 2." *The Historical Journal* 25, no. 3 (September 1982): 649–670.

Balace, Francis. "Le 'réseau Dr. Martin' en Belgique 1945–1948 de la contre-subversion à l'intoxication." In *Subversion, anti-subversion, contre-subversion*, edited by François Cochet and Olivier Dard, 165–186. Paris: Riveneuve éditions, 2009.

Bruce, James B. "Making Analysis More Reliable: Why Epistemology Matters in Intelligence." In *Analyzing Intelligence: Origins, Obstacles, and Innovations*, edited by Roger Z. George and James B. Bruce, 171–190. Washington, DC: Georgetown University Press, 2008.

Bruce, James B. and Roger Z. George. "Introduction: Intelligence Analysis – The Emergence of a Discipline." In *Analyzing Intelligence: Origins, Obstacles, and Innovations*, edited by Roger Z. George and James B. Bruce, 1–15. Washington, DC: Georgetown University Press, 2008.

Central Intelligence Agency. "The OSS in Asia." www.cia.gov/library/publica
tions/intelligence-history/oss/art09.htm.

Chipman, Fanny. "Interview." The Association for Diplomatic Studies and Training,
July 22, 1987. https://adst.org/wp-content/uploads/2013/12/Chipman-Fanny-S
.pdf.

Costigliola, Frank. "After Roosevelt's Death: Dangerous Emotions, Divisive
Discourses, and the Abandoned Alliance." *Diplomatic History* 34, no. 1
(January 2010): 1–23.

"'Unceasing Pressure for Penetration': Gender, Pathology, and Emotion in
George Kennan's Formation of the Cold War." *The Journal of American
History* 83, no. 4 (March 1997): 1309–1339.

Creswell, Michael and Marc Tractenberg. "France and the German Question,
1945–1955." *Journal of Cold War Studies* 5, no. 3 (2003): 5–28.

D'Almeida, Fabrice. "L'Américanisation de la propagande en Europe de l'ouest."
Vingtième Siècle Revue Histoire 4, no. 80 (October–December 2003): 5–14.

Di Biago, Anna. "The Establishment of the Cominform." In *The
Cominform: Minutes of the Three Conferences 1947/1948/1949*, edited by
Giuliano Procacci, 11–34. Milano: Fondazione Giangiacomo Feltrinelli, 1994.

Dittmer, Jason. "Everyday Diplomacy: UKUSA Intelligence Cooperation and
Geopolitical Assemblages." *Annals of the Association of American
Geographers* 105, no. 3 (2015): 604–619.

Elliott, Mark. "The Soviet Repatriation Campaign." In *The Refugee Experience:
Ukrainian Displaced Persons after World War II*, edited by Wsevold W.
Isajiw, Yury Boshyk, and Roman Senkus, 341–359. Edmonton: Canadian
Institute of Ukrainian Studies Press, 1992.

Eustace, Nicole, Eugenia Lean, Julie Livingston, Jan Plamper, William M. Reddy,
and Barbara H. Rosenwein. "'AHR' Conversation: The Historical Study of
Emotions." *American Historical Review* 117, no. 5 (December 2012):
1486–1531.

Ferris, John. "Coming in from the Cold War: The Historiography of American
Intelligence, 1945–1990." In *America and the World: The Historiography of
American Foreign Relations Since 1941*, edited by Michael J. Hogan,
562–598. Cambridge: Cambridge University Press, 1995.

Forbush, Ramsey, Gary Chase, and Ronald Goldberg, "CIA Intelligence Support
for Foreign and National Security Policy Making." *Studies in Intelligence*
(Spring 1976).

Garthoff, Raymond L. "Foreign Intelligence and the Historiography of the Cold
War." *Journal of Cold War Studies* 6, no. 2 (Spring 2004): 21–56.

Gellner, Ernest. "The Sociology of Robert Montagne, 1983–1954," *Daedalus*
105, no. 1 (Winter 1976): 137–150.

Girard, Pascal. "Le Plan Bleu." In *Complots et conspirations. En France du
XVIIIe au XXe siècle*, edited by Fréderic Monier, 119–138. Valenciennes:
Presses Universitaires de Valenciennes, 2003.

Hilsman Jr., Roger. "Intelligence and Policy-Making in Foreign Affairs." *World
Politics* 5, no. 1 (October 1952): 1–45.

Hughes, Gwilym. "Intelligence in the Cold War." *Intelligence and National
Security* 26, no. 6 (2011): 755–758.

Immerman, Richard. "Intelligence and Strategy: Historicizing Psychology, Policy, and Politics." *Diplomatic History* 32, no. 1 (2008): 1–23.

Jackson, Peter. "Intelligence and the State: An Emerging 'French School' of Intelligence Studies," *Intelligence and National Security* 21, no. 6 (2006): 1061–1065.

Jervis, Robert. "Introduction." *H-Diplo/ISSF Roundtable Reviews III*, no. 6 (2011): 3–7.

Johnson, Walter. "On Agency." *Journal of Social History* 37, no. 1 (Autumn 2003): 113–124.

Kamissek, Christoph and Jonas Kreienbaum. "An Imperial Cloud: Conceptualising Interimperial Connections and Transimperial Knowledge. *Journal of Modern European History* 14, no. 2 (2016): 164–182.

Lacroix-Riz, Annie. "How to Manage the Peace: When America Wanted to Take Over France," *Monde Diplomatique* (May 2003).

Lacy, Sharon Tosi. "Smith vs. Smith." *HistoryNet*. www.historynet.com/smith-vs-smith.htm.

Laurent, Jean-Pierre. "Paul Vignaux, inspirateur de la 'Deuxième gauche': récits d'un exil français aux Etats-Unis pendant la Seconde guerre mondiale." *Matériaux pour l'histoire de notre temps: Les Etats-Unis et les refugies politiques européens: des années 1930 aux années 1950*, no. 60 (2000): 48–56.

Ludlow, Piers. "No Longer a Closed Shop: Post-1945 Research in the French Archives," *Cold War History* 2, no. 1 (2001): 158–163.

Lundestad, Geir. "Empire by Invitation? The United States and Western Europe, 1945–1952." *Journal of Peace Research* 23, no. 3 (1986): 263–277.

Mistry, Kaeten. "Approaches to Understanding the Inaugural CIA Covert Operation in Italy: Exploding Useful Myths." *Intelligence and National Security* 26, no. 2–3 (April–June 2001): 246–268.

Patti, Archimedes. "Interview." WGBH Media Library and Archives, April 1, 1981. http://openvault.wgbh.org/catalog/vietnam-bf3262-interview-with-archimedes-l-a-patti-1981.

Peterson, Neal H. "Intelligence and US Foreign Policy, 1945–1954." *Studies in Intelligence* 28, no. 4 (Winter 1984): 67–78.

Prados, John. "Certainties, Doubts, and Imponderables: Levels of Analysis in the Military Balance." *Intelligence and National Security* 26, no. 6 (2011): 778–790.

Propas, Frederic L. "Creating a Hard Line on Russia: The Training of State Department Soviet Experts 1927–1937." *Diplomatic History* 8, no. 3 (Summer 1984): 209–226.

Soutou, Georges-Henri. "General de Gaulle and the Soviet Union, 1943–1945: Ideology or European Equilibrium?" In *The Soviet Union and Europe in the Cold War, 1943–1952*, edited by Francesca Gori and Silvio Pons, 310–333. New York: St Martin's Press, 1996.

Specter, Ronald. "Allied Intelligence and China, 1943–1945." *Pacific Historical Review* 51, no. 1 (1982): 23–51.

Stearns, Peter. "Emotions History in the United States: Goals, Methods, and Promise." In *Emotions in American History*, edited by Jessica Gienow-Hecht, 15–27. Brooklyn: Berghahn Books, 2010.

Stout, Mark. "The Pond: Running Agents for State, War and the CIA." *Studies in Intelligence* 48, no. 3 (2007): 69–82.

Stout, Mark and Katalin Kadar Lynn. "'Every Hungarian of Any Value to Intelligence': Tibor Eckhardt, John Grombach, and the Pond." *Intelligence and National Security* (2015). http://dx.doi.org/10.1080/02684527.2015 .1088691.

Tenenbaum, Elie. "Une odyssée subversive." PhD diss. Sciences Po, 2015.

Treverton, Gregory F. "Intelligence Analysis: Between 'Politicization' and Irrelevance." In *Analyzing Intelligence: Origins, Obstacles, and Innovations*, edited by Roger Z. George and James B. Bruce, 91–104. Washington, DC: Georgetown University Press, 2008.

Villatoux, Marie-Catherine. "Les militaires français et la menace de subversion." In *Subversion, anti-subversion, contre-subversion*, edited by François Cochet and Oliver Dard, 63–77. Paris: Riveneuve éditions, 2009.

Wall, Irwin. "The PCF, Stalinism, and the Cold War." *Romanic Review* 92 (January–March 2001): 13–20.

Weiss, Valentine and Thierry Guilpin. *Fonds Geneviève Tabouis 17 AR 1-269, Répertoire numérique détaillé*. Paris: Archives Nationales, 2010.

Werner, Michael and Bénédicte Zimmerman. "Beyond Comparison: *Histoire Croisée* and the Challenge of Reflexivity." *History and Theory* 45 (February 2006): 30–50.

Wilford, Hugh. "Still Missing: The Historiography of U.S. Intelligence." *Passport: The Society for Americans of U.S. Foreign Relations Review* 47, no. 2 (September 2016): 20–27.

Woodman, Conor. "The Imperial Boomerang: How Colonial Methods of Repression Migrate Back to the Metropolis." *Verso* (blog), June 9, 2020. www.versobooks.com/blogs/4383-the-imperial-boomerang-how-colonial-methods-of-repression-migrate-back-to-the-metropolis.

Books

Acheson, Dean. *Present at the Creation*. New York: W. W. Norton, 1969.

Adams, Henry H. *Witness to Power: The Life of Fleet Admiral William D. Leahy*. Annapolis: Naval Institute Press, 1985.

Aderath, Maxwell. *The French Communist Party: A Critical History (1920–1984) – From Comintern to the Colours of France*. Manchester: Manchester University Press, 1984.

Agulhon, Maurice. *C.R.S. à Marseille, la police au service du peuple 1944–1947*. Paris: Presses de Sciences Po, 1971.

Aldrich, Richard J. *Intelligence and the War against Japan: Britain, America and the Politics of Secret Service*. Cambridge: Cambridge University Press, 2000.

Ambrose, Stephen. *Ike's Spies: Eisenhower and the Espionage Establishment*. New York: Random House, 1981.

Andrew, Christopher. *For the President's Eyes Only: Secret Intelligence and the American Presidency from Washington to Bush*. New York: Harper Collins, 1995.

The Secret World: A History of Intelligence. New Haven: Yale University Press, 2018.

Andrew, Christopher and David Dilks, eds. *The Missing Dimension: Governments and Intelligence Communities in the Twentieth Century*. Champaign: University of Illinois Press, 1985.

Andrew, Christopher and Oleg Gordievsky. *KGB: The Inside Story of Its Foreign Operations from Lenin to Gorbachev*. London: Hodder & Stoughton, 1990.

Andrew, Christopher and Vasili Mitrokhin. *The Mitrokhin Archive: The KGB in Europe and the West*. London: Penguin, 1999.

The Sword and the Shield: The Mitrokhin Archive and the Secret History of the KGB. New York: Basic Books, 1999.

Auriol, Vincent. *Journal de Septennat*. Paris: Armand Colin, 1970.

Bartholomew-Feis, Dixie R. *The OSS and Ho Chi Minh: Unexpected Allies in the War against Japan*. Lawrence: University of Kansas Press, 2006.

Bidault, Georges. *Resistance: The Political Autobiography of Georges Bidault*. Translated by Marianne Sinclair. New York: F.A. Praeger, 1967.

Bidussa, David and Denis Peschanski, eds. *La France de Vichy: Archives inedites d'Angelo Tasca*. Paris: CNRS, 1986.

Byrnes, James F. *Speaking Frankly*. New York: Harper, 1947.

Blum, Léon. *L'Oeuvre de Léon Blum*. Paris: Éditions Albin Michel, 1958.

Breitman, Richard and Norman J. W. Goda. *Hitler's Shadow: Nazi War Criminals, U.S. Intelligence, and the Cold War*. Washington, DC: National Archives and Records Administration, 1999.

Breitman, Richard, Norma J. W. Goda, Timothy Naftali, and Robert Wolfe. *U.S. Intelligence and the Nazi*. Cambridge: Cambridge University Press, 2005.

Brocheux, Pierre. *Ho Chi Minh: A Biography*. Translated by Claire Duiker. Cambridge: Cambridge University Press, 2007.

Brogi, Alessandro. *Confronting America: The Cold War between the United States and the Communists in France and Italy*. Chapel Hill: UNC Press, 2011.

A Question of Self-Esteem: The United States and the Cold War Choices in France and Italy 1944–1958. Westport, CT: Greenwood Press, 2001.

Bruce, David K. E. *OSS against the Reich: The World War II Diaries of Colonel David K.E. Bruce*, edited by Nelson Douglas Lankford. Kent: Kent State University Press, 1991.

Bruce, James B. and Roger Z. George, eds. *Analyzing Intelligence: Origins, Obstacles, and Innovations*. Washington, DC: Georgetown University Press, 2008.

Buton, Philippe. *Les lendemains qui déchantent: le Parti Communiste Français à la libération*. Paris: Presses de la Fondation Nationale des Sciences Politiques, 1993.

Byrne, Jeffrey James. *Mecca of Revolution: Algeria, Decolonization, and the Third World Order*. Oxford: Oxford University Press, 2016.

Caute, David. *Isaac and Isaiah: The Covert Punishment of a Cold War Heretic*. New Haven: Yale University Press, 2013.

Cave Brown, Anthony. *The Last Hero: Wild Bill Donovan*. New York: Times Books, 1982.

Cesari, Laurent. *L'Indochine en guerres 1945–1993*. Paris: Editions Belin, 1995. *Le Problème diplomatique de l'Indochine*. Paris: Les indes savantes, 2013.

Connolly, Matthew. *A Diplomatic Revolution: Algeria's Fight for Independence and the Origins of the Post-Cold War Era*. Oxford: Oxford University Press, 2002.

Costigliola, Frank. *France and the United States: The Cold Alliance since World War II*. New York: Twayne Publishers, 1992.

Courtois, Stéphane and Marc Lazar. *Histoire du Parti Communiste Français*. Paris: Presses Universitaires de France, 2000.

Courtois, Stéphane and Marc Lazar. eds. *Cinquante ans d'une passion française: de Gaulle et les communistes*. Paris: Editions Balland, 1991.

Creswell, Michael. *A Question of Balance: How France and the United States Created Cold War Europe*. Cambridge, MA: Harvard University Press, 2006.

Crossman, Richard, ed. *The God That Failed*. London: Hamilton, 1950.

Devillers, Philippe. *Histoire du Viet-Nam de 1940 à 1952*. Paris: Editions du Seuil, 1952.

Donovan, Robert J. *Conflict and Crisis: The Presidency of Harry S. Truman 1945–1948*. Columbia: University of Missouri Press, 1977.

Drew, Allison. *We Are No Longer in France: Communists in Colonial Algeria*. Manchester: Manchester University Press, 2014.

Du Bois, Cora. *Social Forces in Southeast Asia*. Minneapolis: University of Minnesota Press, 1949.

Duiker, William. *Ho Chi Minh*. New York: Hyperion, 2000.

Dur, Philip F. *Jefferson Caffery, Ambassador of Revolutions: An Outline of His Career*, revised edition. Lafayette: University of Southwestern Louisiana, 1998.

Faligot, Roger and Pascal Krop. *La Piscine: Les services secrets français*. Paris: Seuil, 1985.

Fauvet, Jacques. *Histoire du Parti Communiste Français: de 1920 à 1976*. Paris: Fayard, 1977.

Fenby, Jonathan. *The General: Charles de Gaulle and the France He Saved*. London: Simon & Schuster, 2011.

Flanner, Janet. *Paris Journal: Volume One 1944–1955*, edited by William Shawn. New York: Harcourt Brace Jovanovich, 1965.

Fleming, John V. *The Anti-Communist Manifestos: Four Book That Shaped the Cold War*. New York: W. W. Norton, 2009.

Flicke, William F. *War Secrets in the Ether: Part III*. Translated by Ray W. Pettengill. Washington, DC: NSA, 1953.

Friedman, Max Paul. *Rethinking Anti-Americanism: The History of an Exceptional Concept in American Foreign Relations*. Cambridge: Cambridge University Press, 2012.

Gaddis, John Lewis. *George F. Kennan: An American Life*. New York: Penguin, 2011.

Ganser, Daniele. *NATO's Secret Armies: Operation Gladio and Terrorism in Western Europe*. London: Frank Cass, 2005.

Gaucher, Roland. *Histoire secrète du Parti Communiste Français : 1920–1974*. Paris: Albin Michel, 1974.

Glantz, Mary. *FDR and the Soviet Union: The President's Battles over Foreign Policy*. Lawrence: University Press of Kansas, 2005.

Glass, Charles. *Americans in Paris: Life and Death under Nazi Occupation*. New York: Penguin, 2010.

Greenwood, John T. "The Designers: Their Design Bureaux and Aircraft." In *Russian Aviation and Airpower in the Twentieth Century*, edited by Robin Higham, John T. Greenwood, and Von Hardesty, 162–190. London: Routledge, 2014.

Grosser, Alfred. *La IVe République et sa politique extérieure*. Paris: Librairie Armand Colin, 1972.

Harris Smith, Richard. *OSS: The Secret History of America's First Central Intelligence Agency*. Guilford, CT: The Lyons Press, 2005.

Heyde, Veronika. *De l'esprit de la résistance jusqu'à l'idée Europe: Projets européens et américains pour l'Europe de l'après-guerre (1940–1950)* Bruxelles: P.I.E. Peter Lang, 2010.

History Project, Strategic Services Unit. *War Reports: Office of Strategic Services Volume II – Operations in the Field*. Washington, DC: Government Printing Office, 1949.

Hitchcock, William. *France Restored: Cold War Diplomacy and the Quest for Leadership in Europe, 1944–1954*. Chapel Hill: The University of North Carolina Press, 1998.

Hogan, Michael J. *Cross of Iron: Harry S. Truman and the Origins of the National Security State*. Cambridge: Cambridge University Press, 1999.

  The Marshall Plan: America, Britain, and the Reconstruction of Western Europe. New York: Cambridge University Press, 1987.

Hoganson, Kristin and Jay Sexton. "Introduction." In *Crossing Empires: Taking US History into Transimperial Terrain*. Durham: Duke University Press, 2020.

Jeffrey, Keith. *The Secret History of MI-6, 1909–1949*. New York: Penguin, 2010.

Jeffreys-Jones, Rhodri. *In Spies We Trust: The Story of Western Intelligence*. Oxford: Oxford University Press, 2013.

Journoud, Pierre. *De Gaulle et le Vietnam: 1945–1969 La réconciliation*. Paris: Editions Tallandier, 2011.

Judt, Tony. *Postwar: A History of Europe since 1945*. New York: Penguin Random House, 2006.

Katz, Barry. *Foreign Intelligence: Research and Analysis in the Office of Strategic Services 1942–1945*. Cambridge, MA: Harvard University Press, 1989.

Kedward, H. R. *In Search of the Maquis: Resistance in Southern France 1942–1944*. Oxford: Oxford University Press, 1993.

Kennedy, Robert. *Of Knowledge and Power: The Complexities of National Intelligence*. Westport, CT: Praeger Security International, 2008.

Kent, Sherman. *The Intelligence Process*. Princeton: Princeton University Press, 1949.

Kritzman, Lawrence D., ed. *The Columbia History of Twentieth-Century French Thought*. New York: Columbia University Press, 2007.

Lacouture, Jean. *De Gaulle: The Rebel 1890–1944*. Translated by Patrick O'Brien. New York: W. W. Norton, 1990.

De Gaulle: The Ruler 1945–1970. Translated by Alan Sheridan. New York: W. W. Norton, 1991.

Lacroix-Riz, Annie. *La Choix de Marianne: Les relations franco-américaines de la Libération aux débuts du Plan Marshall, 1944–1948.* Paris: Messidor, 1986.

De Munich à Vichy: L'assassinat de la Troisième République 1938–1940. Paris: Armand Colin, 2008.

Langer, William L. *In and Out of the Ivory Tower.* New York: Neale Watson Academic Publications, 1977.

Lawrence, Mark Atwood. *Assuming the Burden: Europe and American Commitment to the War in Vietnam.* Berkeley: University of California Press, 2005.

Lazitch, Branko. *Biographical Dictionary of the Comintern.* Stanford: Hoover Institution Press, 1986.

Le Bailly, David. *Le Captive de Mitterrand.* Paris: Stock, 2014.

Leahy, William D. *I Was There: The Personal Story of the Chief of Staff to Presidents Roosevelt and Truman Based on His Notes and Diary at the Time.* New York: McGraw Hill, 1950.

Leffler, Melvyn. *A Preponderance of Power: National Security, the Truman Administration, and the Cold War.* Stanford: Stanford University Press, 1992.

Logevall, Fredrick. *Embers of War: The Fall of an Empire and the Making of America's Vietnam.* New York: Random House, 2012.

Loustaunau-Lacau, Georges. *Memoires d'un rebelle.* Paris: R. Laffont, 1948.

Lowenthal, Mark. *Intelligence: From Secrets to Policy,* 2nd ed. Washington, DC: CQ Press, 2003.

Lundestad, Geir. *The United States and Western Europe since 1945.* Oxford: Oxford University Press, 2003.

Mandel, Maud. *Muslims and Jews in France: A History of Conflict.* Princeton: Princeton University Press, 2014.

Marcou, Lilly. *Le Kominform: le communisme de guerre froide.* Paris: Sciences Po, 2013.

Marr, David G. *Vietnam 1945: The Quest for Power.* Berkeley: University of California Press, 1997.

Vietnam: State, War, and Revolution (1945–1946). Berkeley: University of California Press, 2013.

McCullough, David. *Truman.* New York: Simon & Schuster, 1992.

Mencherini, Robert. *Guerre froid, guerre rouge. Pari communiste, Stalinisme, et luttes sociales en France, les grèves 'insurrectionnelles' de 1947–1948.* Paris: Editions Syllepse, 1998.

Milward, Alan. *The Reconstruction of Western Europe, 1945–1951.* Berkeley: University of California Press, 1984.

Miscamble, Wilson. *George Kennan and the Making of American Foreign Policy 1947–1950.* Princeton: Princeton University Press, 1992.

Mistry, Kaeten. *The United States, Italy, and the Origins of the Cold War: Waging Political Warfare, 1945–1950.* Cambridge: Cambridge University Press, 2014.

Moch, Jules. *Une si longue vie.* Paris: Robert Laffont, 1976.

Morgan, Ted. *A Covert Life: Jay Lovestone: Communist, Anti-Communist, and Spymaster.* New York: Random House, 2011.

Reds: McCarthyism in Twentieth Century America. New York: Random House, 2003.

Mortimer, Edward. *The Rise of the French Communist Party 1920–1947.* London: Faber & Faber, 1984.

Murphy, Robert. *Diplomat among Warriors.* New York: Doubleday, 1964.

Nolan, Mary. *Transatlantic Century: Europe and America, 1890–2010.* Cambridge: Cambridge University Press, 2012.

Offner, Arnold. *Another Such Victory: President Truman and the Cold War, 1945–1953.* Stanford: Stanford University Press, 2002.

Patti, Archimedes. *Why Vietnam? Prelude to America's Albatross.* Berkeley, University of California Press, 1982.

Persico, Joseph. *Roosevelt's Secret War: FDR and World War II Espionage.* New York: Random House, 2001.

Philby, Kim. *My Silent War.* New York: Grove Press, 1968.

Pillar, Paul. *Intelligence and US Foreign Policy: Iraq, 9/11, and Misguided Reform.* New York: Columbia University Press, 2011.

Pisani, Sallie. *The CIA and the Marshall Plan.* Lawrence: University Press of Kansas, 1991.

Porch, Douglas. *The French Secret Services: A History of French Intelligence from the Dreyfus Affair to the Gulf War.* New York: Macmillan, 2003.

Procacci, Giuliano, ed. *The Cominform: Minutes of the Three Conferences 1947/1948/1949.* Milano: Fondazione Giangiacomo Feltrinelli, 1994.

Raghavan, Srinath. *India's War: World War II and the Making of Modern South Asia.* New York: Basic Books, 2016.

Robertson, Charles L. *When Roosevelt Planned to Govern France.* Amherst: University of Massachusetts Press, 2011.

Rockefeller, David. *Memoirs.* New York: Random House, 2002.

Rota, Emanuel. *A Pact with Vichy: Angelo Tasco from Italian Socialism to French Collaboration.* New York: Fordham University Press, 2013.

Scaglia, Ilaria. *The Emotions of Internationalism: Feeling International Cooperation in the Alps in the Interwar Period.* Oxford: Oxford University Press, 2020.

Scott-Smith, Giles and Hans Krabbendam, eds. *The Cultural Cold War in Western Europe, 1945–1960.* London: Frank Cass, 2003.

Selverstone, Marc. *Constructing the Monolith: The United States, Great Britain, and International Communism, 1945–1950.* Cambridge, MA: Harvard University Press, 2009.

Sewell Jr., William H. *Logics of History: Social Theory and Social Transformation.* Chicago: The University of Chicago Press, 2005.

Seymour, Susan C. *Cora du Bois: Anthropologist, Diplomat, Agent.* Lincoln: University of Nebraska Press, 2015.

Smith, Bradley F. *The Shadow Warriors: OSS and the Origins of the CIA.* New York: Basic Books, 1983.

Statler, Kathryn. *Replacing France: The Origins of American Intervention in Vietnam.* Lexington: University Press of Kentucky, 2009.

Thorez, Maurice. *Fils du Peuple.* Paris: Editions Sociales, 1970.

Tønnesson, Stein. *The Vietnamese Revolution of 1945: Roosevelt, Ho Chi Minh and de Gaulle in a World at War*. London: SAGE, 1991.

Trachtenberg, Marc. *The Craft of International History: A Guide to Method*. Princeton: Princeton University Press, 2006.

Truman, Harry S. *Memoirs. Volume 1. Year of Decisions; Vol. 2. Years of Trial and Hope*. New York: Doubleday, 1955–1956.

   Off the Record: The Private Papers of Harry S. Truman. Edited by Robert H. Ferrell. New York: Harper & Row, 1980.

   Where the Buck Stops: The Personal and Private Writings of Harry S. Truman. Edited by Margaret Truman. New York: Warner Books, 1989.

Tucker, Spencer C. *Instruments of War: Weapons and Technologies That Have Changed History*. Santa Barbara: ABC-CLIO, 2015.

Vinen, Richard. *Bourgeois Politics in France, 1945–1951*. Cambridge: Cambridge University Press, 1995.

Wall, Irwin. *French Communism in the Era of Stalin: The Quest for Unity and Integration, 1945–1962*. Westport, CT: Greenwood Press, 1983.

   The United States and the Making of Postwar France, 1945–1954. Cambridge: Cambridge University Press, 1991.

Weil, Martin. *A Pretty Good Club: The Founding Fathers of the U.S. Foreign Service*. New York: W. W. Norton, 1978.

Wieviorka, Oliver. *Orphans of the Republic: The Nation's Legislators in Vichy*. Cambridge, MA: Harvard University Press, 2009.

Winks, Robin. *Cloak and Gown: Scholars in the Secret War, 1939–1961*, 2nd ed. New Haven: Yale University Press, 1987.

Yergin, Daniel. *Shattered Peace: The Origins of the Cold War and the National Security State*. Boston: Houghton Mifflin, 1977.

Young, John. *France, the Cold War, and the Western Alliance, 1944–1949: French Foreign Policy and Postwar Europe*. New York: St. Martin's Press, 1990.

Yu, Maochun. *The OSS in China: Prelude to Cold War*. New Haven: Yale University Press, 1996.

Zahniser, Martin. *Uncertain Friendship: American-French Diplomatic Relations through the Cold War*. New York: John Wiley & Sons, 1975.

Index

France (cont.)
  aspiration for social reforms, 40
  attitude to civil war, 40
  center-periphery relations, 13
  coalition governments, 4
  Cold War and, 9
  colonialism, 5, 8, 13, 79, 81, 101,
    118–119, 189–190
  communist influence, 15, 18, 37–38, 108,
    110, 124, 126–127
  constitutional referendum, 86, 123,
    130–131
  economic development, 131, 166
  foreign policy, 15, 50, 72
  German occupation of, 17, 19
  leftist turn in, 66–67
  legitimacy vacuum, 4
  liberation of, 17–18, 28
  national elections, 60, 68
  political development, 6, 9, 34–35, 37,
    139, 148, 152, 166, 181, 200
  pro-American orientation, 9, 50, 139,
    188
  pro-Soviet sentiments, 34, 65, 71
  social cleavages, 49
  socio-cultural atmosphere, 12
  War in the Pacific and, 98
Franco, Francisco, General, 149
Franco-American relations
  assessment of, 18
  colonial issue and, 13, 134
  communist factor in, 47, 61, 66–67,
    76–77
  evolution of, 12, 30, 91, 192
  improvement of, 46, 65, 72–74
  intelligence role in, 2, 46–47, 203
  primary sources, 11
  scholarship on, 12
  Soviet factor in, 69
  tensions in, 5, 18, 33–36, 70–71, 74
Franco-Soviet relations, 44–45, 69, 71–72,
  75–76, 129
Francs-Tireurs et Partisans (FTP), 36
French Army
  communication with U.S. officials, 23
  fear of Soviet invasion, 127
  leftist influence in, 116
  reports on communist infiltration in,
    150–151
French colonies
  American perceptions of situation in, 161

anti-colonial movements in, 146
communist influence in, 120, 159–160,
  191
"right of divorce", 174
French Committee of National Liberation
  (CFLN)
  American view of, 45
  communists and, 34, 41–44, 113
  criticism of, 23
  formation of, 27
  influence of, 4
  members of, 26
  political agenda, 41
  pressure for recognition of, 24
  struggle for political leadership of, 23
French Communist Party (PCF)
  alliance with de Gaulle, 4, 43, 49, 69
  American view of, 58, 65, 78–79, 140,
    198–199
  attack on headquarters of, 125
  colonial policy of, 43, 86, 88–89, 136,
    146, 160, 162, 174
  Cominform and, 196
  criticism of, 4, 41, 169
  demonstration against "fascists",
    125–126
  economic agenda, 63, 154
  expulsion from the government, 15, 159,
    191, 200
  foreign policy agenda, 33, 69
  French officials' view of, 149–150
  Gaullists and, 41–42
  influence of, 4, 41–43, 55, 57–59, 108,
    154–155
  intelligence reports on, 57, 61, 140
  June 1946 elections, 125, 139
  Marshall Plan and, 157, 170
  membership growth, 64
  methods and tactics of, 42, 50, 58, 67,
    115, 173, 187
  in municipal elections, 54, 171
  Muslim population and, 41, 84
  nationalist movements and, 80, 82,
    85–86, 138, 145
  nationalists and, 42
  North African communist parties and, 83
  as opposition party, 158–159
  parliamentary politics, 11
  participation in the government, 28, 34,
    62–65, 68–69, 113
  political alliances, 4, 64

Index